First published in 2019 by Sansom and Company,
a publishing imprint of Redcliffe Press Ltd.,
81g Pembroke Road, Bristol BS8 3EA
www.sansomandcompany.co.uk | info@sansomandcompany.co.uk

ISBN 978-1-911408-58-1

British Library Cataloguing-in-Publication Data
A catalogue record for this book is available from the British Library.

Cover design by Carina Dicks.
Printed and bound by Akcent Media.

Sansom & Co is committed to being an environmentally friendly publisher.
This book is made from Forest Stewardship Council® certified paper.

CONTENTS

Photo: Peter Clark

INTRODUCTION

*T*he Chap was founded at the end of the 20th century in a pub in South London by two men who felt they were not being served by the men's magazines of the time. The so-called 'Lads Mags' didn't feature any advice about which cravat to wear, where to buy a monocle or how many olives should go into a Creole Scream.

So the decision was made to start a pamphlet proposing Anarcho-Dandyism, a satirical response to the absurdity of men who dressed like teenagers and a society that seemed to have cast the gentleman into obscurity. The first edition of *The Chap* was published in February 1999, a rather fanzine-looking pamphlet in a print run of 100 copies, photocopied in Prontaprint. Contents for the second edition had not even been considered, until a feature in the *Daily Telegraph* yielded 750 requests for subscriptions. It seemed that more people than Gustav Temple and Vic Darkwood craved the spirit of Anarcho-Dandyism. Letters from readers poured in, decrying the absence of hat stands in pubs and the paucity of cocktails on the menu at McDonald's.

Photo: Soulsealer Photography

The first edition was hastily reprinted to higher standards (yet maintaining a cover typo), and offices secured on a rear table at the New Piccadilly Café in Soho. *The Chap* quickly grew into much more than a magazine, attracting an assortment of men and women who already favoured tweed over denim and who held no truck with the vogue for wearing sportswear off the sports field (or on it).

The magazine grew in size and scope and began hosting events and parties. The Chap Olympiad started as a modest gathering in a corner of Regent's Park into an annual fixture on the London summer festival scene, attracting 1500 immaculately dressed souls to compete in Umbrella Jousting, Hop, Skip and G&T and Cucumber Sandwich Discus. This was the first-ever sporting event to place a ban on sportswear, and when the real Olympic Games were held in London in 2012, the Chaps were invited to stage their own Tournament of Tomfoolery in the Olympic Park. No sportswear was worn, though the chaps were asked to deposit their sword sticks with security.

As fashions evolved during the early years of the millennium and youths started wearing more expensive pantaloons de Nîmes, abandoning the use of belts entirely, the fashions featured in *The Chap* remained constant, although much less difficult to acquire. Items previously only available in charity shops and thrift stores began to enter the high street, and by 2014 one could purchase a Harris Tweed jacket in Primark – manufactured in China, of course.

The Chap style had become fashionable, helped by television series such as *Peaky Blinders* and *Boardwalk*

Empire. But while tweed, herringbone and moleskin were now freely available on the open market, one still couldn't order a Pousse Café in Burger King, so there was still work to be done.

When Abercrombie & Fitch proposed to open a store on Savile Row, *The Chap* staged a civilised protest, swarming around the Row chanting 'Give Three-Piece a Chance'. It was a heartfelt and elegant plea that fell on deaf ears, but luckily the opening of the children's T-shirt emporium practically bankrupted Abercrombie & Fitch.

The Chap Magazine continued to flourish, expanding in size and returning to a quarterly format in 2017. Spin-off books were published, beginning with *The Chap Manifesto* in 2001, the most recent being *How To Be Chap* in 2016. The magazine's place in society was assured when, in an episode of *Midsomer Murders*, a copy of *The Chap* was seen on the dashboard of the vintage Daimler belonging to a rather louche, caddish character who naturally turned out to have dunnit.

The Chap has published 102 editions so far and the book you are about to read contains a selection of the very best features from the last 20 years, from the earliest black and white editions to the more recent quarterly format. Hopefully you will notice the evolution from advice being given to prospective dandies, fops, boulevardiers and raffish gentlemen in the earlier editions, to interviews and photographs of fully formed versions of the same character types. If the original purpose of *The Chap* was to introduce a little more panache, elegance, eccentricity and bonhomie into society, I hope you'll agree that this ambition was successful.

Gustav Temple, 2019

The Semiotics of Smoking

Whiling away the vast tracts of time that lie between dawn and dusk should never present itself as a problem to a chap of imagination. Lengthy bouts on the chaise longue coupled with elaborate grooming rituals should be adequate to fill most of one's waking hours, but sometimes a fellow may be inspired to experiment with leisure pursuits of a slightly more demanding nature. One such pastime is the semiotics of smoking.

A chap with a cigarette, cigar or pipe in hand, when keenly observed, will within a matter of minutes unwittingly divulge not only his social status and current state of mind but also vital information about temperament, reliability, employability, marital status, sexual proclivities and prowess, family background and literary tastes. Much pleasure may be gained by sashaying through the throng or dallying in public houses, notebook in hand, attempting to build up detailed psychological profiles of one's fellow man. Non-smokers who hold no truck with the tobaccotine arts have already revealed themselves to be beyond contempt and are therefore worthy of no serious consideration.

With this brief at-a-glance guide, the layman will merely be able to scratch the surface of a science that is as frighteningly deep as it is majestically long. But with a little application and additional research, he will find the semiotics of smoking an invaluable insight for use socially, in business and for pleasure.

THE IMPOTENT OR CUCKHOLD

An ostentatious panache can sometimes mask the grief caused by a wife's philanderings, but this fellow's multiple cigarette usage coupled with an awkwardly affected smoking technique speak volumes about inadequacies in the trouser department.

THE PUB POLITICIAN

From time to time a fellow can be gripped by an urge to put a point forcefully. Although usually of vulgar usage, the 'two finger prod' can be highly effective in driving an argument home, especially when debating with members of the lower orders.

THE NOUVEAU RICHE

Trying too hard is a social faux pas virtually impossible to excuse. The unattractive affectations of lottery winners and self-made persons of trade are the tell-tale signs of social inferiority, and as such can have no place in polite society.

THE SENIOR MAN

The man who is happily assured of his own worth can decently allow himself the luxury of a less than overtly masculine smoking technique. Generations of seniority have left him oblivious to the taunts of the hoi poloi.

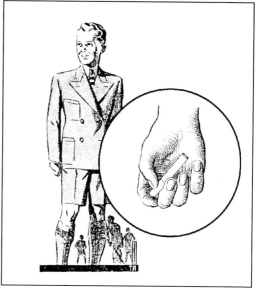

THE EMPIRE

Contemptuous of modern concepts of democracy and self-determination, 'The Empire', whilst rendering a man seductive and charismatic, should best be avoided, as it has been known to lead to acute muscle fatigue and fisticuffs.

THE DECADENT SCHOOLBOY

From its modest beginnings behind school bike sheds this grip has steadily become a national institution in areas where misguided authority has contemptuously disregarded a man's fundamental right to smoke.

THE EXQUISITE

Now almost exclusively the preserve of young women in the lower echelons of advertising and homosexuals, this classic stance deserves wider currency as a signifier of a singularity of mind and a certain opulence of the soul.

THE CLOSET LOTHARIO

This ineffectual-looking cove may look like the boy next door, but a closer inspection of his expertly cupped hand reveals a cunningly concealed prophylactic. The man is obviously an animal.

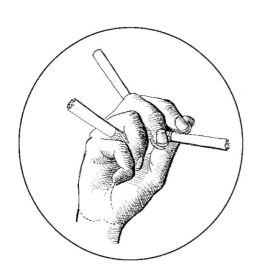

THE RUM COVE

There is a certain brand of wilfull contrariness that is often resultant of inbreeding or an art college education. The aspiring host should think very carefully before inviting 'creative' persons to dinner parties.

THE EXTROVERT

This fellow has clearly taken leave of his senses. In a miscalculated bid to court the attention of his chums he has taken the noble pursuit of smoking and thrown it in the mire. He should never be trusted with any position of authority.

THE OVERLY CONSIDERATE

Efforts to pander to the prejudices of the non-smoker will only earn you the opprobrium of all right thinking people. A man who smokes with confidence and pride will find himself both respected by his colleages and admired by the ladies.

THE PERVERT

This blighter seems to be wearing women's clothing. If it weren't for the fact that he smokes Dunhill Internationals and that his father owns half of Carmarthenshire, he would find himself excluded from all but the most 'theatrical' of cocktail parties.

THE SOBRANIE

These young blades express a natural and healthy friendship through a shared enjoyment of Sobranie Cocktail cigarettes. A public school education has trained them to be at ease with male camaradarie and make the most of their bachelor days.

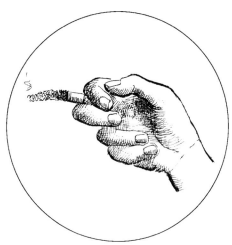

THE NONCHALANT OR SLOVEN

The subtle art of 'long ashing' should be attempted by none but the most experienced of smokers. A crucial combination of poise, steely nerves and split second ashtray technique make all the difference between universal admiration and ignominy.

Gentlemanly

AILMENTS

SISTER MILICENT FOND

1. RACONTEUR'S WRIST.

Excessive gesticulation during the recounting of an amusing or exciting tale is apt to produce undue strain on the radio-ulnar joint. Frequent bathing of the afflicted wrist in a lukewarm solution of laudanum, champagne and Epsom salts is advised. This treatment is most effective if administered whilst the patient reclines on a chaise longue, reading Romantic verse.

3. COCKTAIL FINGER

Though admirably maintained by sophisticated persons during the imbibement of cocktails, the extended finger at the base of a glass can produce strain on the meta-carpals, thus rendering the bon vivant sadly handicapped in quaffing potential. To occupy oneself exclusively with the smoking of a cigar, for part of the evening, will allow the weary digit to rest, though do beware of 'Smoker's Thumb'.

2. HANDSHAKER'S THUMB

Caused by vigorous clasping of a friend's or acquaintance's hand during greetings or farewells. The cure is, in short, to cease shaking hands for a spell. A slight elevation of the hat is prefectly acceptable in polite society, especially if passing on the street. If handshaking is reserved solely for close chums, the thumb will gadually heal itself.

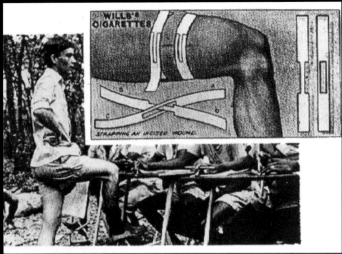

4. IMPERIALIST'S KNEE

The principal victim of this perfidious ailment is the travelling gentleman, who cannot resist the opportunity, of striking a pose for his attendant photographer at every available location. The leg being raised upon a convenient surface (to denote civilised superiority over the inhabitants of foreign parts) can put unnecessary strain on the tibia. A temporary ligature can be easily fashioned from some cut-up shirt collars, as illustrated.

5.FOX-TROT FIBULA

This is caused by unnecessarily vigorous dancing. The cure is simple: cease dancing, and, instead, indulge in witty conversation and smoking.

6.ARMPIT SCORCH

The result of holding forth on matters of the day while standing regally before the fireplace. The armpits are especially vulnerable if the arm is raised to emphasise a point, with the expansive flourish of the *bon vivant*. Treatment: the patient should be gently led to a chair or sofa, taking particular care if he is in mid-*bon mot*; oxygen should be administered directly to the armpit via a sturdy pair of bellows.

7. PICNICKER'S NECK AND ELBOW

The unfortunate result of prolongued reclining on a flat grassy surface, whilst absorbed in leisurely exchanges with pals during a picnic. The cure is to bathe in the nude in the nearest lake or river, whilst maintaining a splendid erection. This will divert the blood supply from the brain, and allow one to return to the gathering feeling somewhat refreshed.

Howard Spent investigates

Trouser Semaphore

In previous issues of The Chap, we (that is, you and I, gentle reader) have probed into the heady realm of Semiotics, wringing out and interpreting the inadvertent symbolism of body language and style affectation. This time around, we take a slightly different tack. Whilst Semiotics deals primarily with an unwitting divulgence of information, what I wish to concentrate on today is a far more calculated form of conveyance.

The acquired skill known as Trouser Semaphore is swiftly gaining currency as the only way for people of quality to communicate in an age of rapidly escalating background noise levels. Typically, at the race track or at unexpectedly rumbustious parties, attempts to make oneself heard above the general hubbub can prove exasperating and, as often as not, utterly futile. Within the space of a week, and with minimal amount of application, it is possible to gain a skill of incalculable worth. Across the floor of a crowded cocktail gathering, you too would be able to convey your innermost thoughts and deepest needs to like minded individuals, using nothing more than flexibility of your physique and the rough pliability of one's trouser cloth. Surely, there is no sight more moving than a man and three square yards of carefully tailored cavalry twill moving in perfect harmony.

After years of practice and much patience, the carefully orchestrated movements can transcend mere practicality and approach a level bordering on art. But no matter to which level you yourself wish to pursue the practice of Trouser Semaphore, on a day-to-day practical level, you will find it an invaluable communication aid, for use socially, in business and for pleasure.

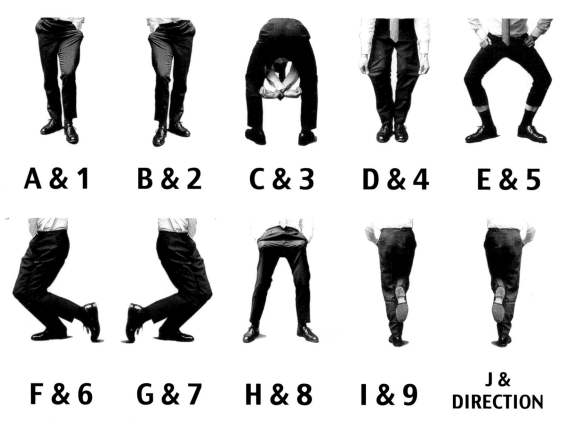

| A & 1 | B & 2 | C & 3 | D & 4 | E & 5 |

| F & 6 | G & 7 | H & 8 | I & 9 | J & DIRECTION |

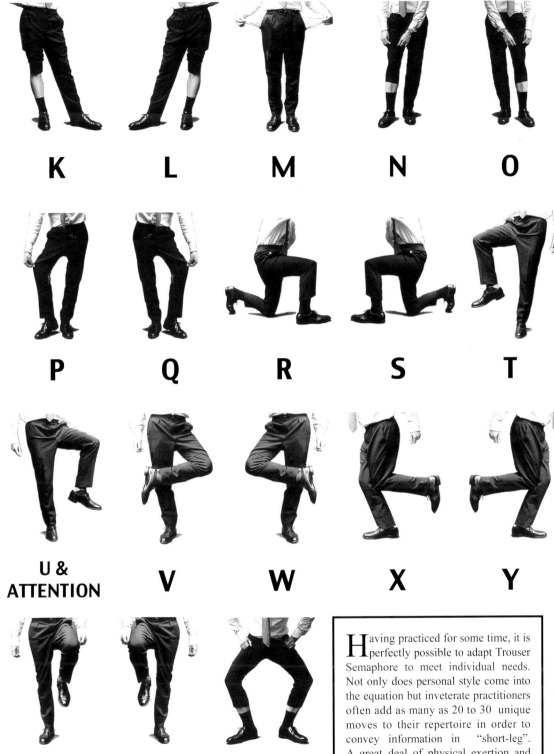

Having practiced for some time, it is perfectly possible to adapt Trouser Semaphore to meet individual needs. Not only does personal style come into the equation but inveterate practitioners often add as many as 20 to 30 unique moves to their repertoire in order to convey information in "short-leg". A great deal of physical exertion and unpleasant bending may be by-passed in this way. Overleaf are some notable examples of this individual approach.

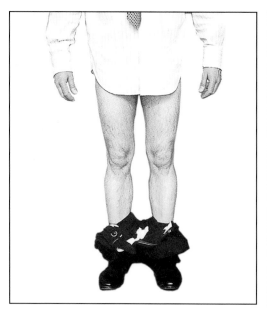

THE SUITOR

Unlike our brusque transatlantic cousins, it can sometimes be difficult for an Englishman to elucidate his inner feelings of affection and bonhomie. Trouser Semaphore enables this rather shy but passionate cove to express himself without consequent loss of face.

THE GAELIC

The 15th Earl of Camardenshire's 'theatrical' temperament has led him towards an ill-judged appreciation of traditional Irish dancing, in which troupes of sturdy-legged colleens wantonly turn the subtle art of Trouser Semaphore into a bare limbed fiasco.

THE MACHIAVELLIAN

Heaven knows what twisted logic has allowed this man to plummet the depths of sartorial knavery. It can only be assumed that by using a cunning ruse known as 'sad-trouser', this tennis player hopes to lure his adversary into unwarranted complacency.

THE PARVENU

The unattractive affectations of lottery winners and self made persons of trade have been alluded to previously in these pages. Untramelled exhuberance is an emotion totally alien to a gentleman and potentially ruinous to a finely stitched gusset.

THE SUBLIME

Spending vast tracts of time wearing one's pyjamas is traditionally associated with a soaring intellect, a singularity of soul and a belief in personal freedom. This man's nonchalant leg crossing says "I am a man apart; a man of worth; a man of dignity".

THE RETROUVE

A wrong-headed notion known as "retro chic" is currently laying waste to our youth, who fondly imagine that by ironically donning the tawdry fashions of the 70's, they are somehow being clever and 'with it'. Nothing could be further from the truth.

THE SELF-ASSURED

Inspired by the self defence mechanism of the European Natterjack toad, this fellow has utilised modern bicycle pump technology to create a look calculated to strike fear into the heart of all but the most determined of muggers.

THE DEMONSTRATIVE

Having words over inadequate service in restaurants can be embarrassing for friends, and altogether unseemly and undignified. Aided by Trouser Semaphore, this chap cleverly leaves staff in no doubt as to his opinion of a draconian dress code.

Spiritual

MALAISE

Sister Millicent Fond tends to the afflictions of the soul which can befall the modern gentleman.

1. YOUTH

The man being helped by his friends has clearly been afflicted with a rather nasty dose of Youth, a disease which can strike at any age, though the middle-aged are particularly vulnerable. This fellow has drunk too freely from the goblet of Adonis, thus rendering him incapable of clear diction and depriving him of the ability to purchase sensible footwear. The best treatment is for the patient to seek membership of a reputable gentlemen's club, there to indulge in large quantities of port, cognac and cigars. This, coupled with voracious reading of the Times, will speed him gracefully into a more dignified age.

2. SPORT

This man has fallen foul of the ravages of Sport. He was found upon a playing field, clad only in breeches, a short-sleeved undershirt and studded boots, clumsily attempting to navigate a leather ball around the field, to the jocular cries of similarly-afflicted comrades. The cure is Baudelaire, of course, or any other poet whose depraved lifestyle resulted in an artistic disease such as TB or syphilis. The sickly stanzas, accompanied to gentle guitar music, will remind the patient that a great poetic mind is best nurtured in the invalid's bed.chamber, not upon the playing field.

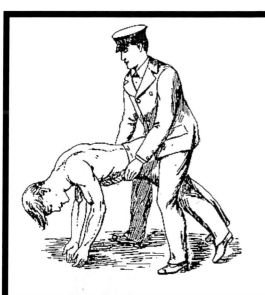

3. HEALTH

There is a common delusion that vitamins and a high-fibre diet can lead to a spiritually enriched life of the mind. The victim of Health has overdosed on products peddled by so-called 'nutritionists', whose sole aim is to get the young hooked on their highly addictive products, thus enslaving them for life to the commode. The patient will first need his stomach drained in the manner illustrated, then fed with large doses of expensive chocolates, eggs and pancakes, and any other foods that will stem the flow of bodily waste. The aim of the treatment should be total constipation.

4. COMMUNITY

The ravages of Community can result in total helplessness, and a dependence on one's friends and neighbours for support in every daily action, such as early morning rising, in this case. The patient has lost all sense of identity, regarding himself solely as a cog

in the grand machine of suburbia. Total abnegation of responsibility has resulted in a 'co-dependent' state, where only by including the whole community in his daily rituals can the patient achieve any sense of his own value. The cure is to spread malicious rumours about the town concerning his nocturnal activities in the park; he will soon learn to keep himself to himself.

5. TRAVEL BUG

The first signs to look out for in this increasingly common ailment are matted hair, the inability to wash, and a large multicoloured protrusion on the back. Victims are apt to disappear for several months at a time, usually to the Orient or South America. They will return with various trinkets, baubles and absurd ethnic headwear, and suffer a form of verbal diarrhoea which renders them incapable of speaking about anything except their travels. The cure is to take them on a tour of the literary taverns of their town's bohemian quarter, pausing to quote from fine English writers such as Johnson, or

Dickens: "It is a most miserable thing to feel ashamed of home." (Great Expectations)

6.FASHION

This is a highly perfidious ailment currently wreaking havoc on the young. The things to look out for are: (1) Tuning the radio to any other station than Radio 3 or Radio 4 (this is usually followed by frequent visits to record stores); (2) an alarming predilection for expensive urban sportswear; (3) the ability to blend inconspicuously with the common herd, with almost total loss of the superego. There is still no complete cure for Fashion, but various palliative treatments can stimulate the patient into a self-healing process. The most important of these is the acquisition of an unusual haircut, which will help to single the patient out from the crowd, and thus reclaim his right to individual expression.

7. CONTENTMENT

The outward signs of this chronic disease begin when the patient ceases to integrate with the real world, choosing instead to gorge themselves on nest-building pursuits such as DIY, gardening and child-rearing. A dullness in the visage, often leading to 'dead-eye', is the first serious symptom. This is usually followed by an alarming expansion of the girth, and a total rejection of sartorial decency, resulting in the wearing of fleecy tracksuits in public places. At this stage the patient should be taken to Paris, and left there with a maximum of 100 francs. They will soon adapt to the realities of life, and hopefully gain an interest in art and poetry, coupled with a healthy weight loss.

PROGRESSIVE EDUCATION. We consulted that redoubtable polymath and man of pleering, Sir Vincent Clowdesley-Shovel, for some advice on the most efficacious and up-to-date techniques, currently being used in the moulding of formative minds. Here are Clowdesley-Shovel's tips on the do's and don'ts of turning out a well-rounded young man.

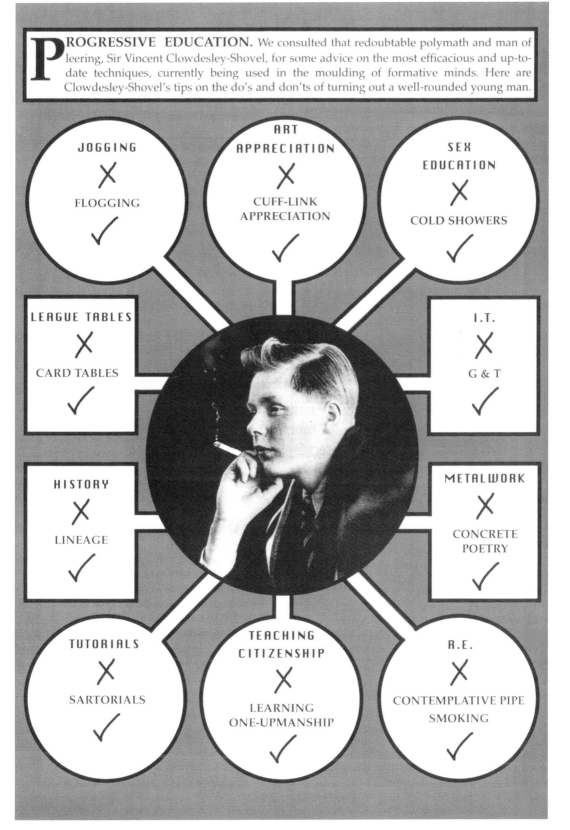

JOGGING ✗
FLOGGING ✓

ART APPRECIATION ✗
CUFF-LINK APPRECIATION ✓

SEX EDUCATION ✗
COLD SHOWERS ✓

LEAGUE TABLES ✗
CARD TABLES ✓

I.T. ✗
G & T ✓

HISTORY ✗
LINEAGE ✓

METALWORK ✗
CONCRETE POETRY ✓

TUTORIALS ✗
SARTORIALS ✓

TEACHING CITIZENSHIP ✗
LEARNING ONE-UPMANSHIP ✓

R.E. ✗
CONTEMPLATIVE PIPE SMOKING ✓

Angur Masonick examines the delicate matter of locating, courting and pleasing the ladies

1. THE MATTER IS CIRCLED, TENDERLY.

It is a truth universally acknowledged that any man in possession of good trousers and firm teeth must seek a lady with whom to share these things. For although we live in very progressive times indeed, many of the finer - and also cruder - aspects of wooing remain as mysterious to a chap as the intricacies of his own digestive system. Younger chaps may find parts of this matter hard to talk about. Others may find them hard to do. That's natural. There have been times when your own correspondent has found it hard, and there have been times when he has not. That's just how it tends to be with the ladies.

But this is not a matter we should approach fearfully. Ladies will not scratch or bite or eat us. That sort of thing exists only in the febrile mind of the adolescent. Ladies should instead be regarded as embodying so much that a chap might wish to claim as his own: kindness, gentleness, finely-shaped hair. And yet perhaps you still feel some fear. Perhaps you have yet to be experienced by a lady. Maybe you have on occasion enjoyed and been enjoyed by a lady,

TOWARDS...
A
PHILOSOPHY
OF
WOOING

but were left with a terrible sense of emptiness, as if you had considered every inch of the world through a highly powered microscope and yet were unable to discern any trace of yourself within it. Well that's just too bad. Sparking up chicks is a hell of a job, so let's just get down to it.

2. AN ENTIRELY HYPOTHETICAL, IMAGINED AND MADE-UP SITUATION IS SUMMONED, AND WITHIN THAT FICTIONAL CONTEXT AN ADVANCE IS MADE.

Let's just say, and this isn't beyond the bounds of credibility, that you know, or know of, a lady. Perhaps you've encountered one at your place of work. Perhaps her name's Veronica, and maybe she sits at the desk in front of you, and you're as familiar with the way her hair sweeps the nape of her perfect neck as you are with the palm of your own greasy, calloused hand. Perhaps you find it hard to talk to her, and that your carefully prepared bons mots dribble wetly out of your mouth, down your chin and on to your shirt, so that she shrinks from your bizarre presence like a lovely little rabbit bolting down a hole. What exactly are you doing wrong here, and how may it be rectified?

3. TWO PROBLEMS.

1. Firstly, you appear to Veronica to be an unnatural and crazy freak. This she finds off-putting. You've done well by deciding in advance exactly what it is you'd like to say to her, but when you speak it sounds like there's a little animal - a vole perhaps - stuck in your throat. Veronica likes all animals, including voles, and in fact at the moment she likes them much more than she likes you.
2. There is a vacuum where your confidence should be. You are like a droopy old vegetable at the bottom of the fridge that not even a student would eat. Veronica must be persuaded that you embody, in a very fascinating way, all the attributes of a gentleman. Your correspondent must be allowed to intervene.

4. YOUR CORRESPONDENT INTERVENES.

"How goes it, Veronica?" I would purr, fixing her with my fully operational eyes. "I gotta tell you babes, you're looking hot hot hot. What say you to a little drinky after work? There's a cosy Pitcher & Piano around the corner. We could be alone."

5. GAUGING THE MOOD, TONE AND VEIN OF A DATE. EARLY PROBLEMS NIPPED IN THE BUD.

Happily installed in a booth, a draught lager in hand, you are in a position to begin wooing Veronica in the old-fashioned way. Look her in the eye. Listen to what she says. Probably you won't understand a lot of it, but nod appreciatively anyway. Keep nodding. Let the conversation develop at its own pace. Interject, interpolate, inveigh if it seems at all appropriate, but bear in mind that this is not the place for expostulation. If you do expostulate prematurely, a polite cough behind your hankie may go some way towards clearing the matter up.

6. THE END OF THE EVENING. THE EXERCISE OF RESTRAINT. A SMALL COMPLICATION.

Veronica is so sweet and lovely that the evening's conclusion approaches like a terrible punishment or even death. Never mind. The purpose of this first encounter has been merely to break the ice, to straddle the gate, to establish a foothold from which we may undertake a more serious ascent of Veronica's fabulously steep slopes. Take your leave gallantly. Part with a chaste peck on the cheek. No matter how she begs, pleads and implores, let the evening end there. She may demand you to satisfy her, again and again, all night long, but resist. See her home, bid her goodnight, and return to your compact bachelor pad, where I will be calmly waiting for a frank account of the evening's proceedings in the full and certain knowledge that Veronica only went out with you in order to get closer to me.

7. WE APPROACH THAT MOMENT IN WHICH MAN AND WOMAN ARE UNITED IN EPIC, SPEECHLESS BLISS.

Let us suppose now that Veronica, for whatever perverse reason, continues in this foolish tryst (God knows why - there was nothing obscene about those poems, it wasn't me who stole her shoes, and I don't understand why they've moved my desk to the other side of the office). Together, you return from a delicious meal at Pizza Hut, your faces greasy with the sheen which food from that particular establishment tends to produce.

"I say, Veronica," you venture. "What about a chipped mug of tepid Nescafé at my place. We could listen to my new Mogwai CD. Or if you don't like Mogwai, perhaps

The Suede. We could fool around." Veronica finds herself enormously unmoved. You have not captured her interest at all. Your correspondent must again be allowed to intervene.

"Veronica," I would say. "I am a man, with all which that implies. You, I suggest, are a woman, subject also to certain basic needs." Here I would pause for effect. "Let's get naked and urgent and let's do it now!"

Pushing open the front door we fall carelessly upon each other. She tears at my very expensive clothes. We move from the sofa to the sink to the scullery to the utility room to the library and reach a breathless conclusion in the lavatory.

"God!" sighs Veronica. I am forced to agree.

Now do you see? Your approach was meandering. Mine was direct. Yours was vague. Mine was clear. Yours was feeble. Mine was audacious. These are the watchwords when wooing a lady. Veronica won't be forgetting your correspondent in a hurry.

ADDENDUM

So it is in these ways that a chap should conduct his affairs with the ladies. He should concentrate on one at a time. He should seek to be there when they need him. He should respect their dimensions and listen to their words, and he should not seek to make a move on Veronica, right? Just tread carefully there, mate, that's all I'm saying.

THE CHAP, PO BOX 21135, LONDON N16 0WW

THE AUTHOR OF THE LETTER JUDGED TO BE THE BEST IN THE NEXT ISSUE OF THE
CHAP WILL RECEIVE THE GENTLEMANLY REQUISITE OF THE CURRENT ISSUE.

SIR,
Do any of your readers find it difficult to obtain a decent Pousse Café? The last time I had one of these delicious Cocktails was from 'Robert' in the American Bar at the Casino Municipal, Nice.

Recently, after an excellent luncheon at the Burger King in Slough I ordered a 'Golden Slipper' and was disappointed to be informed that this was not available as they were fresh out of Eau de Vie de Dantzig, which as you know is Dantziger   Goldwasser.

Bad show all round, don't you think?

DAVID LE NOBLET OF PRESTON, LONG CREDON,
AYLESBURY, BUCKS

SIR,
I count it as a great personal triumph that the ghastly continental practice of drinking black coffee in my workplace has recently been supplanted by taking tea, indeed, obscure leaf teas, made properly in a teapot. Moreover there is talk of procuring a silver cake stand in the not too far distant future. It is these tiny raindrops that will turn the tide and open the floodgates. I cannot sufficiently express how gratifying was the realisation that I am not alone.

C.M.G.RYAN, CASSIOBURY, WATFORD, HERTS

SIR,
Recently I witnessed a mischief-maker of the lower classes pelt a wood pidgeon with an apple. How is the gentleman to act when faced with acts of such depravity?

P.J.MARTIN, PALMERS GREEN, NORTH LONDON

SIR,
In days gone by I seem to remember that in gentlemen's conveniences there used to be notices by the egress saying "Please remember to adjust your dress before leaving". Surely, in these days of an ageing population whose memories may not be so sprightly as they once were, these useful reminders should be reintroduced. They would undoubtedly prevent much social embarrassment and nights spent in the cells of Streatham, and other, police stations.

MAJOR BETRAM BURBERRY -MACINTOSH,
LONDON SW16

SIR,
I recently purchased a copy of the Chap from my local branch of Borders in Brighton and was appalled to find that someone had inserted a note inside. Obviously some devious tick had taken it upon himself to 'spike' your marvellous mag with an itchy little display of underhand sabotage.
Written, in cheap ballpoint as one could find in the lesser respected turf accountant, was the word 'W**KERS' and on the reverse; 'PILLOCK'. I was shocked and dismayed and my only solace was in the fact that I had discovered it before someone of a lesser stomach had.

Anyhow, I removed the note and placed it between the pages of a well known amateur photographers publication, feeling that there it may be better appreciated.

DUX VESPASIAN BELLORUM

Howard Spent investigates

THE SEMIOTICS OF DRINKING

Some years ago now, in the heady days that might loosely be referred to as my 'youth', to my eternal shame I used to frequent one of the more louche drinking holes in the heart of Soho. Of all the soiled and tragic habitués of this resort, one member of the throng sticks in my mind to this day. Unfortunately, I never discovered his name but his essence still haunts my soul to its innermost core. As a budding observer of the human condition, his attitude struck me at once as epitomising the triumph of laconicism over adversity. Constantly in a state of alcoholic ineptitude, he would wander about the pub enunciating but one intelligible word. That word was "Shostakovich". It seems that through the course of a cultured and no doubt rich life, this fellow, faced with impending alcoholism had gradually condensed his entire existence, with its aspirations and triumphs, into a simple four syllable expression. To some this may have seemed a failure, but to me it represented an achievement close to Zen enlightenment. The masterful selection of one sibilant word, easily pronounceable in a state of advanced intoxication but at the same time of high cultural value, singled him out as a fellow journeyman of erudition and panache.

This is but one example that the squalid world of drinking has to offer, of how complex meaning can be condensed into a brief readable form known as semiotics.

Striding manfully into any place of adult refreshment, one only needs an ounce or two of perspicacity and the eyes in one's head to read the truth of people's lives merely through the way they act. In case you lack either of these qualities, dear reader, there follows a brief summary of my own observations that represents the result of many gruelling months of laborious field work, propping up bars in highly disreputable venues, chatting to ladies of questionable virtue and quaffing stunning quantities of virulent liquor. My suffering is your gain. I humbly offer you the fruits of my labour.

Read and gain insight, for quite rightly did Pliny the Elder pen the eternal words 'In vino veritas'. I exhort you to absorb and memorise these pages for use socially, in business and for pleasure.

THE CONNOISSEUR

This ludicrous looking fellow might know a thing or two about vintages, tails and chocolatey aromas but appearing too finickity and fastidious has never been, and never will be, calculated to win the hearts of ladies. Expertise is often the mask of impotence.

THE SUBLIME

The man who throws his life and soul open to malt whisky, undiluted and sans glace, is a man of rare distinction and impeccable character. More a religious vocation than a drink, ancient malt ordains its imbiber as the heir to dionysus's sacred mantel.

THE VULGARIAN

This demented guttersnipe obviously thinks that he is hip and with-it to drink foreign lager straight out of the bottle. Such an assumption is as sickening as it is wrong-headed. He richly deserves a good thrashing and a savage kick in the billingsgate.

THE ARRIVISTE

A glass filled with a lurid concoction, piled high with fruit and novelty items, singles this man out as a social inferior who imagines that distinction and cachet can be bought by the ounce. His profession in sales is wholly incompatible with being a gentleman.

THE LOVERS

Sweethearts in the first flush of romance are liable to throw all caution to the wind and attempt risky manoeuvres involving drinking whilst linking arms. Such moves are highly foolhardy, may result in serious injury and in rare cases can prove fatal.

THE REAL ALE MAN

There is no shame for a man of sensibility and sophistication to indulge, on occasions, in an honest pint or twelve. By imbibing malty brews and guffawing loudly, this fellow gains the common touch, and, thus, the respect and trust of the hoi polloi.

THE SERIOUS DRINKER

A slight over dependence on the stimulating effects of gin are not a worrying matter, but more a sign of generosity of spirit, and a robust and forthright approach to life. This fellow's highly admirable behaviour makes him a prince among men.

THE SENIOR MAN

To the civilised man about town, indecision as to what to drink should never present a problem. At all times of the day the noble Martini can be regarded as a haven in a fickle and turbulent world. Sexual gratification at this man's hands is virtually guaranteed.

THE UNDER-AGED

Sometimes it can be difficult for a publican or owner of an off-license to spot an under-age drinker attempting to flout the law. This young turk dupes his adversaries by the fiendish ruse of donning a frighteningly convincing facial appendage.

THE DEVIANT

The 15th Earl of Camardenshire's colossal fortune and rather outré temperament might legitimize his theatrical tastes in clothing, but nothing can possibly excuse his drinking of 80's embrocations with names such as 'Taboo', 'Mirage' or 'Zapatista'.

THE TANKARDEERS

Although they are unrelated, Robert and Julian have developed a deep and trusting father-and-son relationship. Their bonding has been helped by a shared love of pewter tankards and frequent cultural vacations to louche resorts on the coast of Morocco.

THE PLAINLY RIDICULOUS

"Sir, there seems to be an extraneous object in the neck of my bottle. Kindly remove it at once". This imported affectation leaves a right-minded fellow irate and perplexed, and is merely designed to disguise the lamentable taste of the lager within.

THE ARTIST

It has long been a tradition among artists and so-called 'creative' people to imbibe cheap but stylish drinks such as Absinthe, Thunderbird and Creosote. Despite ceaseless mythologising about the dangers of such beverages, there is no evidence of long term harm.

THE SINGULAR ADVENTURES OF CECIL DE CASHMERE.

It had all been a bit too much for poor old Cecil, what with flying carpets, trips into space and evil villains from far off lands.

He took to his bed for several weeks, and mulled over his life thus far....

Brought up among servicemen, Cecil had learnt from an early age that life is what you make it..

He was fortunate enough to have been blessed with fairly enlightened parents

AH, THE SOPORIFIC FRAGRANCE OF WINTER'S MELANCHOLY DAWN. ERE WOULD I LAY MY HEAD IN ITS EVERLASTING SHROUD OF GLOOM ...

Even the servants were sources of somewhat unconventional nuggets of wisdom ...

I MAY BE THE BUTLER, SIR, BUT WE ARE ALL SERVANTS OF BEELZEBUB

DON'T LISTEN TO YOUR FATHER, CECIL. DON'T LISTEN TO ME EITHER. WE CAN'T TEACH YOU ANYTHING YOU WON'T FIND OUT FOR YOURSELF. LEARN TO BE THE MASTER OF YOUR OWN DESTINY.

Eccentric uncle Theo was a regular visitor chez de Cashmere. He would turn up with all of Cecil's cousins, and often bring one of his special friends ...

RIGHT KIDS, THIS IS FRANK, AND WE'RE ALL GOING TO PLAY 'HUMILIATE THE CONSTABULARY'

Cecil soon understood the nonsensical nature of material things, much to the horror of less enlightened sorts, such as the poor ...

When experimentation with hallucinogens was all the thing at boarding school, Cecil was more comfortable with the effects than some of his peers.

The more progressive teachers gave him private tuition in Dada poetry

O MAM RE DE MI KY WE HAVE ESCAPED THE WAHHA HO HO

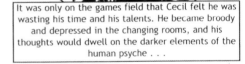

It was only on the games field that Cecil felt he was wasting his time and his talents. He became broody and depressed in the changing rooms, and his thoughts would dwell on the darker elements of the human psyche . . .

He preferred to sneak out of the school grounds and visit galleries showing modern art.

Cecil became such a singular pupil that his form masters could not even analyse his handwriting

THE WAY HE LOOPS HIS G'S SHOWS A CLEAR INDICATION OF . . . WAIT A MINUTE, THIS IS IN ARABIC!!!

Cecil's singular manner and his contacts in the underworld won him plenty of friends by the time he reached the fifth form.

DON'T WORRY OLD CHUM, BY THE TIME MADAME X HAS FINISHED WITH YOU, YOU WON'T BE ASKING ME WHAT AN ASSISTED SHOWER IS!

Their situationist sound sculptures in the nearby village didn't go down very well with the locals .

Cecil and his chums soon developed a healthy disregard for authority

YOU TWO RUFFIANS GOT A LICENSE FOR THAT SOAP BOX FULL OF SHIT?

EXCREMENT TO YOU, MY DEAR FELLOW!

Some of the scenes of adult behaviour he witnessed might have traumatised any ordinary child

But for Cecil, every deviation from the norm was an exciting new challenge . . .

A NEWSPAPER WITH TOTALLY BLANK PAGES. HOW THRILLINGLY AVANT-GARDE!

Cecil and his pals were lucky enough to be introduced to tobacco by one of the tradesmen in the village

TABS, SNOUT, HARRY RAG - CALL IT WHAT YOU WILL, IT'S GREAT STUFF. HERE, TRY SOME!

Cecil's gilded youth was only marred by the magnetic attraction he held for weirdos, freaks and perverts...

A YOUNG MAN CAN OFTEN FEEL VERY ALONE, SIR...

His accidental meeting with his doppelganger proved to be the turning point in Cecil's spiritual development

UNDERSTAND ME AND YOU WILL UNDERSTAND YOURSELF!

Cecil's bohemian credentials weren't much help when it came to searching for gainful employment...

MARSUPIAL EVENSONG OF BEDSHEET RETROGRADE - SPERM, ALABASTER, ROSTRUM

But he always took comfort from the words his father had said to him as a young boy, when they took opium together . . .

DON'T WORRY OLD CHAP. ONCE YOU'VE GOT PAST THE VOMITING STAGE YOU'LL FEEL HEAPS BETTER!

END

CONSUMPTIVE
COSMETICS

Good morning Muse, what's wrong?
Something you saw last night is left in your hollow eyes;
Your colour's bad, your cheeks are cold
With horror, with madness! - and you don't say a word.

The Sick Muse   **Charles Baudelaire**

We can always rely on good old Charlie Baudelaire to articulate a sentiment so subtle, so complex, so recherché, that ordinary folk would not recognise it if it walked up and boxed their ears. And is it any wonder that the muse was as prey to sickness as the poet, when you consider the lifestyle he led? By the age of forty, a combination of syphilis, strokes and hard living had reduced him to a physical and mental wreck, on the verge of insanity and paralysis.

Had Baudelaire been the picture of health, with ruddy cheeks, a robust frame and hearty manner, it is doubtful whether he would have been taken very seriously as a poet. In the 19th century, the fashionable look among bohemians was the wan and sickly pallor of the tubercular poet. "When I was young, I could not have accepted as a lyrical poet anyone weighing more than 99 pounds," Théophile Gautier tells us. A celebrated femme fatale of the period, Princess Belgiojoso, strolled along the boulevards of Paris as gaunt and pale as death in person. But this was not the result of bulimia, or a steady diet of Evian water, cocaine and lettuce leaves such as today's ladies of fashion maintain. Tuberculosis produced 'the look' without any effort at all on the patient's part. The disease's victims were many, though it seemed to favour sensitive, artistic temperaments. "TB was thought to etherealize the personality, expand the consciousness, to aestheticize death," according to Susan Sontag. "The TB sufferer was a dropout, a wanderer in endless search of the healthy place." With TB being very difficult to catch these days, and relatively easy to cure, how can we cultivate the wasted demeanour of the consumptive, and thus impress upon our friends the sensitive, aesthetic nature of our souls? The answer lies in cosmetics. Gentlemen, prepare to rummage through a lady's handbag, or, better still, her bedroom cabinet. Ladies, prepare to make yet another visit to the chemists with a gentleman's funds (the very mention of the words 'ladies' requisites' will have him shielding his eyes while handing you wads of fivers).

The most important aspect of a consumptive's demeanour is the face. Start with an all-over layer of foundation. Add a touch of green to the palest shade you can find, to emphasise the sickliness. A delightfully feverish sheen can be added by daubing Vaseline on the forehead and cheekbones. Now to the eyes: use an eyebrow pencil to draw rings around them, rubbing the black until it blends smoothly with the pale foundation. Some dark mascara, with a touch of Vaseline, will give the eyelids a deathly hue. To the lips, apply a hint of blue, suggestive of a man about to breathe his last. The tongue should appear dull, matt and coated. A black coating can be achieved by regular consumption of red wine, producing a nice dark contrast to the pallid visage.

Excessive smoking should encourage a hacking cough. Increase the strength of your brand to help this, or, better still, smoke cheroots and inhale them. It is all the more effective when you cough if the whole body rattles.

Spend all your waking and sleeping hours clad in pyjamas and dressing gown. Throw all your other clothes away, so you won't be tempted to get dressed. Make sure visitors call in the middle of the afternoon, to emphasise that you are completely inactive. Always receive visitors in bed, under an exaggerated amount of bedclothes. A few additions to your room can encourage the heady aroma of the invalid's bedchamber. Leave the tops off bottles of medicine, allowing their clinical odours to seep into the room. Used bandages, swabs and cotton wool can be left in sinister mounds near the bed, allowing your friends to conjecture the worst.

Your social niceties will need radically rethinking. Be vague about remembering people's names, and pretend to have forgotten they were coming to see you. Act as if every meeting could easily be your last - make melodramatic gestures and grand statements. Languish on a huge pile of pillows, one arm tragically outstretched, while you quote the stanzas of Shelley and Keats you would like to have read at your funeral. Generally try to give the impression that, unlike ordinary people, you are in a heightened state of lyrical sensitivity, inhabiting an ethereal plane of existence which straddles life and death. Emphasise this by allowing some of your sentences to trail off . . . Pretend to fall asleep when being told a fascinating tale. When your friends try to rouse you, stare at them uncomprehendingly for a minute, as if you were looking into the eyes of God or the Devil.

BEFORE

AFTER

Photographs showing an aspiring poet before and after the judicious application of cosmetics

HANDSOME

Vladimir Shokov embarks on a crusade against vulgarity, making some new friends in the process.

An acquaintance of mine recently found himself in need of a public convenience, having just refreshed himself with several light ales in a West End tavern. He had the misfortune to be within the vicinity of Piccadilly Circus, the only conveniences being those situated in the bowels of the underground station. Upon entering the gentlemen's unit, my acquaintance received something of a shock. The entrance of the lavatories was carpeted with various pools of human effluence of a particularly nasty odour; a vagabond appeared to be performing a cursory grooming ritual at the filthy enamel sink, and, worst of all, a young fellow seemed to be pleasuring himself at one of the urinals.

Now, my acquaintance is rather a sophisticated sort: he never leaves his rooms without an exquisite suit of clothes, a pair of gloves and an ebony cane. It fairly brought tears to my eyes when I pictured his elegant figure forlornly micturating at one of the urinals, amid this scene of frankly Rabelasian dimensions. To call it Sodom and Gomorrah would be to bestow it with far more glamour than it deserves. It was, in short, a scene of the most abject vulgarity.

When this experience was described to me, I could only nod my head in mute recognition of all-too-many similarly depraved sights which I had witnessed within this city. I realised that vulgarity, as opposed to the more popular evils such as biological warfare, genetically-tampered foodstuffs and Johnny Foreigner's noxious cheeses, is by far the greatest threat to the future of humankind.

Perambulating through the chilly thoroughfares of this city, my home and my nemesis, I began to observe the scale with which vulgarity had crept into the lives of the townsfolk. A young fellow, clothed in a rather unattractively cut suit with an outrageous four-button jacket, was dashing along Shaftesbury Avenue. He had clearly missed a luncheon appointment, perhaps due to becoming engrossed in one of the city's fine 17th century church façades; in his hands he was clutching a tin-foil container, from which he was spooning into his mouth some revolting oriental concoction, while maintaining an ignoble canter along the pavement. I immediately felt pity for the poor fellow, having myself missed many a luncheon appointment due to architectural appreciation, so I offered him help.

"Discard your perambulatory snack, sir," I said to him, "and join me for a light repast in a pleasant eatery."

His reply cannot be repeated here, but suffice to say it contained a rather unnecessary series of profanities. I shook my head in dismay as I watched him merge with the passing throng, hardly pausing to toss his spent foil container into the gutter.

I had little opportunity to reflect upon this display of vulgarity, before being confronted by another example. As I turned into Great Windmill Street, a young lady stepped into my path, wearing pancake make-up, fishnet stockings and a single piece of red patent leather obscuring her modesty from the world. Without so much as a by-your-leave, she invited me to avail myself of her body, adding that her residence was in the vicinity. Now, my libido is as powerful as the next man's, but I must confess a certain fondness for the subtleties of formality and subterfuge which normally precede a visit to the courts of Venus.

Needless to say, my second offer of luncheon was flatly refused.

I decided on a rare solitary lunch, and proceeded in search of a modestly priced though refined eatery. I found myself upon The Oxford Street, which I believed to be the home of such establishments. However, the friendly little restaurants offering simple home cooked meals that one could wash down with a glass of ale were nowhere to be seen. In their stead were a succession of establishments whose function I found it difficult to determine. Loud music emanated from within the cavernous interiors, where flashing lights illuminated scores of youths, many of whom sported a curious type of headset with a black stick

pointed at their mouths. It was the middle of the afternoon, yet these youths disported themselves in a manner one associated with evening revelry. That is to say, they shouted, jostled one another for attention, gyrated their hips to the thumping music, and loitered around the cubicles at the back of the establishment. All in all, it was a scene of the most obscene vulgarity. I hastened to escape, only to find a succession of similar emporia lining the street.

Curious as to whether I had been mistaken in my geographical calculations, I ventured into another of these establishments to enquire. I approached a spiky-haired youth wearing a headset, and asked whether any charming little eateries still existed on The Oxford Street. The question seemed to confuse him, and he responded with something of a non sequitur: "What size are you, mate?"

Reflecting upon this for a moment, I surmised that it was an indecent proposal of a thoroughly depraved nature. I left the place without comment.

he
c A
P N
a

Droplets of rain had begun to fall; much of the crowd surged into the glittering emporia to seek shelter. I, for my part, remained alone on the pavement, a light drizzle moistening my brow. A half-remembered line from a forgotten film suddenly came to mind: "Someday a real rain is going to come and wash all this away..."

---- ∞ ----

Over the next six months, I immersed myself in a rigid training schedule. Surrounded by the 'vagueness with precision' of Fauré's sonatas for violin and piano, I concocted intricate blends of India and China teas, and spent sleepless nights sampling them, perfecting my cup and saucer control. I mastered new and complex knots for my enormous collection of ties; I starched my shirt collars till they nearly cut my cheeks. My personal grooming routine would last for hours, until I had perfected dazzling acrobatics with a cut-throat razor. I studied cigarette lighting techniques, until I was able to successfully light four cigarettes in a few seconds, with various lighters concealed about my person, including one which shot out of my shirt-sleeve on a species of metal pulley.

Finally, the day arrived when I knew I was ready. Armed with my collection of cigarette lighters, a slim volume of Symbolist verse and some 67 bons mots, I set out for the West End of London.

You must understand that I was in something of a frenzied state of mind. Perhaps I was not quite in full control of my faculties, but my purpose was clear: I felt that I had been selected by the gods of elegance and sophistication to begin the crusade against vulgarity. My subsequent actions, I believed, would clean up the city once and for all, paving the way for the practitioners of virtue, beauty and refinement.

My first stop was Chinatown, where I located the establishment most popular with the yuppies (Oh yes, I now knew what they were called, for I had studied their habits in the newspapers). Discreetly placing myself to one side of the take-away counter, I waited for my 'friend' to appear.

Sure enough, up he trotted, or rather sprinted, in search of his tin foil container of comfort food. He was just about to fling his credit card at the diminutive oriental behind the counter and bark out his order, when I gently touched him on the sleeve. "I think it is time for lunch," I said with a smile, opening my jacket just enough for him to see the cut-throat razor nestling there.

"I see," was his brief reply. He clearly understood, and swiftly pocketed his credit card. We walked side by side to Great Windmill Street, where it took a short time to locate the address of the harlot (Yes, I now knew her moniker, too). We ascended the two flights of stairs, and I knocked on the door. At this point, the yuppie tried to make a dash for it, but I halted him by whipping out my volume of verse and reading him a stanza of Verlaine. This held him rooted to the spot until the door opened. "Well, hello!" said the harlot, "do come in." She tried to show us some sort of price list, but I counteracted with a few witty bons mots, before thrusting her my card and inviting her to lunch.

The three of us strolled up to The Oxford Street, where, with some difficulty, I managed to locate the particular emporium of depravity which I had previously entered. I found the be-headsetted urchin I had spoken to (whom I now knew to be a vendor of poorly-made, overpriced factory clothing). "My good man," I said to him, "I believe it is time for your lunch break!"

He clearly had some difficulty in understanding me above the infernal din in the shop. I shouted directly into his plastic mouthpiece, using a cheap ruse to lure him out of the shop: "My size isn't in stock," I shouted, "You'll have to go to the other branch." He flung off his headset and dumbly followed the three of us out of the shop. Of course, I had already decided where we would go for lunch. I planned to leave nothing to chance on this day of reckoning. I led the dumbfounded trio to 'Laurelei', a delightful little eatery in the heart of Soho, happily untouched by the creeping tentacles of vulgarity.

I let them order whatever they wanted, not that there was much choice (an integral part of the rehabilitation process, for I have noticed that too much choice in consumer-related commodities leads inevitably to vulgarity). I managed to engage the three misfits in a fairly successful trialogue during the meal. Yuppie found that Harlot and himself had attended the same school, and Youth had apparently sold Yuppie a pair of trainers once.

When the meal was over, I demonstrated my skills in the tea-making milieu, having previously arranged this with the proprietor of Laurelei. The trio were visibly impressed. Harlot asked some intelligent questions, such as whether the variable annual rainfall in Ceylon affected the flavour of the teas. We got on to the subject of personal grooming, and Youth brought up the tricky sub-genus of personal hygiene. Harlot was able to enlighten him on one or two scores, and then Yuppie launched into an eloquent tirade against expensive safety razors, resulting in a round of applause from all of us.

It was during coffee and liqueurs that the ice really began to melt. Harlot got out her B&H Superkings (by now, she had graduated to the more acceptable 'Monica'); Yuppie (Philip) whipped out a rather splendid Havana cigar, and Youth (Gary) surprised us with a willingness to smoke at all, drawing out a packet of Marlboro Lights from his tracksuit trousers. Ah, how we smoked! How we laughed! My collection of lighters proved useful, particularly during a tricky moment when all four of us put a tobacco product to our lips at the same time. Philip was the recipient of my swing-motion double-action Zippo, deftly executed at the flick of a wrist.

We adjourned to the Fox and Hounds, next door to the Laurelei, for a few rounds of cognac. By then, I knew that my work had been done. With a few simple lessons in civilised living, I had shown a trio of dormant souls that we did not need vulgarity to foul up an otherwise beautiful existence. It was our divine right to simply say No Thank You to vulgarity and Yes Please to refinement.

---- ∞ ----

I still bump into Philip occasionally on Shaftesbury Avenue, as he leisurely ambles back from a 3-hour lunch at the Laurelei, and we pause to exchange a few lines of Verlaine in front of a splendid Georgian portico.

Monica is now the manager of a delightful little patisserie in Soho, where I often drop by for a cup of tea and some petits fours.

The last time I saw Gary, he was cocking a snook at a brigand of sportswear-clad ruffians on The Oxford Street. They were wearing Nike; he was wearing a Hawkes worsted three-piece and sporting a magnificent cane. The foppish delivery of Gary's acerbic witticisms soon had the better of the ruffians, whose bovine attempts at one-upmanship merely sucked them deeper and deeper into their quagmire of vulgarity.

THE LOST ART OF DOF

**By our etiqutte correspondents
Torquil Arbuthnot and Nathaniel Slipper.**

We live in a world where, sadly, too many gentlemen no longer wear hats. By hats I mean, of course the trilby or the Homburg, the bowler or the Panama, and not the baseball cap worn forwards, backwards or sidewards, nor the Patagonian goat-herd's bonnet (as worn by the embarrassing, yet not embarrassed inhabitants of Camden Town). With the decline in hat wearing has come a concomitant, and regrettable dwindling in the elegant art of doffing. It is not just a question of lifting one's hat from one's head and then replacing it, as if lifting a saucepan lid to check the devilled kidneys are coming along nicely. That different social situations demand different doffs should be as well known as the etiquette of holding a polite conversation with one's ne'er-do-well brother-in-law.

The standard doff (or the "Watson") is used when encountering those who are perhaps not one's social equals, but nevertheless worthy of a gentleman's acknowledgement, for example the bank manager, the vicar, the local bobby. In this situation grip the crown of the hat lightly in the right hand, lift an inch or so with a forward tilting action, and replace immediately in one smooth motion without breaking your stride. Imagine that the brim of your hat contains a barely manageable amount of milk, and you wish to pour a little into a tea cup, without spilling a drop of it of it or slopping any over the sides.

If the "doffee" is some distance away, such as the far side of a croquet lawn, then the hat should be lifted completely from the head so that the doffee can see daylight 'twixt hat and head (the "Chamberlain"). A variation of this doff, (the "delayed Chamberlain") whereby the hat is held aloft for several minutes, is used when standing on the deck of a colonies-bound P&O steamer, bidding adieu to those on the quayside. N.B. When wearing a soft hat, lift by the crown; hard

FING

hats (the bowler, the topper) should be lifted using the brim.

On meeting one's equals or, should such people exist, one's betters, use the Watson doff but lift the hat the merest fraction of an inch. This doff (the "Salisbury") should, of course, be accompanied by a greeting and a comment on the weather, perhaps with an apposite quote from Baudelaire or Mallarmé.

The appropriate greeting to chaperone the doff is of course, "how do you do", said as a statement rather than asked as a question. To one's lessers, one should initiate the greeting. Always allow one's superiors to greet first. The correct answer to "how do you do" is "how do you do", with the slightest of emphasis on the word "you". This is all that is truly necessary, all is well with the world, and one can now continue one's perambulation without continuing the conversation, and not appear even the slightest bit rude.

When meeting ladies on the street, remember that it is incumbent upon the ladies who know you to make the first gesture of acknowledgement, and for ladies unknown to you to proceed with their business as if you were never seen.

Whilst in the bloom of youth, and still a dashing bachelor, should a pulchritudinous young lady pass one in the street, it is just permissible to doff one's hat "gallantly" (the "Logan") (Fig. 1). The right arm should be raised so the upper arm is perpendicular to the pavement, then the hat doffed completely till the lower arm is vertical. The whole arm should then assume an aesthetically pleasing L-shape.

On rare occasions one can utilise the simultaneous doff-and-usher gesture (or the "Shuttleworth-Robinson gambit"). This should be used when taking a blushing debutante to dinner.

One removes the hat completely and segues the doff into a sweeping gesture while simultaneously opening the door (of one's roadster or of the eating establishment) and ushering the young lady therein. However, there is, it must be said, something raffish about this doff, and it should, perhaps, be restricted to those males who affect suede shoes and have a penchant for loud waistcoats.

One is never too young to start doffing. Schoolboys should not raise their caps or boaters: the "Harry Wharton tug" (Fig.2) is the correct way of doffing the cap or boater. With right forefinger and thumb, simply tweak the peak or brim downward a half-inch or so. There is no need to resettle the headgear to its original position, as a young stripling's hair's natural springiness will, providing the youth is not too enamoured of brilliantine, accomplish this unaided.

Distressingly, one will encounter in public certain persons one does not wish to encounter; persons who, for reasons best known to themselves, H.M. Constabulary have not yet put in "chokey." Good manners prescribe one should acknowledge them rather than affect not to see them or make a vulgar and pagan gesture. In such a situation the briefest of schoolboy tugs on the brim, accompanied by one's best military stare and a curt inclination of the head, (known as the "Pierrepoint"), is the correct response. Do not, however, flick the brim of your hat with your forefinger while favouring the ruffian with a narrow-eyed glare: one is not Mr John Wayne encountering Mr Lee Marvin in the high street of Dodge City, and one may find oneself in the unflattering position of chasing one's hat down the street in the manner of the droll Mr Chaplin.

Finally, on no account accompany the doff with any kind of bow, be it a Prussian neck-click (der "von Leese") or a Mediterranean doubling-over (il "ferissione"). This sort of behaviour is not seemly in an Englishman, but is the province of, respectively, the unfeeling Nordic type and the excitable Latin.

Suggestions for further reading:

Gerard de Nerval: Reflexions sur l'Enlevements des Chapeaux
Anon: Tailor & Cutter Vol. 23, Spring 1942 'Correct Deportment of Military Headgear'
Robert Burton: Anatomy of Doffing; an analysis of what Doffing is, its kinds, causes, symptoms, prognostics, and several instances of it; Philosophically, Medicinally, and Historically.
George Du Maurier: Trilby

Fig. 1. **The Logan** - Note the aesthetically pleasing L-shape formed by the right arm.

Fig 2. **The Harry Wharton tug** - The correct mode of doffing for a stripling youth.

THE CHAP, PO BOX 21135, LONDON N16 0WW

THE AUTHOR OF THE LETTER JUDGED TO BE THE BEST IN THE NEXT ISSUE OF THE
CHAP WILL RECEIVE THE GENTLEMANLY REQUISITE OF THE CURRENT ISSUE.

SIR,
I feel I should bring to your attention the horrendous level of service I received at a new lunching house in my village, which appeared to be owned by one Ronald McDonald Esq. Upon entering, no-one took my hat or cane, I was instructed to extinguish my Carey, and there was no table service. Instead they held with a disgusting practice of ordering one's own food from an open kitchen at the back of the premises! As it was breakfast time, I ordered a brace of kippers, four devilled kidneys, a dish of kedgeree and a pot of Darjeeling. When the pimpled knave behind the counter began to titter, I demanded to see Ronald McDonald immediately, but to my horror they produced a deranged simpleton who they had cruelly made up as a clown.

I have since learned that Mr McDonald intends to open another such establishment in the neighbouring village of Westgrove Belmont. Alas! And so the Darkness spreads!

BRIGADIER GORDON VOLANTE, PUDSEY, LEEDS

SIR,
I travel by motor-scooter frequently and my chosen protective outfit is tweed hacking jacket, snowy corduroy trousers and silk scarf. Nothing unusual about that I hear you cry! I still believe that a little more flair could be added.

I had considered spats, do you think this wise? They may raise a snigger amongst the gaudily clad "teddy boys" as I believe they are called, I am however immune to their vulgar grunting that passes for speech.

ADAM FULLER, THE BRITISH MUSEUM, LONDON.

SIR,
I have a young son, and in order to protect him from the hazards of modern day life I have taken to reading him excerpts from your Internet site before bed. Hopefully the magazine itself will be more manageable. Smoking a cigar, drinking a fine malt and operating a ridiculous device with one hundred and five buttons is more than his four-year-old mind can cope with.

DAVID PARSONS, ABOYNE, ABERDEENSHIRE

SIR,
Please thank Sister Millicent Fond for informing people about the joys of consumption. As an opera singer, I have enjoyed many an evening dying slowly, tragically and, most importantly, tastefully. I must say it fires one up.

LADY VON TWEED, BRIGHTON, SUSSEX

SIR,
On my travels about my local town I saw several individuals staving off the potentially hazardous rays of the sun with pairs of spectacles featuring dark, frosted lenses. I proceeded to the nearest optician in the hope of procuring a similarly darkened monocle. Imagine my dismay upon discovering complete incomprehension of my plight in every establishment I visited.

MAJ GEN SL ST LEGER, CANTERBURY, KENT

SIR,
I wish to protest in the strongest possible terms!
In haste,

MAJOR BERTRAM BURBERRY-MACINTOSH

BREAKING A LEG WITH PANACHE

Torquil Arbuthnot and Nathaniel Slipper investigate the art of treading the boards without the incumbent loss to one's dignity displayed by today's young thespians.

"All the world's a stage, and all the men and women merely drink a great deal, commit fornication and get up late" - Holinshed, How's About It, Act 3 Scene IV.

No-one seems to enjoy a more ebullient lifestyle than the actor. Fretting little and strutting oft, he makes his deep-voiced way from club to club, being lauded and spoilt by all he meets, having only to impart scurrilous gossip in return, pausing only to attend lavish awards ceremonies and entertain the matinée masses at the Royal Shakespeare Theatre every other Wednesday in the summer. A recent Oxford University survey revealed that actors have the highest ratio of agreeable claret consumed to actual hours spent at work than any other profession. So which is it to be then, a sober nine to fiver in an uninspiring cubicle in a dismal office in a building that smells of November, or the raffish, easy life of the actor, a life sans alarm clocks, sans cheap suits, sans commuting, *sans la vie en grise*? I thought as much. Step this way please...

So, how to enter this gentle world of Bacchanalian indulgence, pipe tobacco and languorous idleness? Unfortunately, the traditional method involves a year at what is laughingly referred to as 'drama school', where one will fritter away one's drinking hours pretending to be a panda bear, wearing ill-advised tight black clothes and ruining Mr Wilde's perfectly acceptable light comedies by setting them in a Siberian gulag, and having a skinny ginger fellow play Lady Bracknell in the nude. The only thing worth learning from these establishments is how to talk in a basso profundo voice, and this can be achieved without setting foot in a 'studio' or 'rehearsal room', but simply by requesting Turkish cigarettes from your local Tobogganist. If asked, one should always claim to have 'learnt my craft at RADA' – happily this can stand for 'Revelling and Drinking Association', 'Rum And Double Absinthe' or even 'Really Amateur Dramatic Arse', as well as anything else.

Yet surely one should learn the skill and the craft of acting? Of course you must. Happily, all the knowledge that you will need to pursue your new career can be gained from the tragic figure of Mr Dominic Leoline-Smythe, whose role in life appears to involve no more than standing outside the main entrance of these self-styled drama schools and bellowing, "you go on, you say your lines, you go off." A seedy vulgarian he may be, but a man of intimate wisdom of the theatrical arts he is too (along with his detailed knowledge of the inner decor of most of the doss houses of central London).

The unsophisticated actor, armed with his acting knowledge, may now opt for admiring the reduced furniture in a leather sofa shop in Wakefield, wearing a scarlet and yellow dungaree combo on *Playaway* or appearing as a mutilated corpse in *The Bill*. If you believe this to be the next step in the thespian career, then you should abandon this gentleman's quarterly now and begin to affect a regional accent, so that you might end up in any of the penny dreadful soap operas that fill our noctovisual screens.

Priority number one must be the accumulation of anecdotes. Without a sprinkling of these glittering tales, people would tire of your three page spread in the *Sunday Telegraph* colour supplement, let alone your company in Whites. One should begin with the one about Tom Baker and the crate of pineapples, and another about Googie Withers and Beerbohm Tree's wooden leg. On encountering other actors, one will immediately exchange these anecdotes, and hey presto, one has four anecdotes. Eventually one should have a mental encyclopaedia of such tales, ranging from the wildly scandalous (usually involving John Gielgud) to the mildly titillating (Sheila Hancock, say, or Dame May Whitty).

Also, by taking part in this anecdote bazaar, one will make the acquaintance of, and become known to, other actors, with whom one can loaf for hours bartering tales. It is worth noting that none of these fables has to be true, and that it is perfectly acceptable to change any names or incidents, if you think there may be others more appropriate or amusing. Always use first names or nicknames when referring to knights and dames of the stage. If in doubt, invent a nickname and precede it with an endearment; thus, "Darling Boffles Sinden" or "Dear, dear, sweet Stinker Dench."

But the wealth, dear boy, from whence comes the wealth? There must, in your younger days, be some board treading, and before one becomes too consumed with the gout one must occasionally perform the same performance daily and perhaps even twice daily, gruelling though this sounds. Happily, there are a number of parts that are crucial to the play, but take up little of your time.

For example, the Apothecary in *Romeo and Juliet*. Enter midway through the second half, a scene alone with Romeo; deliver your six lines, hand over the poison, exeunt in pursuit of a gin and tonic. Three minutes of your time ensures a comfortable living. Each play will have such significant parts, too important for you to have to play another part, but not important enough that you must be sober for the curtain call. Whilst waiting backstage for your moment *sous les lumières*, you can rehearse your anecdotes for after-show imbibing, as well as picking up some new ones along the way.

And then of course, the film career, and Hollywood. Sadly all the great films have now been made, and rather than seek intelligence, wit or even a good story, modern films simply introduce you to rough ragamuffin creatures who will remove their clothes, drive too quickly and then blow things up, accompanied by needless profanity and the moronic throb of the 'soundtrack'. One staggers from the cinema trying to clap hands over eyes and ears at the same time. Thankfully, there is a shortcut to becoming a film legend, and that is simply never to appear in films. And not appearing in films by being too drunk.

When offered a starring role in a film, along with the fee, you will be offered all manner of sweeteners, perhaps a small Moroccan boy to sort your tobacco for you, or the use of a personal 'Jim' (whatever one of these mysterious items might be). Ensure your contract contains nothing but absinthe, vermouth, champagne (even if it be non Premier Cru), a man to mix you a perfect vodka martini, gin, Pimms, one bottle of Indian tonic water and one lemon. If you begin six hours before shooting, then by the time you stagger in to position, you will continue to stagger until you are in a position on the next film. This is also the perfect time to make wise alterations to the script

(In *En Vacances, En Seine*, Matthieu Severiou's famous entry into the restaurant was such a moment, and the priceless look on Francesca Mangette's face is genuine). Perhaps swinging from the chandeliers, or emerging from the ocean in a white bikini? Happily you will be thrown off set until sobriety arrives. As long as you ensure it never does, you will soon be given a pleasant severance handshake and thrown into the next stage of the actor's life, the anecdotee.

Once an anecdotee, an actor is at the height of his powers, and will never need to work again. People will gather in huddles in green rooms everywhere to recount your latest adventure, before whispering 'No, really?!? Did Sir Ralph ever get the stains out of his waistcoat? Still, you've got to admire the old beagler, haven't you?' And on seeing you in the streets, erstwhile colleagues will propel you to fine eating establishments to hearken at your denials, all the time adding the tale to their anecdotes, and exaggerating it tenfold the next time the tale is told. Likewise with fellow anecdotees, you should wrap up by a warm fire, ingest some vintage port and morphine for the gout, and simply laugh; words will not be necessary, for you have partaken in the finest your profession can offer.

And so to the final curtain, and lighting the way to dusty death. The actor's death is unimportant; you could be run over by a milk float whilst dashing to the vintner's for a hogshead of sweet cider in naught but pyjama bottoms. The importance of the end is the reaction. The country should fall into a grief and wailing as if you were one of the family, as if a national treasure has left for that great proscenium arch in the heavens, and even the lights of the working men's' clubs of the North will be dimmed in respect. And so the obituaries. A typical quote will be, 'He was always so alive, so vibrant', or 'He wanted nothing but to bring joy and enlightenment' and 'But he was more than simply a fellow actor, he was a true and kind friend'. All that these kind and honest recollections really mean is that you toped a great deal and told droll and scandalous stories about people they knew. The lights may be dimmed, but your name will live on, and all for a grand total of no more than six hours' work in your twenties.

So leave behind the life of off-the-peg suits and cartoon character ties, marketing projects and 'dress down Fridays', throw off the veneer of the respectable working life, fire up a Sobranie, curl up with a splendid bottle of gin and turn to a friend, open eyed and hushed of voice, and enquire, "I say, did you hear about Julian Glover on the set of *Mason and Dixon*?"

Howard Spent investigates

BODY ODDIFICATION

In this issue, dear reader, I intend to depart slightly from our usual remit of probing the symbolism and significance of things, and instead turn our attention from the semiotic to the ethnographic. As you well know, my jolly capers in the abstruse gardens of semiology have taken me, at times, far from the hallowed soil of Blighty and into that fearful realm known as 'abroad'. You are probably less aware that during these forays into foreign climes I have compiled an exhaustive library of the ways and customs of many forms of man. Chief among my observations has been the tendency of fellows of many races to alter their physiques and decorate their bodies through a whole host of techniques known collectively as 'body modification'.

Although the modern gentleman might associate the term 'body modification' with the attention seeking antics of so-called 'youth' or the outlandish excesses of the circus freakshow, he should take some time to think again. The fashion for tattooing, for example, took off after Captain Cook's first jaunt to the South Pacific in 1769. Initially the domain of rough-hewn sailoring types, it soon after gained currency in elevated circles. In 1862, when the Prince of Wales visited the Holy Land, he had the Jerusalem Cross tattooed on his arm. His sons followed suit. When the Duke of Clarence and the Duke of York (later King George V) made a visit to Japan in 1882, Edward VII instructed their tutor to take them to the studio of celebrated master Hori Chiyo, who tattooed dragons on their arms.

Today's dandies are once again reclaiming the marginalised territory currently occupied by body modifiers and cleaning up the rather shabby and perverse reputation that 'eco warriors', masochists and other perforated riff raff have given to the art. Going back to the tribal origins of physique tailoring and transforming it into a new chappist discipline known as 'body oddification', the chap now has a wide choice of adjustments he can make to his person that can prove practical as well as decorative. A serious interest in tailoring your physique is guaranteed to make you more memorable and effective socially and in business, but more than that will provide you with endless hours of intense pleasure.

THE QUIZZICAL EYEBROW

Any decadent rake worth his salt will have mastered the technique required for raising a quizzical eyebrow, but sometimes the sheer physical exertion of being arch can lead to neuralgia or even migraine. By replacing one eyebrow with a skillfully trompe l'oeil tattoo, this sterling fellow is assured of a permanent demeanour of knowingness.

THE WASP WAIST

A competent tailor can work miracles in concealing the inadequacies of a fellow's physique, but the effects of a tightly laced corset are difficult to emulate by any other technique. This chap has trained his waist to an elegant girth of 19 inches in order to render his torso an artwork of considerable beauty.

THE TERRY-THOMAS

A natural and wholesome admiration for that screen cad, Mr Terry-Thomas, may lead an impressionable fellow to attempt to emulate the star's irregular dentation. The front teeth may be driven apart through the introduction of a gradually increased quantity of cocktail sticks during the hours of sleep.

THE LIP SAUCER

Inspired by the antics of the Mursi people of Southern Ethiopia, this daring cove has trained his lower lip in a handy teacup holding device. Experienced 'lip saucerers' of an exhibitionist bent have been known to delight all and sundry with a spot of hands-free Oolong consumption.

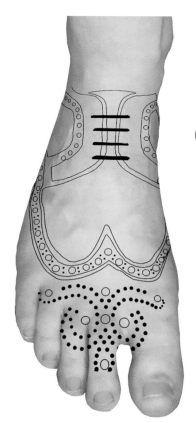

THE CUFFLINK

A man of individuality might blanche at the rather predictable locating of studs and rings in nose, eyebrow or lip. A piercing skewered through the soft flesh on the underside of the wrist is both a subtle and convenient location, enabling a fellow to sport items from his vast collection of cufflinks even when in his bed, the sauna or the bath.

THE INNER BROGUE

The spiritual origins of marking one's skin with needle and ink are maintained in this 20th century classic. 'Finding the inner brogue' is arguably the most important mission a gentleman can indulge in. This tattoo signifies to one and all that the high quality of his footwear is merely the external signifier of a psyche brimming with transcendentalism.

THE GIRAFFE NECK

The 15th Earl's continuing fondness for ladies attire is disturbing enough for his parents and the country set of Camardenshire, but his present obsession with the neck ringing propensities of the Karen Padaung tribe of the Myanmar boarder in Thailand augurs very badly indeed for discreet and inconspicuous attendance at the vicar's annual garden party.

THE CHEEK PIERCING

Pushing knitting needles through one's chops is an outré pastime best left to the itinerant fakirs of India, but, with a little ingenuity, cheek piercings may easily be adapted to the needs of an Englishman. Twin perforations will allow for dual pipe smoking without demobilisation of the mouth, leaving it free for conversation, gormandising or love.

THE SUIT FRONT

This delightful combination of tattooing and subcutaneous button implant is guaranteed to provide the bashful chap with a swift escape route from abject nakedness and its associated realms of rudery. Sartorial elegance even when in the buff is the hallmark of the true gentleman.

THE EXTENDED EAR LOBE

The Amazonian Indian habit of extending the earlobe to unfeasibly large proportions can provide a resourceful chap with handy storage space for essential grooming items such as a shaving brush, a cut-throat razor or (as illustrated here) a comb.

A YEAR IN CATFORD

Provençal viticulturists DIDIER and VERONIQUE CAUDILLON did what their Aix neighbours had only ever dreamed of – buying an authentic South London council flat and living in *Le Style Anglais* for a year. This is the first instalment of their diary for that unforgettable year in Catford, London SE6.

The 2002 Gault-Millau guide describes the Catford franchise of Dixy Fried Chicken as 'the nearest the French traveller is likely to get to the authentic *Catfordois* dining experience.' A posse of teenage girls enjoying a post prandial cigarette in the entrance, their pale *embonpoints* sagging out of nylon tracksuits, was testament to the restaurant's popularity with the locals.

We passed below the neo-modernist *façade* composed of large slabs of brightly coloured Perspex with a comical tricolore chicken motif (though the colour scheme referred to America's finger-lickin' deep south), to be greeted by the maitre d'. This was a middle-aged gentleman from the Levant, whose moustache, sleek with airborne lipids, quivered with puzzlement when we announced that we had reserved a table for two. We wondered whether, like Maison Lefevre in our Provençal home, Dixy operates on a first come, first served basis. Like all the best restaurants, Dixy has few tables – in fact there is only one, which was occupied by a rugged old *clochard* of Scottish descent enjoying a tin of the local moonshine. After a spot of good-natured badinage with the maitre d', he surrendered his table to us.

When we asked to view the menu, the maitre d' merely raised his eyes heavenwards, and above his head we saw a charming fluorescent display of the day's fare, accompanied by helpful colour illustrations. We have always adopted a 'when in Rome' policy on our gastronomic voyages, so we asked the maitre d' what the *plat du jour* was. He motioned a bandaged thumb towards an illustration bearing the enticing sobriquet of 'Family bucket chicken nugget mega meal'.

Within a few seconds, a pimpled youth put his head over the counter and said, "D'you want coke or Fanta with that, mate?"

"*Attendez, monsieur*," we said, consulting our Gault-Millau for guidance. We read that it is an English custom to serve a complimentary beverage with meals such as these, so we grasped the opportunity of sampling the local tipple and plumped for the coca-cola. We received a generous plastic beaker each, and immediately experienced the world-famous numb teeth sensation that accompanies this diabetes-inducing beverage. The food was superb: breaded *brochettes* of reconstituted *poulle* with *porc* traces drizzled with *sauce tomate*, with deep-fried shards of potato-flavoured monosodium glutamate, accompanied by *juliennes* of cabbage, carrot and onion in a sweetened *aioli*, all served in a rustic cardboard bucket.

As our first English luncheon battled its way into our digestive systems, we realised what an adventure it was going to be adapting ourselves to South London gastronomic customs over the coming year.

Like so many Provençals, we had often returned from our customary annual *soujourn* in London with the feeling of having only scraped the surface of that wonderful city. It was like being wrenched away from an urban paradise, making our life

on a 34-acre farm in the Luberon Mountains seem hum drum and monotonous. Our modest vineyard, our three goats, our olive oil press, our swimming pool with views over the mountains, lunches with neighbours that lasted all afternoon under cloudless azure skies – they were all very well, but we often yearned for a life more steeped the edgy, gritty urban authenticity that can only be found across the Channel. So one year we thought we'd make a go of it. Rent out our six-bedroom farmhouse in Provence to some gullible Britons, take a little maisonette in Catford and see what Providence threw at us.

The estate agents we contacted in Catford seemed more than eager to help us find a 'typical' abode in the area, and after viewing several *chi-chi* apartments in nearby Blackheath, we soon found exactly what we were looking for: a dilapidated ex-local authority two-bedroom flat on the Dregnor Estate, just between Catford Shopping Centre and the Catford Gun Company.

The flat needed a few repairs, for the previous tenants seemed to have left in rather a hurry. There were curious scorch marks up the walls, the doors had large holes in them, and the floor was a carpet of empty beer cans and hypodermic syringes. The fixtures and fittings had all been removed, so effectively we would be buying a blank canvas to decorate as we wished. "*C'est vraiment charmant!*" we shouted to the estate agent, knocking on his

locked car window. £250,000 and a surprisingly small amount of paperwork later, number 23, Dregnor House, Catford was ours.

Since our vision was to abandon our simple Provençal ways and immerse ourselves in the authentic British Metropolitan existence, we wanted to decorate the flat entirely in *Le Style Anglais*. We would spend a year eating, drinking and sleeping exactly as the Catfordians did, and after a year, *qui sait?* We might even settle here for good.

The first step was to have the water, gas, electricity and telephone reconnected. We were asked to supply monumental amounts of identification, birth certificates, blood tests etc, before any negotiations took place. The previous tenants must have been a lively lot! Life at Dregnor House must have been one long party – and we were determined to keep things on a similarly crazy footing!

We purchased a large fridge, several cases of lager, a CD player and some discs by local musicians. Matching nylon tracksuits completed the picture, and we spent the first evening of our new life in a whirl of Tenents Super, Pringles (wafer-thin slices of pan-fried starch marinated in essence of shallot and *fromage*) and the evocative strains of 'So Solid Crew'. The neighbours, drawn to the sounds of music and good cheer emanating from our flat, were eager to introduce themselves, and soon the flat was a medley of friendly faces.

In the spirit of good neighbourliness, we kept up a steady supply of lager to our new friends, trotting up and down the seven flights of stairs to the off licence that never seemed to close.

In the ambience of cordiality, one of our neighbours must have mistaken our stereo for his own, as it was missing by the morning. But here was the joy of council flat dwelling: we would only have to put the word out, and we felt sure that soon the mistake would soon be rectified.

We soon realized that social life in our block tended to revolve around the sound system. Our neighbours rather quaintly tried to outdo each other throughout the day by cranking up the dials on the stereo equipment. We lived among the perpetual rattle and boom of competing sound systems, leading to constant headaches and small piles of brick dust in the corner of the living room. We loved it. This was *La Vie de Riley*.

It was clear that the essential requisite for an authentic Catfordian lifestyle – the SE6 equivalent of our four-metre stone outdoor dining table in Provence – was a state-of-the-art sound system. But how would we find *le chose authentique*? We consulted advertisements in shop windows and local newspapers placed by local disc jockeys on their uppers. After making a few calls, we found ourselves in the tiny bedroom of a fellow who called himself MC Muthafukka for a living – although his parents had addressed him as Otis when ushering us into his boudoir.

Otis/Muthafukka had an impressive array of machinery, which the constraints of an impoverished background and being fifteen had not appeared to hinder. We returned to our flat with over £3,000-worth of audio equipment and Badman's assurance that it would produce some 'mongin' sounds.

For the remainder of our home décor, we set off on Sunday morning to one of South East London's famous markets. Sedgehill Field Boot Sale takes place every week from 6am in a muddy field off Southend Lane. The boot sale is as much a social occasion as an opportunity to trade household items. A powerful smell fills the air, a blend of strong tea, fried onions, cigarettes and last night's booze. Couples manning the stalls mainly consisted of a rotund lady swaddled in pink nylon, sucking on a Raffles king size and putting on a brave face, while her hungover-looking husband lurked near his car reeking of old pub and probably wishing he were dead. We breakfasted in *Le style Catfordois* –

tranches of *porc fumé* in a griddled *brioche* drizzled with *sauce brune*.

Searching in vain for the type of stall you find in Provencal markets, piled high with pungent cheeses, fresh fruit and tasty viands, the nearest we found was one old costermonger selling family packs of Wagon Wheels. Most of the stalls specialized in second hand clothes, toys and bric-a-brac, some peddling indispensable requisites such as novelty lighters, large smoking papers and Duracell batteries.

This was an opportunity of decorating the flat with genuine Catfordian cast-offs. We ended up with a marvellous collection of souvenir plates from Mallorca, some plastic-framed prints of puppies and kittens, a couple of copper reliefs depicting village scenes and some horse brasses. When it came to clothes we were spoilt for choice. There were tracksuits – *de rigueur* among the Catfordian populace – in every size, shape, colour and style, whose brand names were all very similar: Tommy Hillfiger, Tony Halfrigger and Timmy Hellfinger.

By the time we had left the market, the hour was inching its way towards one o'clock, which could only mean one thing.

This particular Sunday we were in the mood to sample the delights of the famous English 'pub lunch'. A number of local places were recommended by the Gault-Millau, but as we drove in search of one we passed a tavern that seemed to epitomize the traditional English pub. Its name was The Green Man. We tossed our Gault-Millau into the back seat of the car and entered it doors.

The saloon style interior was instantly appealing. At several of the tables sat clusters of wounded young soccer *aficionados* nursing the previous day's scars in Stella Artois, sucking on Benson & Hedges for added comfort. At the bar, their middle-aged counterparts (their parents?) swaggered about displaying their enormous *embonpoints* and their sunburned tattoos, engaging in playful badinage richly peppered with their coarse *argot*.

We took a table and ordered a round of chilled lagers to whet our appetites for a stupendous Sunday feast. Much like Les Deux Garcons in Aix, The Green Man has no menu. At Les Deux Garcons this is because the day's delicious fare is the spontaneous creation of the eccentric 3-Michelin-starred chef, Laurent Desoux. At Catford's The Green Man, the reason there is no menu is because there is no food. Our requests for the bill of fare were greeted with much hilarity by the fellows ensconced at the bar. So we asked them to suggest

to us what the typical Catfordian would do for his Sunday luncheon.

"Stick around mate, we'll show you how it's done."

This seemed like a good opportunity to discover the local customs at first hand, so at their invitation, we joined the hearty fellows for a lager or two more. As the guests, we felt that etiquette demanded that we pay for the drinks, and soon the jovial gathering had swollen to fifteen or twenty locals.

There is a not unpleasant (though not wholly pleasant) numbing around the temples that is the result of several flagons of draught lager. With persistent consumption, a further sensation begins to occur which can best be compared to having one's eyeballs removed, allowing someone to play table tennis with them, then wrapping them in sandpaper and replacing them in the skull. By eight pm, with only a packet of salt and vinegar crisps under our belts, we asked our new friends when the aforementioned 'bite to eat' would take place. "Don't worry about that mate – you don't wanna waste valuable drinkin' time. Mine's a pint of Fosters and a double Southern Comfort."

At half past ten we finally emerged, swaying from the Green Man into the chill night air. Our friend led us towards what they promised would "make you wish you'd drank a few more lagers!"

We sincerely doubted it, as they bundled us into an establishment named 'Best Turkish Kebab'. The smell within was too overpowering for us, so we waited outside.

Presently our friends emerged carrying armfuls of paper packages, two of which they handed to us. We copied our acquaintances by tucking into them right there in the street, under a light drizzle, our faces lit by the glare of neon and passing car headlights. The repast turned out to be the most delicious meal we had ever tasted. A *pain levain* filled with slices of a spit-fired lamb-flavoured offal *terrine*, which we could see blistering in the window of the establishment, with a julienne of *salade tiede* and a unique chili *jus*. Every mouthful seemed to fill some aching chasm created by the volumes of lager inside us.

Although we were used to long lingering lunches of seven or eight courses, accompanied by several different wines and punctuated by a *trou Provençal* – a light serving of sorbet to cleanse the palate between courses – the English tradition had its own peculiar charm. The afternoon had been one long *trou Catfordois* between a long-forgotten breakfast and this Middle Eastern midnight repast.

At a grand total of 164.76, including an afternoon's worth of lager, a large doner kebab for each of our hosts and several packets of Benson & Hedges, lunch *a-la-Catford* had not come cheap, but it had certainly been an authentic English experience.

CLASSIFIED

SITUATIONS VACANT

Picturesque hermit, with at least 3 years experience, required. An exciting opportunity to work with the landscape gardening team at Floodsbury House, Wiltshire. Must be in possession of long white beard and able (when tracked down) to entertain visitors with rare nuggets of bucolic insight. Preference will be given to the candidate who can demonstrate an ablity to survive on a diet of woodland fungi, frog spawn and small rodents. Dank cave supplied. No vegetarians. Telephone Floodsbury 045

Houseboy required for large rambling mansion in Wigan. Duties to include basic errands, housework, parlour games and Mexican wrestling. Would suit almond-eyed Turk of no fixed abode. Accommodation and weekly rations of Vermouth, Gentlemen's Relish and body lotion provided. Call Wigan 249.

Assassin. Disinherited peer, inexperienced in such matters requires the services of a professional hitman to 'cash in the chips' of close family member. Five-figure payment as soon as title and deeds to extensive estates have been transferred to own name. Confidentiality guaranteed. Contact: Julian, 12th Viscount of Tiverton (pending), on Tarvin 905

PET SERVICES

AVUNC-U-LIKE uncle walking service for tired, lonely or depressed uncles. Our walkers are fully trained in pipe filling, Times Crossword assistance and leather elbow-patch maintenance. Uncles are walked in groups of maximum six in local parkland, with a visit to a pub. Their tweeds get an airing, they get to meet other uncles, and they are given a listening ear to their half-baked theories on space travel and bovine telepathy. Call Preston 064.

Panther Hire. Make an impression the next time you visit the opera or a film premiere. Hire one of our range of big cats as the ultimate fashion accessory. Diamond studded collars and insurance on request. Phone Stroud 499

CHILDREN'S ENTERTAINERS

"MR BEAST" – unique magic act for children's parties, featuring Black Mass, devil-worship, hobgoblin invoking and sinister chanting. Kids will love this dark night of the soul; guaranteed emotional instability for a lifetime. Call Hounslow 666.

"MAD" MALCOLM THE CLOWN, for birthdays, christenings, circumcisions. "Mad" Malcolm is a clown with a difference – he isn't funny! Look, kiddies, who's that lurking in the garden with too much mascara and a ginger wig, sharing a bottle of Teachers and a packet of woodbines with little Simon – it's "Mad" Malcolm! Contact Malcolm at Secure Unit, HMP Belmarsh.

HOUSEHOLD SERVICES

MR BEAU CRUMPLE. Break in newly tailored suits, trousers and jackets the easy way. Our staff of fully-qualified suit trainers can give your pristine attire that 'lived in/died in' look much favoured by the English aristocracy. We employ only tried-and-tested techniques such as thrashing about on heather moorland or sleeping in gutters. Satisfaction guaranteed. Scarborough 277

EXOTIC SHEDS. Tired of pottering about in your shabby, dilapidated garden shed? Let us convert it into a Turkish bath, an Indian marble pleasure palace or even a fully staffed Moroccan Souk with a realistic desert surround! If you've recently had a few complaints from your neighbours about the height of your hedge – give them something to really witter about! Call Stockport 351.

Howard Spent investigates

THE SEMIOTICS OF EYEWEAR

Some time ago, a reader of this august periodical wrote to me, suggesting that I turned my semiotic observations towards the realm of eyewear. The reader (whose name I am sadly unable to recall) rather flippantly suggested that the title could be Semioptics. Though such blatant tomfoolery would be enough to alienate most serious men of science, I pride myself on never dismissing the musings of the layman merely because they may initially appear ill-hewn or irritatingly jocular. Indeed it will no doubt strike seasoned readers of this section that the appraisal of a man's human condition, social status and psychological profile merely through the optical instruments he chooses to secure to his face is an eminently reasonable avenue of semiological enquiry.

The eyes, if we are to believe popular sentiment, are the windows to the soul and act as dual conduits by which we perceive and are perceived by the outside world. Our language is peppered with phrases relating to our eyes. Gents often see eye to eye or endeavour to brow beat one another, and as far as the ladies are concerned, making eyes, winking or maintaining a mischievous glint are all essential weapons in the art of wooing. It is beyond the scope of this article (and indeed this publication) to venture too deeply into the abstruse (and often disturbing) ways of womanhood, but it might be noted in passing that ladies are far more adept at realising the full potential of their ocular orbs than we are. The eyes to the average female are what the sting is to the scorpion - a formidable weapon, ever poised and pregnant with deadly allure. Much time

and effort is taken to attract attention to them through the use of gaudy pigment and false eye lashes. It is telling indeed that Saint Lucy became so aware of the attracting power of her own dainty orbs that she was prepared to tear them out, rather than subject herself to the ravishings of a potential suitor.

But, dear reader, I find myself teetering on the edge of digression into an area better left to a future article. For the moment, let us return to the gentleman and the way in which he chooses to frame or otherwise enhance his visual apparatus. All fellows at one time or another have found it useful or necessary to adopt optical equipment to improve their eyesight or appearance. From the jeweller's eyeglass to the many species of spectacle; from Innuit snow goggles to monocles, whatever contraption a chap elects to wear, it is bound to speak volumes about his state of mind, his future hopes and his stolen dreams. If the eyes are the windows to the soul, then then a pair of spectacles or other ocular adherence may act as the gaily-painted shutters, the elaborate pediments, the ornate stucco work, or, indeed, the veritable window-boxes of a man's psyche.

So keep a sharp eye out for the varieties illustrated in the following pages. A keen observation of one's fellow man in the realm of opthamological enhancement will provide you with a head start in the game of life, and will allow you instantaneously to judge the difference between decent fellow and utter scoundrel. The semiotics of eyewear is guaranteed to prove an invaluable aid for use socially, in business and for pleasure.

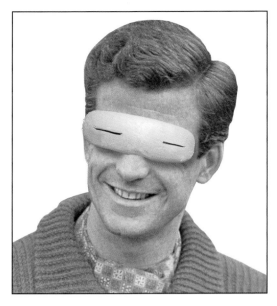

THE PRETENTIOUS

Hand-crafted Innuit snow goggles are apparently a-la-mode with the indigenous peoples of Alaska, but such eyewear is infra dig when donned as as 'ethno-fashion' by those who inexplicably decide to dwell in the inhospitable wastes of Notting Hill.

THE THEATRICAL

The 15th Earl of Camardenshire's family are willing to turn a blind eye to his 'artistic' tastes in clothing, but are dismayed that his choice of spectacles demote him from the haughty echelons of genuine peerage to the lowly role of pantomime dame.

THE LOUCHE

Regarded by some as the apogee of ocular apparatus, the lorgnette is a perfect choice for the exquisite or decadent gentleman. It is particularly suited for lascivious ogling as bedouin boysevants gyrate shamelessly to the intoxicating rhythms of Beelzebub.

THE POST-IRONIC

By self-consciously donning a pair of 'nerdy' glasses and replicating the fashion errors of his forefathers, this fellow believes that he is being 'with it' and knowing. Slavish adherence to the dictates of fashion is a degenerate's method of bolstering flagging self-esteem.

THE PROSTHETIC

A chap of bravado and spunk won't allow a simple war wound to diminish his usefulness. The possession of a glass eye is something that all young turks can aspire to. It is particularly efficacious in keeping children entertained at parties or whilst babysitting.

THE ADENOIDAL

Pince nez are secured to the face by the touchingly literal Gallic expedient of 'pinching the nose'. This optical item has long been associated with the avant-garde intelligentsia, which no doubt accounts for the particularly nasal tones of the French tongue.

THE SUBLIME

The universal badge of seniority and savoir-faire, the monocle is the hallmark of the man to be reckoned with. Its effectiveness is somewhat diminished, however, if sported in conjunction with well-meaning but crudely-crafted items knitted by one's maiden aunt.

THE VULGAR

Common-or-garden rock stars or has-been disc jockeys sometimes imagine that the wearing of sunglasses is enough to render them masculine, sexually potent and youthful. Concealing the direction of one's gaze is the first refuge of a scoundrel.

THE STUDIOUS

This pitiful acned boffin would rather strap a jeweller's glass to his eye and ponder the mating habits of ants than seek the love of a robust young lady of child-bearing age. The rarefied world of academe is all too often a disguise for sexual inadequacy.

THE RIDICULOUS

Moral bankruptcy and a dearth of imagination can lead to a fellow trying to win favour by wearing novelty sunglasses of outlandish proportions. This nincompoop fondly imagines himself to be rather eccentric and 'off the wall'. He most definitely is not.

THE CALCULATING

This stylish cove is acutely aware of the importance of being correctly equipped for a night at the theatre. Opera glasses are an essential viewing device for 'casing' the priceless baubles laying atop the perfectly framed contents of a burgeoning décolletage.

THE VAIN

A fellow can find himself so intoxicated by his own physical beauty that he is unwilling to pollute his features with spectacles. This deluded specimen might be better advised to jettison his contact lenses altogether lest he stray too close to a mirror.

ALUMNUS ELEGANTIS

Torquil Arbuthnot and *Nathaniel Slipper* *advise the university student on ways to ensure that his seat of learning is a sedan chair of opulence and debauchery*

Whilst this magazine offers much advice and counsel to those people to whom Chappism does not come naturally, it is vital that attention is paid to the next generation of gentlemen. Callow-faced youths may be too easily distracted from the path of dignity and sophistication by the barbaric caterwauls of popular music, or worse, the lure of denim and nylon. They may never know of the joy of the briar, the sparkle of a vodka martini or the pleasure of relieving Mr Ladbroke of 60 guineas after the 3.15 at Doncaster. The young are at their most vulnerable on fleeing the security of the family home or the public school, and being surrounded by like-minded ingrates who may have the audacity to assume that seventeen pints of "snakebite" in a sticky floored "nightclub" is the essence of existence. Thus, this guide is aimed at those young people thinking of or already attending university. By following these instructions, a member of the younger generation can maintain their respect and be looked upon by the general public as an example of unbridled panache and *élan*, rather than a tax-dodging, bedizened loafer.

There is, of course, only one university in Britain, and that is Oxford. Many other cities and towns claim that they also have similar establishments, but a true chap would blush from spending three of their formative years in some concrete monstrosity of the Midlands, or the dark satanic mills of the North. One is not to be fooled either by members of the royal family who opt to join the arts-and-craft communities of our Caledonian cousins. Intelligent homosexuals are permitted to attend the University of Cambridge, which offers a variety of courses on espionage leading to worthy careers working for the KGB in mysterious buildings south of the Thames.

Oxford, as you are doubtless aware (but those you wish to influence may not be) is made up of a number of colleges, and it is essential to choose appropriately. Otherwise one will be mired in some Stygian examination-factory full of northern scholars and other low personages, and one will but hear rumours of gentle sophistication, and occasionally catch a glimpse of fine fellows clad in finest tweed in retreat from lecture theatres in search of splendid beverages. Christ Church and Keble come highly recommended, Keble particularly, as it has high church connections, which always come in useful when explaining one's actions to the magistrate. Lincoln is also tolerable, and possibly Magdalen (although our old scout warns us that they admit what he calls "grungy sorts" as well these days). If these fail, then St John's, Trinity, University, Worcester and St Benet's Hall will suffice, although you will be in a minority, and must treat your time there much as a nineteenth century missionary would have in attempting to spread the Chappist credo. Sadly, even Oxford has its hot-beds of all-embracing

An undergraduate should ensure that his modest accomodation is furnished in a style that befits a gentleman.

Symbolist poetry. If one's finances run to it, employ an amusing dwarf to pass round the cocktails; but if one is financially embarrassed, make do with a pet badger with a tray of canapés strapped to its back.

A miniscule proportion of your time at these temples of education could be spent desperately trying to complete assessments or cram for examinations, so it is essential to choose a course that will pose no intellectual challenge whatsoever (and where you may also meet like-minded gentlemen). Therefore, at all costs, one must choose an Arts subject that one is already vaguely knowledgeable about. No interesting books have been written since Mr Rider Haggard's splendid *King Solomon's Mines* in 1885, so English literature is unlikely to expand in the near future. Likewise, History has remained fairly stagnant since the Relief of Mafeking. Foreign languages are also a gentle option, as it matters not if one graduates without being able to speak a word of a foreign lingo, *The Chap* having recently begun a policy of scattering copies of this august publication overseas. Therefore not only will Johnny Foreigner speak the Chap's English, they will also be able to advise on the nearest establishment where one's moustache can be appropriately waxed.

The sciences are to be avoided at all costs. Not only are they exceedingly difficult and require a gentleman to spend inordinate amounts of time in a laboratory staring blankly at the periodic table, but also one will be surrounded by the strangest sort of creature one would fear to meet. These fellows (there are no ladies in the world of the scientist) will have a complexion that appears never to have seen sunlight, hair that has never been in contact with a barber's implements, nor even a plunge of brilliantine, and their garb will consist of ill-fitting black "t-shirts" bearing extraordinary messages, such as "Napalm Death" or shiny acrylic garments bearing the legend "Sunderland FC". A true chap will never gain a degree in science, as the horror of these forced-upon companions will send him fleeing from the building to settle in a dingy cellar for three years' contemplation with the hookah.

The main dangers to which one's dignity will be exposed will come from other people. Sadly, as ever in this brave new world, not

radicalism and rent strikes which must be avoided at all costs: for example Pembroke, and to some extent Wadham, Somerville, Exeter, Hertford and Queen's. Balliol can have its over-enthusiastic students, but has enough of a tweed-clad contingent to make it bearable.

On arrival at one's college, one must immediately redecorate one's rooms with black leather wallpaper, peacock fathers, a sheaf of assegais over the chimneypiece, several daguerreotypes of oneself on safari, a collection of shrunken heads, a Nantucket harpoon ("went whaling in me gap year") and leather-bound, travel-bruised editions of 'Sapper', John Buchan, Biggles, "artistic" magazines, Thesiger (Ernest, not Wilfred) and volumes of everyone lives on a diet of couth manners, esoteric literature and impressive liqueurs, and at university one will be exposed to these others, therefore one should choose one's friends with more care than normal. When joining societies, it is imperative that future implications are considered. What may at first seem like an elegant collection of young gentlemen of the Hellfire Society may soon become a pathetic collection of pock-marked specimens comparing episodes of American television programmes set in outer space and bemoaning the continuation of their virginity in little over two months. However, when one inevitably becomes President of the Union, using nefarious methods made traditional by the least civilised members of the Empire, the opportunity to surround oneself with the most sparkling minds, and perhaps a dazzling lady to make the tea and begin your biography, will present itself. It is at this point that one will require the elimination of the dreadful fellows that were met during the early days of term, with their "I did rather well in my A-levels, two Cs and a D"; "after Coventry I went travelling to Leicester, but it's simply too commercial and popular these days, so we hitched to Derby and travelled there for a while" and "I do miss my mum, I want to go home, where's teddy?"

Should the Chap not wish to attend Oxford, the only other establishments worth frequenting are the Universities of Heidelberg and Ruritania.

At the former one can obtain duelling scars, blood-brotherhood, Palatinate beer and flaxen-haired maidens; at the latter one can wear funny hats, partake in comic-opera revolutions, and end up as Minister of Culture (where one can make statutory the Noonday Absinthe Power Nap). Do not make the mistake of going to the Sorbonne. Instead of sipping a Pastis and swapping *bons mots* with Henri de Montherlant, one will find oneself ripping up the agreeable cobblestones of the Boul' Mich' and lobbing them at blue-chinned riot police – scarcely the way a gentleman wishes to spend his education.

At the end of the academic year, one will spend a few hours in a fractious hall, easing through the examinations, where, in three hours, one will produce more written work than has been done in the whole of the previous nine months. Contrary to advice, one should never read the exam questions too closely, but simply write all that one knows about a particular subject, and assume that, in the midst of it, a fusty academic will discover that you are far too clever for his silly questions and award you the highest mark imaginable.

The true *ur*-chap will, however, never set foot in an examination hall, having contrived to be rusticated mid-way through his final year for stoning the college swan to death with empty gin bottles.

PIPE SMOKER OF THE YEAR

This year Stephen Fry won the coveted title of Pipe Smoker of the Year, an award created in 1964 by the The Pipesmokers' Council to honour a distinguished pipesmoker and to raise money for charity. Mr Fry's name now stands alongside such luminaries as Sir Harold Wilson, Peter Cushing, Sir Patrick Moore, Tony Benn and Dave Lee Travis. The Chap had the pleasure of meeting Mr Fry at the lavish award ceremony at the Savoy Hotel in London, where Gustav Temple put some pertinent questions to him on the position, both moral and political, of the pipe smoker in modern society.

Mr Temple: What signals would you say are given out by smoking a pipe as opposed to smoking a cigarette?

Mr Fry: **A pipe gives a man an air of authority and purpose. Unlike, say, the French, we British are ashamed to show any signs of individuality. Smoking a pipe marks one down as a dangerous eccentric, an image which most British people are not comfortable with. The French are unafraid of being perceived as bourgeois, so they will adopt external symbols of it such as pipes and hats quite readily.**

Mr Temple: Can smoking a pipe be used as a seduction tool?

Mr Fry: **Indeed. Many ladies are drawn to the image of a pipe smoker as a trustworthy, dependable individual. The patron saint of pipe smokers, Sherlock Holmes, has created an association between smoking a pipe and possessing mental acuity. Not only that, but the pipe also has pacific connotations, which the ladies find reassuring. There is nothing aggressive about a pipe.**

Mr Temple: Is the use of a pipe clenched between one's teeth, as featured in many 1950s DIY manuals, conducive to manual labour?

Mr Fry: **The pipe clenched between the teeth of the DIY enthusiast signals that he has put his boy racer days behind him and is ready to settle down. I personally would be inspired with far more confidence in a builder if he smoked a pipe. Then perhaps one wouldn't find so many roll-up butts scattered all over the floor when he has finished.**

Mr Temple: Would you ever consider laying floorboards while smoking a pipe?

Mr Fry: **I would rather smoke a pipe while watching someone else lay them.**

Mr Temple: Would it make any sense to allow pipe smoking in zones where cigarettes are banned?

Mr Fry: **There are certainly many restaurants which do not allow the smoking of a pipe, whereas they quite happily permit their customers to smoke cigarettes. Interestingly, it is more the *idea* of the pipe that such establishments fear. Once presented with the beautiful aroma of some choice tobacco, such restaurateurs soon lower their objections.**

Mr Temple: What single situation in your life would have been far more pleasant if you had been in possession of your favourite pipe?

Mr Fry: **Recently I have been directing a film, a very stressful process in itself, especially in pre-production. Everyone seems to be firing all manner of questions at me the whole time, expecting immediate answers – what colour tie, where should this go, and so forth. As was Harold Wilson's habit, I find the deployment of the pipe very useful as a way of gaining a few extra moments to consider my answer. If I begin the process of filling the bowl and lighting the pipe, I am not perceived as evading the question, and I am then able to give a satisfactory answer.**

LETTERS

THE CHAP, PO BOX 39216, LONDON SE3 0XS

PATUM PEPERIUM
IN MARE INTERNUM
THE GENTLEMAN'S RELISH
The Original
1828 Recipe
DELICIOUS ON HOT TOAST

THE AUTHOR OF THE BEST LETTER WILL RECEIVE A POT OF PATUM PEPERIUM: THE GENTLEMAN'S RELISH. CAPTAIN ROSCO 'BISCUITS FRUIT' VAN NOOTE IS THIS ISSUE'S WINNER.

SIR,
I should be grateful for a soupcon of advice (as our Gallic cousins would say – if they spoke imperfect English) regarding a matter of some domestic urgency. I have over the past few months been cultivating a lifestyle that one would, with the benefit of operatic referends, describe as bohemian. To wit, I have decided to become a writer of some languor and frivolity and have, to that end, endeavoured to contract tuberculosis, as is befitting of all such decent chaps.

However, after introducing a small colony of rodents into the boudoir, I have received a number of complaints from Her Majesty's Inspectors of Public Sanitation. My efforts have unfortunately been extirpated in the interests of the stalking menace of hygiene in the clean living echelons of my neighbourhood. My question, Sir, is this: are there any other methods by which one may acquire a fatal disease in keeping with the ambience of a dusty garret that would not infringe upon the baser needs of one's neighbours?

SIR ARTHUR WYKEHAM-SPATS, LONDON

SIR,
Having seen all the fuss made in the penny dreadfuls of the supposed "grooming" of youths by pederasts, I have been keeping my eyes peeled for the results. So far I have not spotted a single youth displaying even a modicum of personal elegance, let alone evidence that he has been in contact with comb, brush or brilliantine in recent weeks. The boys in my neighbourhood continue to sport the scruffy clothes, unruly haircuts and coarse manners to which I have reluctantly become resigned over the years.

I do wish the gutter press would not get one's hopes up!

Yours,
VISCOUNT MONTAGUE SEBASTIAN URQUHART
KNOCKHOLT, KENT,

SIR,
I was drinking in my usual haunt when a most attractive lady in Salvation Army uniform engaged me in conversation, promising a life changing experience should I accompany her to a meeting. Initially disappointed to find it was a Bible meeting, I was soon gripped by the telling of the parables, though less taken by the exhortation to forgo alcohol.

Looking for my car afterwards, my new-found fervour was soon put to the test when I saw a man groaning in the gutter. He was outside a low drinking den and I presumed his attackers were inside spending the spoils they had robbed from him. Should I *pass by on the other side?* No, I would be the *good Samaritan!* I lifted him in my arms and asked his name. His mumbled reply sounded like *"Mind your own flock,"* a clear reference to the parable of the lost sheep! I *set him on my own ass*, actually the back seat of my ageing Riley. There is no reference to how the good Samaritan should react to the victim being sick on his ass, but I decided to *turn the other cheek* and open the window.

I took the man home and put him to bed, then fell exhausted on my own. Rising earlier than usual the following day, I was astounded to find no trace of the man. It was not until later that I realised I had witnessed a miracle, for *every trace of alcohol had disappeared from my home*!

Your repentantly,

PERCIVAL CHOLMONDLEY-PRATT,
CHUDLEIGH KNIGHTON, DEVON.

SIR,
It was some months ago that, upon recommendations received through your peerless publication, I happened to procure one fine badger shaving brush. However, at each and every attempt to approach the badger with said brush and trusty pearl-handed cut-throat in hand, I'll be blowed if the blighter doesn't attack me in a most violent and righteous fury.

I am now deficient to the tune of three digits and a significant portion of my left ear. Perhaps the instructions were somewhat amiss? On the bright side, I anyway long ago resolved never to learn the piano, lest it interfere with my self-refreshment schedule. Also, the stump where my right index finger used to be serves as an excellent pipe tamper.

Gratefully yours,

BACCY-BARON-BURCHER,
HMP LATCHMERE HOUSE, SURREY.

SIR,
I was taking time out of my schedule of studying the architectural merits (aesthetics and fortification), or lack of them, of the Kremlin and St Basil's Cathedral, when some impudent urchin had the temerity to take the enclosed photograph and demand 10 roubles for his trouble. My first thought was to give the young cove a sound thrashing, but it then occurred to me that said image might interest your readers. With this in mind I settled for administering a swift clip round the ear, a stern warning as to the consequences of interrupting an Englishman from his trusty briar and copy of *The Chap*, and sent the hapless lad packing.

Yours,

CAPTAIN ROSCO 'BISCUITS FRUIT' VAN NOOTE,
CLIVE BARRACKS, SHROPSHIRE

ALISTAIR CROOK'S LETTER FROM T'NORTH

Alistair Crook and his amusing chum Hankinshaw investigate
the curious northern pastime of Association Football

As winter takes its brutal hold on these dark, satanic and appallingly cobbled streets, my mission to explore the t'North and all its delights continues. I find myself spending most mornings warming my hands on a brazier by the ironworks, accompanied by my travelling companion Miles Benedict F. Hankinshaw (who is warming his hands on a brassiere).

In the rare occasions when it is not so cold that our mouths are frozen shut and ice begins to form on our extravagantly coiffeured eyebrows, we ponder the mysteries of this unusual underworld. One such strangeness in the air is the disappearance of the t'North's menfolk from 2.00 pm until 5.15 pm each Saturday. We have inspected waiting rooms at the railway station, small antechambers in the ruins of the abbey and even Ladbrokes, but with no success, until it dawns upon us – they are at association football.

I am not as afraid of association football as I once was. This is thanks to that roguish spendthrift Hankinshaw, who for my birthday treated to me to an evening watching football outside Mr Rumbelow's Electrical Supplies boutique on the High Street. I was told, by one of his "cousins" with the ability to lip read, that some of the football audience were singing, "sit down, and behave yourselves", which makes me feel that they must be handing out copies of The Chap on trams and trolley buses.

Thus, one fine Saturday afternoon, as the rain screams into our faces from a sideways direction, and the sky turns a dark shade of coal, we don exceedingly thick woollen scarves, bobble hats, mittens and cummerbunds. Having injected each other with cognac-enhanced morphine, and filled our hip flasks with morphine-enhanced cognac, we set off with slow, reluctant steps for the family seat and ancestral home of Northtown United, for an outing to the t'football.

Our request for two seats in the stalls but not too close to the orchestra pit is met with blank incomprehension by the troll in the box office, who also refuses to take our cloaks, and confirms to our horror that we will have to spend the afternoon in an outside position. For amusement, we purchase a small yet extraordinarily expensive Chap-sized magazine called "The Programme", which includes a cast list (from which we are disappointed to learn that Mr David Beckham will not be singing tonight). However, rather than a series of humourous lifestyle articles, it consists of many daguerreotypes of young men running round wearing short trousers and vulgarly coloured shirts.

Imagine our surprise when association football turns out to be just this. A number of young men in short trousers appear, and then proceed to run after a large billiard ball which they boot into the air, whilst kicking, scratching and gouging at their fellow actors while the gentlefolk around us turn into braying, swearing oafs. Like most modes of employment, each player has his role, which we suppose they try and do as well as they can. Unlike most modes of employment, it is a free house to shout out comments on their performance. For a job well done, a fellow receives a warm round of applause, but for any mistake, the same people are on their feet, guffawing, pointing and making all sorts of extraordinary hand gestures. It later becomes clear to us that there are two lots of these sporting johnnies, one set against the other!

It is certainly worthwhile mentioning the astonishing wardrobe of this congregation. The shiny nylon that is on display everywhere could set off an electrical charge at any moment, and the fact that although it is possible to wear either a cravat or a finely crafted tie with the shirt, no-one has chosen to do so. Each of the players has had his mother sew his name to the back of his shirt, along with the number of his cloakroom peg. Even that notorious scarecrow Hankinshaw refrains from asking the names of their tailors.

At the interval, I am distressed to realise that my drinks order seems to have been ignored (four quadruple Highland Parks, three vodka martinis and a pint of dry-roasted bitter, with a strawberry milkshake for Hankinshaw). My dissolute chum is aghast by the lack of ice creams, but is happily mollified by the frozen centre of the "meat" pie, which not only do we have to fetch ourselves, but also have to eat straight from its tin foil container, our ivory handled cutlery having been removed by some burly frighteners on the way in.

Eventually we perceive that the entertainment is over, noticing both the lack of spectators and the fact that the lights have been turned off. For those who have an interest in this sort of thing, and who may have lent some money to Mr William Hill on its outcome, the final score was, let's say, 0-0. Or 1-0. Or 6-3 4-6 6-4. Or 276-4 declared. Frankly we are beyond caring, as we slink away in the night, frozen to our sock-garters, keeping to the shadows to avoid the ruffians inflicting fisticuffs upon each other. We have learned enough about the sporting activities of the gentlemen of the t'North, and in future will avoid them at all costs and concentrate our research on one of their indoor pursuits.

Next issue: A Working Men's Club

CHARIOTS OF COCOA

It has been four uneventful years since men lacking in substance dusted down their flannels, polished their rosewood briars and embarked on a rigid training schedule under a table in the Lamb & Flag. But, as Torquil Arbuthnot and Nathaniel Slipper report, the 17th Chap Olympics look set to put Regent's Park back on the A-Z

"**B**ring me your tired, your poor, your sick, and make them run around and jump up and down," goes the Olympic motto; and once again the four-yearly cycle has turned and it is time for the great athletic event. However, a true gentleman, rather than being forced to sprint around some Greek building sites in tight clothing, sweating and getting muddy knees, will make his way gently to Regent's Park, home of the 17th Chap Olympiad. This we are delighted to take part in, for, despite the use of false passports, moustaches and aeroplanes, we have been unable to sneak through customs of the Hellenic paradise where we ouzoed away much of our lamentable youth.

Once again, it is with great pride that dear old Blighty is asked to host this momentous event, and the only request that one puts to Lord Olympic is that, in return, no competitive Americans are allowed to enter.

The Olympiad itself is akin to the beloved sports days of our youth, even down to the be-flannelled teachers wandering around the greensward with clipboards, desperately trying to finish things off before sloping to the Wagon and Horses. In appropriate fashion, the Chap Olympics are not about winning, but trying to avoid taking part. Happily most of the events take up very little effort, and, to the dilettante gentleman, training is akin to cheating.

Usually at the counting up of the baubles and medals at the end of the afternoon, it is a clean sweep for Britain. It has to be noted that all the events take place in only one competition, and are then entirely replaced for the next competition. This is to prevent our Australian cousins from spending the next four years and their entire scientifical budget on practising and becoming good at any of these fine sports. As a people, they show an inappropriate level of competitiveness that is not becoming on this chivalrous occasion.

The games open with the lighting of the Olympic pipe, which is filled with an agreeable mixture of Greek Shag and Captain Cavendish's Premium Aromatic. The pipe is then ceremoniously paraded around London Zoo by a variety of gentlemen, pausing only to buy an ice-cream cornet. And then the mighty contest begins.

The opening event is the relating of anecdotes, the traditional opening line of which is: "I say, that reminds me, gentlemen, of a rather amusing story I should like to impart." The judges keep a keen eye on the quality of the punchline, the amount of guffaws received during the telling of the tale, and the ability to end the same story that was begun, rather than changing anecdotes several times.

This is followed by the 10-yard saunter. Fellows still huddle in corners and talk about the proud moment when Sir Nicholas Seabeggar broke the fourteen-minute barrier for this event. At the time it was feared that Sir Nicholas might explode or his skin fall off, but the world record he set in 1932 has yet to be beaten.

Throwing the quill is the next exciting event, which sees fiery-haired poets gently bowl their quills onto the park, with cries of "Alack, alas, woe is me, I am rent asunder," and other such melancholy mouthings. Next, the royal party, where dukes and barons take part in the Fabergé egg and spoon contest, in which they amble round showing off their wealth and looking intolerably smug. This soon ends, when the judges make great play of having to inspect these expensive gewgaws before scarpering with them. Inevitably they turn out to be cheap forgeries, and one of the morals of these games is that the landed gentry are not to be trusted.

The apathy marathon is one of the definitive events of the Chap Olympics. This begins with gentlemen examining their pocket watches and murmuring to each other that the pubs have now opened. Once ensconced in a snug with pints of foaming ale, a careful analysis of the games still to be played takes place. This can last for at least an hour longer than the remaining events would have taken. Eventually, to much nodding of the head, the rest of the Chap Olympics are cancelled and the party move on to the Lamb and Flag for all round celebrations.

And so for another quadrennium, the athletic event of the season retreats to an elderly man's briefcase, to gather dust in his attic until 2008. Another glorious triumph and many golden medals for plucky Britain and a yah boo sucks to anybody who believes in training and going without fine red wine and Turkish gaspers. Meanwhile, in the pub, the committee, comprising of all those still vaguely upright, begins squabbling over which events will take place in the next competition. This can last for several days and will be utterly forgotten within fifteen seconds of the end of the conversation.

OTHER EVENTS IN THE 2004 CHAP OLYMPICS

Hat doffing (the most number of different doffs within a timed minute).

Who can shout loudest at a foreigner and still come away without having bought stamps/tobacco/a glass of Madeira.

Shooting the cuffs.

Making a glass of brandy and cigar last for as long as possible while the competitors sit in armchairs discussing politics and economics.

The Raffles Event, where the Chap has five minutes in which to shin up a drainpipe in full evening dress, clamber through a sash-window and empty a dowager's jewellery box.

100-yard crawl through bushes, whilst evading one's creditors and/or a prospective father-in-law bearing a shotgun. Fisticuffs with ruffians who snigger at one's attire. The ruffians' arms are bound to their bodies for their own personal safety.

Discus (involving a plate of cucumber sandwiches as the implement to be wafted through the air without spilling a single sandwich).

Dressage event - accompanying a lady into Simpson's department store (competitors will be penalised for foot-faults, refusals, errors in deportment and sheer caddishness).

The Gentleman's Excuse-Me: an opportunity for the Chap competitor to 'scratch his name from the racecard' at the last moment, upon realising one has a prior engagement with one's tailor/turf accountant/mistress.

The training ground for events such as the 10-yard saunter. Note the particularly difficult home stretch, after consuming 17 straight single malts in the leather armchair on the right.

Training for the Chap Olympics can be excessively demanding, which is why there is very little of it. But, as Nathaniel Slipper found out when he was shown around the Chap Olympiad training centre in a room above the Lamb & Flag, contestants do not enter the competition entirely unprepared.

Athletes often require initial assistance with unfamiliar positions such as standing up

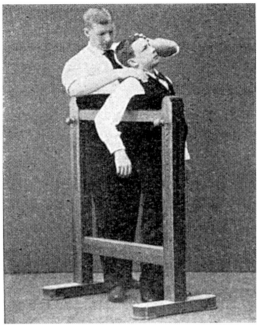

Good mantelpiece posture can vastly increase one's chances in the Relating of Anecdotes

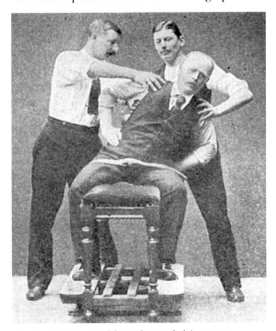

Trainers put an athlete through his paces for the gruelling cigar and brandy event

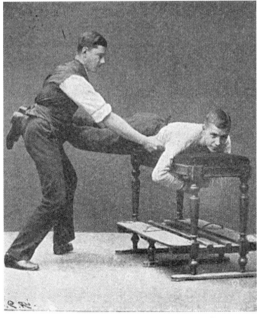

An athlete is prised off the apparatus after rigorous training for the 24-hour snooze

THE SILVER VIXEN

Miss Martindale offers observations and advice to the fair sex from the Ladies' Smoking Room

Welcome to the Ladies' Smoking Room – and you must welcome me too, for with my appointment as your Resident Ladies' Columnist, I make my debut into the world of the Woman Worker. Well, not quite *debut* exactly, for I did on one other occasion receive what I believe is known as a "pay-cheque"; but now, it seems, I am to receive one regularly, four times a year. It makes one feel quite *bourgeois,* but I take solace in the fact that writing has long been considered a lady's occupation. And in any case, the iron discipline of turning out a thousand words or so four times a year 'on the dot' will prevent me from becoming lazy.

But let us pass on to other matters. The thought of all this routine and time-keeping is starting to make me feel faint.

THE UPPER HAND IN GLOVE

A question I am often asked is this: "I choose my outfits carefully, but I still worry that I do not look completely out of place in the 21st century. Is there any one thing I can do to ensure utter *chic*?"

Well, for once in this dreary old life, there *is* a Magic Solution. Wear gloves. It is as simple as that. Not the sort of gloves dreadful people wear to keep their hands warm (what do you think fur muffs are for?) but the sort of gloves ladies wear even when they need to flutter a fan to keep cool. Black gloves or white gloves, long gloves or short gloves, gloves of soft calf-leather or of simple cotton. Gloves are the touch the phoney forgets. Gloves, worn with the right outfit, separate the doves from the pigeons and the New Lady from the New Woman. Gloves lift an *ensemble* from the aspiring to the inspired.

Until recently, no lady would dream of leaving the house without hat and gloves. Then (some time around 1950) the rule was softened to gloves only. To anyone who imagines that the rule has been softened beyond that, the answer is: *only for oiks.* No doubt some anarchist will, at this point, wheel out the example of some member of the royal family. To forestall such impertinence, let me remind you that members of the royal family are also coached at great expense by the Commissariat to *speak* like modified oiks. You weren't thinking of doing that too, I trust? Well then.

BOTTLE FEEDING

In a moment of irascibility – I do have the occasional irascible moment – I chanced to remark that people who drink out of bottles should have them kicked down their throats. I was treated, for my pains, to a pious little homily about how some reasonable people might on certain occasions drink from bottles. I feel therefore that I should clarify my exact position on the subject.

I am compelled to agree that there are some exceptions to my rashly-stated rule. In the case of small babies, for example, the practice of drinking from bottles appears to be so well established in tradition and custom that an exception must be made. In the case of a person dying of thirst in the desert who comes by chance upon a bottle of water, I feel that Dire Necessity can reasonably be pleaded and that, after a suitable period of penance, she may very possibly be re-admitted to the human race.

In other cases, I will grant that some instances are slightly more culpable than others, but I reiterate the substance of my initial point: that people who, in restaurants or public houses, where perfectly good glasses (or even inferior ones) are freely available, nonetheless, of their own free will, choose to drink out of bottles, should have said bottles kicked down their throats.

I realise that this will seem to some a harsh punishment, but desperate times call for desperate measures, and since I am sure that such action would give offenders occasion to pause before repeating the offence, I fail to see how the end cannot be said to justify the means.

For the sake of completeness, I should add that it has been pointed out to me that the piratical practice of swigging rum from bottles (usually followed at least by the common courtesy of wiping their mouths with the back of their hands, frequently neglected by the pub bottle-drinker) is also hallowed by custom and tradition. To this I must reply that pirates do not count. Pirates are exceptions to many rules, even such simple and uncontentious ones as the rule that men wearing earrings should have their ears cut off. Hard cases make bad law, and pirates are well known for being hard cases.

You may write to Miss Martindale at **silvervixen@aristasia.co.uk** *Further feminine wisdom may be found at* **www.aristasia.co.uk**

GILBERT and GEORGE

Banny Poostchi takes tea with the immaculately tailored East End artists

A s the days begin to shorten, I find it a great comfort to look through my holiday snaps, whence at a glance I am transported back to the glory days of summer. In June this year, I journeyed to Venice to board the ferry to Croatia. Imagine my delight when, strolling along the quayside of the Grand Canal, I chanced upon two other English gentlemen, also enjoying their summer hols in that wondrous city—Gilbert and George, who happened to be there for the Venice Biennale.

So pleasurable was their company that, upon my return to London, I could not resist calling on them at their elegant townhouse in Spitalfields. There was just one hitch. I had inadvertently mislaid their calling card. Then I hit upon an ingenious solution. I would look them up in The Yellow Pages, just as one would look up a purveyor of fishing rods. The next day I was happily ensconced over tea with Gilbert and George, and chanced to remark on my good fortune that they were listed under "Artist" in the telephone directory.

Gilbert: The Yellow Pages just did that.

George: They did that without asking us. It was a long time ago.

Gilbert: We had a shop.

George: We never stocked anything.

Gilbert: Nobody ever phoned up.

How marvellous. So it was a happy accident?

Gilbert: Ah yes, we liked that. But the result was nil. Nobody ever phones and says, "I've just seen you in the Yellow Pages". One lady called for a tombstone once.

Have you thought of dispensing with "Gilbert and George" and simply calling yourselves "Artist"?

George: That would be like a Socialistic, Nazi or Communistic thing.

Gilbert: Collectivism is the thing we are most allergic to. It reduces the potential of the individual. It stifles the individual. They become perverse! They become ill! Mentally ill!

George: And they all become dictators in the end!

Gilbert: They get locked up! All totalitarian regimes always lock up the artists. The western world is dangerous enough in that way—if you think of how many numbers every individual has now, a street number, telephone number, a VAT number, a car licence, dog licence, gun licence, passport number! Extraordinary!

So how did you come to acquire the tag "Gilbert and George"?

Gilbert: We thought it was simpler and more friendly to art. People just say "grandma", don't they?

George: We wanted to be like CORNFLAKES, you know, like a title: GILBERT AND GEORGE. It was all based on simplifying and making ourselves visible.

Gilbert: We even did that with a royal coat of arms for a while. To make ourselves appear more established than we actually were. You have to remember that at that time [the 1970s] the idea that you could go on to succeed as an artist was an impossible idea. Unthinkable! Very, very few people had. The fallout from art colleges was enormous, nearly all of them ended up teaching, or becoming a pop star, or running dad's pig farm.

Was the royal coat of arms intended to be ironic?

Gilbert: No, I think we actually wanted it to look formal. Because art at that time was very scruffy, and grubby, and everything was to do with mucky stuff and we wanted to be clean and normal and classical, so we wouldn't alienate vast sections of the population, because a lot of the art that was being done then only meant something to a very small elite group, and if you showed it to your mother she wouldn't like it.

George: Scruffy art in some way.

Gilbert: Grubby…

Has your unusual name helped your art?

Gilbert: Yes. Because we are our art.

George: Because you go to Venice and you walk up and down and they all know "Gilbert and George". The moment that they see us, they see our art.

Gilbert: We are our art and it's a democratic art. And that's why it's good to dress normally because all the artists wanted to dress in a weird way. Paint all over them or strange whiskers or strange hairstyles. That only alienates people.

George: Our art is talking about being alive today. It's a language that is part of everybody. Like happiness. Everyone understands that.

Gilbert: Sex, money, race, religion.

George: Everyone understands that.

Gilbert: Those are the main things there are in the world anyway—everyone's circling around those things. So why should an artist do something so obscure that people go to museums and look at the fire extinguisher and wonder whether it's a work of art?

George: You don't know where the art

starts and where it...

Gilbert: ...whether it's a bench or whether it's an artwork. That's why it's so silly.

George: Ha ha! But don't tell them! Ha ha ha!

And as you are so attached to your name, are there any other names you are especially fond of?

George: Spunk.

Why spunk?

Gilbert: Well it's a nice word, that's all. When people take group photographs, and the cameraman says, "Say cheese" it doesn't really work—but if he says, "Say lesbian" then everybody laughs!

George: And everybody smiles. So lesbian's better than cheese!

How important is the name of each of your artworks to the art itself?

Gilbert: We always say it's like if you're in a bookshop and there are two books and you've got to run for the train in two seconds, and one says *Murder at the Vicarage* and the other one says *Orgy at the Vicarage*, everyone has a big choice immediately.

George: And we know what people would prefer.

And what would people prefer?

Gilbert: Oh I think everybody would prefer *Orgy at the Vicarage*—it's more unusual. They've all read *Murder at the Vicarage*.

WHY I LOVE MY SPATS, BY EARL OKIN

Popular bossa nova crooner Earl Okin has been wearing spats for as long as he can remember, but no-one has ever asked him why. The Chap finally popped the question.

The origin of the spatterdash was to dash the spatter on one's military boots, in the days when washing linen was easier work than the "spit and polish" required to see one's face in one's boots. Nevertheless, it was when these incomparable and quintessential parts of a true gentlemen's wardrobe were miniaturized toward the end of the 19th century that their true worth was realized.

Firstly, especially in those days of gas-lit streets, white or pearl-grey spats were so useful when perhaps one had overdone the port. One could look down and see much more clearly where one's feet were. Such a useful pair of garments!

In those days, only true gentlemen wore them. Now, I am being generous and including foreign gentlemen, for everyone from international Royalty to Italians such as Puccini and Caruso, and Russians such as Chaliapin, wore spats.

Later on, the adoption of spats became the symbol of aspiring upward mobility to the rank of "gentleman". For example, Charles Chaplin, when off-screen, wore spats and even Americans (or colonials, as I prefer to call them) such as Fred Astaire and Duke Ellington wore them. And it wasn't just the good guys either, for Al Capone wore them too.

In other words, spats were the mark of being at the pinnacle of whichever world one inhabited. Naturally, this habit of upwardly mobile people pretending to be gentlemen began to "devalue the currency", and the habit of spat-wearing died out. After all, the status of a true gentleman is a somewhat exclusive club. It's not just a matter of monetary success.

So why do I choose to wear spats? I feel that now (after a decent interval) might be the time to bring them back, and I'm constantly amazed at how often, walking about in the world, I'm complimented on my spats. Naturally, non-gentlemen do not fully understand what spats are, hence their quaint cry of "Nice shoes, mate", but even such people innately understand the spat-wearer's superiority.

For me, spats epitomise style, especially in conjunction with the classic three-piece suit or frock-coat, bowler or top hat and, of course, the dress cravat. However, spats do present occasional drawbacks.

I was in the country recently and had no access to plus fours and brogues, so was wearing my spats. The rain was particularly intrusive that day, and the earth over which I was walking was soon turned into a slippery muddy quagmire. One managed to avoid any ignominious slipping over on to one's posterior, but I was forced to admit, while getting into my Rover at the end of the day, that spats cannot always be relied on to dash the spatter!

AM I CHAP OR NOT?

Readers are invited to have their Chappist potential assessed. Send your photos to Am I Chap? PO Box 39216, London SE3 0XS, or post@thechap.net

Left: Sir, you have donned the raiment of the Victorian gentleman without resembling an awkward wedding guest in hired nylon from Moss Bros. But what really makes you a Chap amongst men, Mr. Horatio Scotney-Le Cheyne, is the expression of utter bewilderment you wear, which suggests an excess of either laudanum or fresh air.

Above: What on earth, Mr. Lee Garland, could quilted jackets, unkempt hair, crew-neck sweaters and cheesy grins possibly have to do with The Chap? You seem to have enticed a perfectly nice-looking young lady into your company, but we wonder whether the relationship has any future, if you continue to take our sartorial advice so lightly.

Right: We're not quite sure who sent us this photo, but if it was the fellow on the right, then we salute your superb moustache and declare you a Chap. Your manservant, however, could do with a new suit of clothes and some lessons in posture.

Left: "Do you like my new raincoat?" writes Hiroki Ohashi, from Japan.
No, not particularly.

Left: Clearly the members of a Rotary Club in Hertfordshire on a day trip to an Owl Sanctuary. Hats—too new looking, not worn at jaunty enough angles; Trousers—too low slung (haven't you heard of braces?); Jackets—unbuttoned?!

CHAPPIST DISPATCHES

GOVERNMENT DENIES GENTLEMEN THEIR FUMATORY RIGHTS

The government has come up with one of its most draconian laws to date: banning smoking in all public places. The new law, contrary to New Labour's Manifesto pledge, includes private members' clubs, and, most shocking of all, does not even exclude the Reform Club.

One wonders what Mr. Churchill would have replied, when asked to stub out his cigar as he entered the premises of his club to mull over his next move against Herr Hitler. Indeed, the Führer himself, a vehement anti-smoker, would have heartily approved of the new law.

Stephen Fry, erstwhile Pipesmoker of the Year and frequent champion of the smoking gentleman, didn't mince his words when he told The Chap: "The new law is not only a violation but a piece of gross impertinence. An embarrassing, foolish piece of legislation that delights only Malvolios and like puritan scum."

A horrible smoke-free cloud of disinfected air hangs over the future of the Sheridan Club, when the new law comes into effect in summer 2007. Will the members be forced underground to found the first of a new generation of "Smokeasies", just like whisky drinkers under

By 2007 these men will be classed as criminals. Even to publish pictures of them will be illegal

Prohibition in the United States?

The Irish, victims of a similar ban for nearly three years, are apparently happy with the arrangement of hovering under giant heated mushrooms outside pubs; but of course the Irish are a more socially robust people than the English. One wonders what will happen when a smoker has to dart away from a conversation with a non-smoker to have a crafty snout outside; will his interlocutor be expected to wait in silence for him to return and for the conversation to resume? Or will the art of exchanging badinage suffer from constant disruption?

Peter Wiseman, of the Pipe Club of London, is not optimistic about his Club's future when the new law comes into effect: "We shan't be able to continue holding our meetings at the Ship Tavern, and none of the members has a house large enough to accommodate us all. The only solution would be to hold the meetings in my garden, but in the winter the club would have to temporarily shut down." The PCoL won't be the only club hit by the legislation; all four of the main other British pipe clubs will have difficulty meeting at member's homes. "The only exception will be the Aylesbury Churchwarden Club," said Wiseman, "as there are only eight members."

WORLD OF SPORT

A monograph by Douglas Kipper and Stafford Grape, with the purpose of educating and informing the uncommon gentleman as to the ways and what-fors of Rugby Union

Like all sports, Rugby is a derivative of golf. The main features that differentiate Rugby from its beautiful and upright sister is that it is played on a much smaller green, the holes are H-shaped, clubs are not used, the golf ball is larger and shaped like a Brazil nut and there are teams of around fifty a side instead of one.

Other characteristics that mark rugby as golf's rather uncouth and backward brother are the lack of intellectually stimulating banter and the game's physical nature, which makes pipe smoking betwixt holes impractical. And while golf daintily promenades towards the ultimate of ultimate goals, the 19th hole, parasol in hand, Rugby crashes into the bins at the back of the club and scours through the refuse for scraps of potato skins and snails.

There are four different types of rugby: Rugby Union, Rugby League, Red Trousers Rugby and Secret Rugby, the latter played only by the foulest sailors in the foulest corners of the globe and of which it is forbidden to speak. Today we shall be looking at Rugby Union. The most important indicator that you are watching a game of rugby union is quite simply the shape of the ball. Some might say the sight of a hundred grown men chucking a giant almond in a field is the stuff of nightmares. Quite so, although there are several other things they could pass around that would be much worse, for instance a kissing-disease such as Herpes.

Rugby, like so many other activities, has its own peculiar language. An etymological analysis of some of rugby's terminology produces one very simple conclusion: it is utter gutter-talk. If we were to pass a random selection of terms such as *scrum, loosehead prop, hooker, side-boot* or *fly half* to the well-trained ear of an etymologist or a Bedlam alienist, they would soon conclude it to be the frantic wordplay of a deranged unfortunate speaking in tongues. Or Cockney rhyming slang, as it is nowadays known. As a precautionary measure, we would advise the players of rugby to hold back on the usage of such terms and, indeed, all speech.

The 'kick off' is probably the most interesting part of the game of rugby. You will often see the referee look at his watch in an exaggerated manner before the match. This act tells all and sundry that the game is about to begin. Finally, he blows a whistle in order that blind men need not ask, "Has it started yet?"

Once all the players are satisfied that everyone has heard the whistle, the game begins. The players spend the duration of the match, which can last up to four days, churning up the mud with their unwieldly frames, which can lead to such dreadful fauxes-pas as showing one's belt or trouser buttons.

During the game a player may putt the ball into the H-shaped hole with his foot-shaped club (not to be confused with a club-shaped foot, which is more attuned to Secret Rugby than Rugby Union). This wonderful thing is called a 'try' and is worth between one and six thousand points, depending on the weather and the colour of the scorer's lower garments. On scoring a try, another gentleman of the team will pat his colleague on the shoulder and skillfully hide his jealousy. You may wonder why it is called a 'try' and not a 'succeed'. The reasons are twofold. Firstly, playing down the significance of success helps to curb the "green-eyed monster". Secondly, and more importantly, it is fundamental to rugby not to seem overly competitive. To the professional rugby player, even scoring a 'try' is enough to make him blush.

It is an oft-spoken truth that rugby is very confusing. It is the only sporting game where the action runs forwards and backwards at the

Recent attempts to unite the world of rugby with the world of fashion have been entirely unsuccessful

TEN THINGS YOU NEVER KNEW ABOUT RUGBY

1. Historically, the Rugby scrum developed from the children's playground game "Cat's Cradle", not, as is sometimes erroneously claimed, "What's the time Mr. Wolf".

2. In Wales, it is forbidden to depict Gareth Edwards in cartoon form.

3. Rugby balls do not make a fizzing sound when thrown, but rugby players often shout "Weeee" when passing the ball, although the crowd can rarely hear this.

4. Rugby league is mentioned in the Bible, but not rugby union.

5. Johnny Wilkinson once ordered "rugby" from the menu in a Lithuanian restaurant, but was disappointed to be served cricket on toast.

6. There are men on either side of a rugby field with flags, who will aid an aircraft if it has to make an emergency landing on the pitch.

7. Jona Lomu's Aunt Toyah has a lazy eye.

8. Nobody likes a clever bugger.

9. The *Puffin Children's Secret Rugby Colouring-in Book* was first published in 1861.

10. In 2007 there are plans for the rugby goal posts' shape to be changed to the letter "W".

same time. As the players run forwards, the ball is passed backwards. Surely this is just a simple case of "robbing Peter to pay Paul"? Indeed, what sane man dashes up the down escalators on the London Underground when he can go up the right way and get there five times as fast and with little or no effort? Perhaps therein lies the beauty of the sport of rugby. Is it an exquisite acting-out of the futility of life? Is it there to remind us that every action, no matter how hard one tries, (nor indeed how many 'tries' one scores) will end up with the same inevitable outcome: death. Looked at this way, any sport is surely an exercise in futility, unless it proffers a reward as treasurable as the 19th hole.

The Reading Room

Lindsay Bagshaw leafs through the season's literary offerings

● ●

SELECTED AUTHORS: ANTHONY POWELL

Mr. Anthony Powell (pronounced "Pole") was born in 1905, the only child of an army infantry officer. Powell's childhood and upbringing were typical for his class: four years at Eton (where his school chums included Mr. Henry Green and Mr. Robert Byron) were followed by three at Balliol, where he was a member of the notorious Hypocrites Club with Mr. Evelyn Waugh and Sir Harold Acton. He accepted a position with the publisher Duckworth in 1926, and published his first novel, Afternoon Men, in 1931. Always on the fringes of the demi-monde, he had an affair with the painter and artists' model Miss Nina Hamnett, a lady prone to exhibiting her breasts and saying "Modigliani always said I had the best tits". He dabbled as a scriptwriter of "quota quickies" for Warner Brothers, and spent a year in Hollywood (where he met Mr. Scott Fitzgerald). He published four further novels in the 1930s: Venusberg, From a View

to a Death, Agents and Patients and What's Become of Waring. During the Second World War, Mr. Powell served with the Welch Regiment and, later, in the Intelligence Corps as a liaison officer.

In 1951, Mr. Powell published the first instalment of what was to become his twelve-volume novel sequence A Dance to the Music of Time, a roman fleuve covering the period 1914 to 1975 and focusing on the world "where bohemia meets Mayfair". This project kept him occupied for another 24 years, during which he wrote a million words stretched over a thousand pages and created hundreds of characters, including the repulsively fascinating Widmerpool. He published four volumes of discreet memoirs and three volumes of acerbic journals. Mr. Powell was friends with many artists (Messrs Daintrey, Burra, Wadsworth) as well as writers (Sir VS Naipaul, Messrs Larkin and Amis). He became friends with Mr. George Orwell (who described him as "the only Tory I've ever liked") in 1941, arranging for the purchase of a smoking jacket while he was in hospital and organising his memorial service. Mr. Powell refused a knighthood in the 1970s but later accepted a CH from the Queen. He died in March 2000, aged 94.

Despite the longevity of Mr. Powell's career, his huge literary output and the critical acclaim with which it was received, he is still relatively unacknowledged by and unknown to a broader readership. Unfortunately, contemporary literary critics have confused his upbringing with his work, and assumed he is a snobbish writer, a calumny which they lazily promote. Fortunately, in this centenary year of his birth, an excellent biography (by Mr. Michael Barber) and an exhibition at the Wallace Collection (co-curated by The Chap's etiquette correspondent, Torquil Arbuthnot) should push this unjustly neglected author back to the forefront of English letters where he belongs.

A Dance to the Music of Time is available in 12 volumes from Random House.
The Wallace Collection exhibition, *The Life and Work of Anthony Powell*, runs until 5th February 2006.

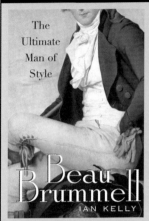

The
Ultimate
Man of
Style

Beau Brummell
IAN KELLY

When Beau Brummell was born, English gentlemen dressed extravagantly and embarrassingly in elaborate wigs, make-up, and garments of garish silk. Mr. Brummell was responsible for the transformation, which still exists today, into clothes that are simple and well cut. Mr. Brummell espoused clean lines in a coat to such an extent that he insisted his tailors hide pockets inside the tail-flaps. "If John Bull turns round to look after you," he said, "you are not well dressed; but either too stiff, too tight or too fashionable."

Mr. Brummell's life is a riveting story of unparalleled fame, fashion and admiration followed by a descent into poverty and syphilitic madness. The man who put Savile Row on the map, who could win friends, political arguments or the favours of women with apparent effortlessness, and who was responsible for some of the wittiest put-downs in history, Mr. Brummell created the myth of the British gentleman typified by wit, style, and the finest tailoring in the world. Mr. Ian Kelly brings the fashions and people of Regency England vividly to life in this excellent biography.

The New English Dandy purports to celebrate "the return of the well-dressed man". Six chapters offer different "takes" on the 21st century dandy: "The Gentleman" (Beau Brummell's direct stylistic descendant, exemplified by a daguerreotype of our esteemed editor); "Neo-Modernist" (Savile Row meets "pop" culture); "Celebrity Tailor" (focusing on individual tailors and their mastery of cut); "East End Flâneur" (what passes for bohemianism in the purgatory that is Hoxton); "Terrace Casual" (overpriced yobbo-chic); and "New Briton" ("new and exciting visual languages" apparently, although it resembles nothing more than attiring oneself from a child's' dressing-up box). Ms Cicolini has, at best, a tenuous grasp on what exactly is a dandy, and labours under the massive misapprehension that spending vast sums on "vintage" plimsolls and "designer" PE kit makes one a dandy.

Many of the daguerreotypes illustrating "Terrace Casual", for instance, show gentlemen got up in garments that resemble those one sees on every ragamuffin in Britain; yet because these anoraks and jeans are from a particular "label" they are breathlessly described as "incredibly subtle" and "a refusal to conform". Fortunately the interviews in this book are excellent, as are many of the daguerreotypes (including ones of Mr. David Piper and Mr Johnny Vercoutre of The Modern Times Club).

The
New English
Dandy

Alice
Cicolini

Thames & Hudson

LETTERS

THE CHAP, PO BOX 39216, LONDON SE3 0XS
post@thechap.net
The author of the best letter will receive a delightful pair of Chap cufflinks. This issue's winner is Sebastopol T. Hawley-Smoot, of Brinkley Court

Sir,

I have just finished reading *Freedom the Spur*, the classic wartime memoirs of Gordon Instone MM, who bravely escaped from occupied France. Within the work is a possibly life-saving tip that should be highlighted for all readers about to venture into dangerous, inhospitable lands—be they run by raving fascists or not.

Instone records how, while laying low in Paris debating his next move, he spent much of his time seated on a park bench smoking his pipe. One afternoon, a middle-aged lady walked up to him and asked, "You're English, aren't you?" Astonished, Instone replied that he was and asked the lady how she knew this. She replied: "Only an Englishman holds his pipe the way you're holding it!" Instone sat looking at the bowl of his pipe "as if it were dynamite". He was lucky, however, as the lady was herself English, but living in France. Instone went on to his freedom, although he had learned the hard way of the dangers of smoking in the "English manner" while on enemy territory.

If any of your readers should find themselves in a similar soup, then for goodness sake adopt a sullen posture, dangle the pipe precariously from the side of the mouth and shrug your shoulders in a nonchalant fashion when asked a question by a member of the public.

Yours,

Sebastopol T Hawley-Smoot,
Brinkley Court

Sir,

I was most heartened to read the letter in which Dickie Winchester discussed the limitations of trouser semaphore whilst wearing the *djellabah*. Having returned recently from Illyria, I find myself roaming the heather-clad hills of home in a heavyweight kilt of hunting tartan (the Gordon). I can now communicate using Winchester's adapted trouser semaphore in Gaelic, as well as all 36 letters of the Albanian alphabet (Gheg dialect). The pleasing results are long conversations across the glens with retired Artillery officers and Kosovans seeking to include Argyll and Bute in their quest for a Greater Albania.

Mirupafshim,

Xhoni McAuley
(Chieftain, Clan Skanderberg)

Sir,

I, as a faithful Chapette of 14 years of age, feel isolated from the Chappish community. Alas, I have never met a Chap or Chapette before in the entire course of my short life. This is because I live in the colonies, namely, New Zealand, where every person I know that understands the meaning of the word 'cravat' was taught it by me. Many females ridicule our classic garment, the skirt, and deny their sex by wearing these new-fangled and mass-produced 'jeans'.

Just last year, my best friend, Miss Larsen, received one of those infernal contraptions, a 'cellphone', for her birthday—and she actually enjoys using it!

Alas! I wade through this un-Chappishness day after day. I am the only Chapette in this tiny country of 4 million people, but I fight! When I wear my cravat with my school uniform and protest that there is no rule against wearing one in the regulations, I am fighting for Chappism worldwide!

Yours in isolation,

MISS HEIDI BOULTER
NEW ZEALAND

SIR,

I would be grateful if any gentleman could show me whereabouts in the Bible it says that an attractive young barmaid is allowed to slap me around the face and then send some muscle-bound giant of a man to rough me up as I leave the King's Arms, simply because I showed her my most attractive smile.

Yours,

MORTLOCK LEANDER
HUDDERSFIELD

SIR

At my local watering hole last Tuesday I was approached by an uncouth looking fellow, who asked, "Do you take the chap?" Well, I must say that I felt quite affronted, as I had always fancied myself as a bit of a ladies' man. As my wrist left the harbour of my Harris Tweed and my fist connected with the end of this blackguard's nose, I realised that he must have espied my cuff attire and leapt to the obvious conclusion. Upon realising the fellow had asked a purely innocent question, I helped him to his feet and confessed, "Yes, I do take *The Chap*, quarterly throughout the year!"

Your servant,

SIMON D. JONES, CLEETHORPES

SIR,

The education system seems unable to provide young ladies with even the most basic instruction in the art of washing and ironing. Specifically, young—and sometimes not so young—women have obviously not the slightest clue about the correct temperature to wash garments of clothing. Almost without exception they are washing blouses, cardigans, trousers and indeed skirts at such a high temperature that they shrink, and thus are unable to decently cover the wearer's midriff.

These poor laundering techniques have inadvertently provided me with an insight into the unfathomable world of the fairer sex. I did not realise that it is the practice for many ladies to carry around with them a spare earring attached to the excess flesh around their navel. Obviously more ladies than I realised experience the loss of an earring on a regular basis.

Yours,

SAM WATTBE-FUDDLED
TUNBRIDGE WELLS

SIR,

Cartoon characters stalking the Dane, and men in black bedlinen writing their own headlines? All very well, but on behalf of the differently saned, I would like to express my outrage at the hijacking of the Lunatic Fringe by these bandwaggonneers. As a partially rational man myself, I am often to be seen wearing elements of my breakfast as I tantalise the fauna of Egham with my golden merkin. I too favour the cloak for its possibilities of sudden revelation. Gentlemen, there the similarity ends. Never in my life have I admitted the taint of an agenda, of any stripe.

These johnny-come-latelys are dragging Mad Pride through the mud, and it is for this reason I call on my brethren in tweed to chew through their straps and join me in a madmen's mutiny.

Yours,

HUGO JERZY-BALLOONGONG IV
THE BANDSTAND, EGHAM.

DEAR SIR,

We are some sofisticated men, who need a club in Denmark.

What are we doing?

Do you know somebody who is interested to make a club in Denmark? We are around 22 persons between 40-50.

Kind regard,

SIR CLAUS JOERGENSEN
DENMARK

AND DAMNED BE HIM

Lord Gawain Douglas, great grandson of the Marquess of Queensberry, discovers the origins of the noble art of Pugilism

"Bottom!" "Bottom?" "Yes, Bottom!" Speaking as one who has none of same, in an age that has little, I tell of those Englishmen who had it in abundance; the bare-knuckle fighters of the golden age of boxing, which shone between 1720 and 1860. This was the age of "Boximania" and "Bottom" meant guts, the absolute refusal to give in; the determination to go on long past any reasonable point. The boxers' names say it all and ring out like their characters of stone: Big Ben Brain,

Bold Bendigo, Deaf Burke, Gentleman John Jackson.

The 18th century bare knuckle boxing scene, The prize Ring, was quite remarkable, peopled by characters whose humour, flamboyance, talent for friendship and astonishing courage gave rise to an ideal of what an Englishman should be like. This ideal was typified by the phrase And damned be him that cries enough, which is engraved on the huge trophy given to Tom Cribb, one of our greatest bare knuckle champions, in 1815. Cribb's fight in 1811 for the English title with the black American champion, Tom Molyneaux, was one of the archetypal battles of pugilism.

Boxing then had its roots in the cudgeling booths of Stuart England, whose most famous exponent was James Figg, first champion of this country and, like Robin Hood, an expert in the use of sword, fist and the quarterstaff. Figg opened a school in London in 1719 to educate gentlemen in self-defence. This was an absolute necessity in Georgian London, and members of the upper classes would think nothing of laying aside sword and wig to correct the disrespectful lower orders.

The use of the clenched fist to settle a dispute, as opposed to the French pistol or the Italian blade, was as natural to every class of Englishman in those times as the growl to the dog. If two working men had a disagreement, they would retire to some quiet place accompanied by their friends, strip to the waist and battle it out. William Cobbett remarked interestingly in 1805, that

THAT CRIES "ENOUGH!"

with such a battle there "Ceases forever the cause whence it arose". Perhaps today we are wrong to discourage playground fights. Figg's pupil, Jack Broughton, "The father of boxing", established the first official rules since the time of the Greeks. He did this because one of his opponents died as a result of fighting him, and Broughton was concerned enough to try and reduce the level of brutality. Three sets of rules have existed: the Greeks', Broughton's and those of my great-grandfather, the ninth Marquess of Queensberry, formulated in 1865.

Boxing is literally as old as the hills, the ancient hills of Greece, where it was introduced in the 23rd Olympiad in 688 BC. The name probably derives from the Greek "Pyx"—with the fist. Later it played out its terrifying drama in the Roman arena. The engravings above show the brutal thongs on the hands and arms of a Greek pugilist of 500 BC, which later degenerated into the lethal Caestus of the Roman arena. And here is a description by Theocritus of a particularly fine fighter of the day:

Torn were his ears by the boxer's blows, and orbed was his monstrous bosom and back with flesh as of iron; like an enormous wrought metal statue he showed...

There is a raw power in these classical descriptions that vaults the centuries. Fight reporting is as old as the game itself, and chaps like Virgil and Homer were rather good at it. There were no ringside broadcasts then, but gripping records were made of the contests. The Romans probably brought organized boxing with them to England, but the first proper mention dates back to King Alfred's day: His soldiers partook of exercises in the form of wresting and fighting which is boxing. Richard III was also "Distinguished as an expert with the clenched fist when opposed to an antagonist". Later we hear that Walter Raleigh and Samuel Pepys both gave tiresome lads a damn good box to encourage them in greater courtesy: "I became angry, and boxed my boy that I do hurt my thumb," says Pepys.

Training for a contest in the days of the bare-knuckle fighters was astonishing by present-day standards, and the regime of modern boxers pales beside that endured by the 18th century "pug". An incredible amount of food and drink was taken, mainly underdone lean beef and legs of fowl. No vegetables or fish were allowed and only the raw yolks of eggs. Liquor was taken neat and beer home brewed and old, but no more than 3 pints a day with breakfast and dinner, and none with supper. Violent purgatives were given daily and vomiting was induced, as were long periods of profuse sweating. Frequent bleeding was administered. It took four months' training for the fighter to reach his best and it was quite common for him to lose three stone in weight. Great store and attention were given to the state of the boxer's skin, by whose quality the standard of his fitness was appraised. Today, a horse is still judged similarly.

An unbelievable amount of roadwork was involved; up to thirty miles a day of walking and running. A rope would be tied about the boxer's wrist and to the tail end of a cart, forcing him to run along and to keep his arm up—a huge physical and mental strain. This was not just to develop wind but also punching power and great power in defence. No modern athlete would submit to such a thing. The boxer would do continuous sparring when not doing road work or eating and the heaviest fighting usually took place at midday.

There was a strong connection between the racing turf and the prize ring in those days and my crazy ancestor, the 4th Duke of Queensberry, was a great supporter of both. He was also patron to one of the greatest boxing champions, Gentleman John Jackson. Jackson was perhaps the first real English sporting celebrity, friend to prince, poet (Lord Byron) and commoner alike. Jackson was also a first rate teacher and introduced the straight left, which had never really been used before. In his Bond street academy he invited pupils to try and land punches on him, but they could never break through his impenetrable guard. The only time he ever lost a fight was when he slipped and broke a leg. However, instead of giving up he made a unique proposal. He begged his opponent that they should sit opposite each other in chairs and continue to fight until one of them quit. His opponent, "The Brewer", who had been losing the battle, wasn't keen and pocketed his fifty guineas. Even so, the bravery of this challenge made Jackson more popular than ever. Bottom!

The third set of rules compiled by my great-grandfather, the ninth Marquess of Queensberry, together with his establishment of different weight categories, ushered in the modern age of boxing, with its three-minute rounds, gloved hands and greater concerns for safety. Concerns which have not always been satisfied, for the gloved fist can have a more concussive effect internally, despite a less damaging external result.

Who were the best, the old or the new? My father Francis, the 11th Marquess, had many chats on this matter with Jake Hyams at the bar of the National Sporting club. Old Jake was in a perfect position to expound, having fought in both styles, bare-knuckle and Queensberry rules. Hyams' first fight lasted a week, and he fought one of the longest first rounds in Boxing history—45 minutes.

Hyams said that under old Prize Ring rules endurance was the main thing; nowadays with twelve rounds stamina is secondary. It made no difference in the old days how far one fighter might be at the end of say, twenty rounds. What mattered was who could "Toe the mark" and fight until his opponent quit, whether it was one hour or three. They trained not for a 20-round sprint but a 200-round marathon. The modern fighter might therefore outbox but could never outlast the old timers. There was no time limit, and a knockout in those days might be administered several times without signalling the end of the fight. The cry, "Enough!" was the only true end.

Modern training, according to Hyams, fell woefully short. His training methods were little different to those described earlier; twenty miles on the road every day, three

square meals, three rub-downs, three bouts of sparring. Between times his hands were continuously in brine to harden them.

My father once asked Jake what justification there could be for boxing in the 20th century. "My Lord," said Hyams laconically, "The boxer fears nothing." Perhaps we who fear most things and dare little should try and find some bottom again.

Daniel Mendoza
1764-1836
English
11 stone 6 lbs
Won 7 fights
A very scientific boxer

John Jackson
1769-1845
English
14 stone
Won 2 fights
A Great Teacher

Bill Richmond
1763-1829
United States
13 stone 8 lbs
Won 11 fights
The First Great
Black Fighter

AM I CHAP OR NOT?

Readers are invited to have their Chappist potential assessed. Send your photos to Am I Chap? PO Box 39216, London SE3 0XS, or post@thechap.net

Right: The turban has enjoyed a recent renaissance, thanks to a bout of unpleasantness in Mesopotamia. Farhan Ali Von Fiza Ullah wisely eschews such an outmoded form of headwear, and shows that a trilby is the only true way to display one's traditionalist allegiances.

Above: "Are we chap material?" write Marina and Kevin. The young lady (who has forgotten her hairbrush) seems to be wearing Kevin's hat, and he in turn wears her scarf. Chaps who swap clothes with Chapettes are nothing but chumps.

Left: We always receive at least one photograph taken at a wedding, where the menfolk seem to think that because they are dressed in formal attire, they qualify as Chaps. This is rather like asking whether one qualifies as a savage jungle predator when wearing a leopard-skin coat.

Dom Galea accompanied his photograph with the aphorism: "Never descend to the ways of your those above you." Don't worry, old sport – you haven't.

Left: Laird Howard Ashley Clarkson S. Torrie's singular use of mediaeval architecture as a clothing accessory is to be commended. He is also correctly wearing a hat out-of-doors. Had he not forgotten to leave the bottom button of his waistcoat undone, he would be perfectly attired for a stroll in a graveyard.

Left: "I am a young man from America," writes Zack Holloman, "and recently I participated as an extra in a movie set in 1940. Please disregard the glasses."

Mr. Holloman, if we start by disregarding the glasses, where will it all end?

Left: "Is my friend Jeremy a bounder?" writes Maxim Adlam. The short answer is no, because a bounder, while lacking in moral and emotional scruples, is always impeccably dressed. Your friend Jeremy looks like the sort of extremely annoying smug fellow one desperately tries to avoid at parties.

Below: Lord Cuthbert of Kitch-en (sic) asks whether he and his chum are Chaps. By removing the background of their photograph one suspects they have something to hide. What the fellow on the left should have hidden is the lining of his coat. And as for loafers with plus fours, bottom buttons done up and cravats tied like bandannas, it really beggars belief.

Above: It is nice to see the animals making an effort. This equine dandy has adorned himself with a smart pair of velvet paniers bearing a royal crest, a superb vintage bridle and a monkey in a riding hat.

Above: Just when you think you can't take any more wedding photographs, along comes a proper Chap. Commander James Renwick (see also Letters, page 46) not only enhances his naval officer's uniform with a half Windsor knot, but he also has the decency to share his favourite magazine with an airman.

MILITARY ATTACHE CASE

In areas of military conflict, British soldiers can be victims not only of bombing raids but open derision and, in some cases, cutting remarks about their uniforms. Nathaniel Slipper and Miles Hankinshaw point out the essential requirements for mortar attack, tedious hours in the trenches and evenings in the local saloons.

Since many shocking things happen in war, which can widen a fellow's eyes so much that his monocle pops out and is lost in the mud, monocle protectors are essential.

If in a position of being both cold of hand and writing a letter, fingerless gloves will keep the majority of the hand warm enough. Wearing thick gloves such as these will not be compensated for by the best writing paper in the world.

The portable oak writing desk, carried in a handy pouch on the hip, is useful for catching up with vital correspondence, such as the 'thank you' letter to Aunt Agatha for her birthday present of a five-shilling postal order.

In order to keep warm in a chilly climate, the military are issued with thermal vests and long johns. However, wearing the vest outside the clothes can give the appearance of someone who performs maintenance on roads and railways.

Trousers should not be tucked into boots, whatever the circumstances. As can be seen, they ruin the cut of a chap's trousers and leave unsightly creases. Moreover, this young private's trousers do not seem to have been ironed. Court martial beckons.

If the cord at the rear of the soldier's helmet is pulled, the Tommy will say a variety of military phrases such as "The Kaiser is a buffoon", "Goering has two but they are small" and "Do we have an exit strategy?"

Always carry a packet of ladies' nylon stockings in your knapsack. When liberating foreign towns, they will endear you to the local young ladies, who will express their gratitude with the touch of their lips.

We often hear tales of a soldier's life being saved by a bible/cigarette case/hip flask in front of his heart. It therefore makes sense to carry at least 12 of these items about your person at all times.

The Sam Browne belt, issued by the army, comes with snuffbox, whistle, tobacco pouch, and waterproof lighter as standard. You will also need to add a cloth for wiping dust off your gramophone records, an inflatable barber's chair and a multiple Time Zone pocket watch, which tells you the time in Mayfair, Whitehall and Ascot.

A small knife can be hidden inside your sock garter, for use in emergencies, such as when a package of Gentlemen's Relish arrives for one of your comrades who has unfortunately snuffed it.

GET THE LOOK
How to Dress Like the World's Greatest Dictators – on a budget
This issue: **KIM JONG-IL**

OVERALLS

The backbone of Kim Jong-il's outfit is a two-piece set of khaki overalls. Naturally, Kim's are bespoke and cost him thousands of Won, but you can get a pair from any good hardware store. Remember to ask for flat fronted trousers with French pleats.

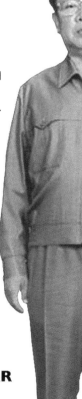

HAIR

Kim's hair maintains its alignment of zero degrees from the vertical through the use of static. Every few minutes, one of his minions rubs his hair with a balloon, then holds the balloon just above the dictator's head. If you haven't got a balloon, a vaccum cleaner will do.

EYEWEAR

Kim's spectacles were made by top North Korean designer Tom Min Sing. He was shot last year for being homosexual, but you can buy a very similar pair at Specsavers.

FOOTWEAR

The secret of Kim's imposing height of 5 feet 2 inches is the platform soles in his smart Hush Puppies. He has them especially made at night by tiny Korean elves, but you can buy a similar pair from any good orthopaedic shoe shop.

UNDERWEAR

The North Korean President is a huge fan of Spiderman. His underpants are in the traditional Y-front style, with a picture of his superhero on the rear. Kim's are made of bulletproof goretex, but you can buy a pack of three cotton pairs at Primark for £3.99.

KNIT YOUR OWN HUSBAND

Below: The advantage of the outdoor type is that once you have finished knitting, there is no more work to do. The result is self-sufficient, and can simply be left in a potting shed overnight. You may find it useful to install a zipper, to make it easier to wash out the sods of earth and stray potatoes.

The suave husband ca[n] be quite decorative a[t] first, giving off a pleasant odour of Brylcreem and vermouth. But you may begin to find flecks of his exquisite angora on your lady friends' clothes, and soon the whole marriage will unravel before your very eye[s]

The double husband requires a knit one, pearl one technique: once you have knitted your husband, you'll also have to knit his lifelong companion, Jeremy. You'll find them both very helpful when it comes to shopping for curtains—but don't expect any heroics in the bedroom, and do not be surprised when Jeremy takes up knitting himself.

Tracey Delauney was so fed up with her ex-husband that she decided to knit herself a new one. Here are some of her tips

Some ladies may wish to experiment by knitting an eccentric husband. The result will be unpredictable and sometimes fun, but beware: he may suddenly want to start a nudist commune in your house, or even join the ranks of Jeremy and Simon (see below left)

The artistic type is easy to knit, since quality is not an issue. However, his main contribution to the household will consist of pottery, and he'll never do the washing up, in case it disintegrates.

The literary husband will require a lot of fiddly work, especially around the spectacles. Once completed, however, he'll be quite content to sit in his study for days on end; his only demand of you will be the occasional help with a crossword puzzle.

Some ladies prefer lady husbands, and who are we to judge? Lady husbands require a lot more work, but the results tend to be more durable.

PASSENGER SAFETY CARD
What Chaps and Chapettes should do in the event of an airline emergency

(1) At the first sign of turbulence, extinguish all half-smoked cigarettes and pipes. Light a fresh one – it could be your last.

(2) Be aware that during turbulence, ladies will be in a state of distress. An offer to light their cigarettes will be gratefully received, and could help prevent hysterics.

(3) Ladies are requested to apply a layer of lipstick before departing the fuselage. Hairbrushes are also provided in the arm of your seat.

(4) The emergency hair driers and curling tongs may be used by the ladies to ensure they are well-presented when leaving the aeroplane.

(5) Ladies are requested to remove any flat-heeled shoes before an emergency evacuation. High heels are more likely to catch the attention of a helicopter crew.

(7) In the case of an evacuation, an emergency trouser press will drop down from the rear of the seat in front of you.

(6) A butler is situated at each of the six emergency exits. He will announce the names of the passengers as they jump out of the fuselage.

(8) In the event of a sea landing, a Gieves & Hawkes inflatable waistcoat is under your seat. This includes a small flask of single malt and a celebratory cigar, in the unlikely event of your survival.

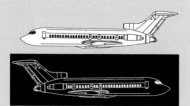

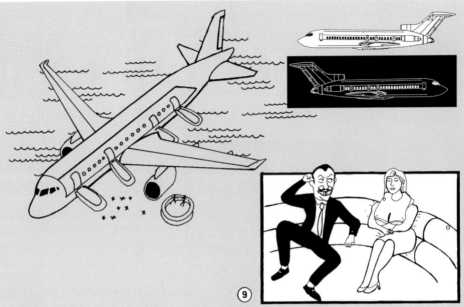

9 The order of precedence for passengers leaving the aeroplane by the emergency slide is: 1)cads, 2)children and ladies, 3)gentlemen, 4)foreigners.

10 In the event of a hijack situation, explain to the hijackers clearly and firmly that you are an English naval officer, and offer yourself up as a hostage.

11 A supply of dress suits, bow ties and collar studs are kept in the cockpit in the event of an evening emergency. Please ask the captain for details.

12 If egress from the aeroplane is impossible, this is the position to adopt in the event of a crash landing.

WHERE THE WILDE THINGS ARE

Sebastian Horsley, raconteur, bon viveur and connoisseur of fine mascara, has published a memoir of his shocking life, Dandy in the Underworld. He gives us his definition of what it means to be a dandy

to creativity passes so close to the madhouse and, indeed, often ends there.

About the most terrifying burden a human being has to bear is a sense of his own isolation. We plunge into pools of shared meaning to escape. We take refuge in shared pastimes and customs and codes. We are all actors. We think we are safe when we hide in our roles. Look at the doctors, the accountants, the preachers the plumbers, the poets and playwrights. They think they are real people. But they are only face paint. And what happens when we stop feeling safe in our camouflage? What happens when we feel the chill winds of uncomfortable truth. How do we then find our place?

A dandy discovers his own distinctive answer. He has looked at the world as so many have seemed prepared to accept it and decided that, in all honesty, it's pretty humdrum. He wants - like all of us do - to be special. But he's prepared to throw down a perfumed gauntlet and fight. So he sets out to write his own rulebook, to make up his own codes, to revel in the glory of his own individuality. The dandy makes explicit an urge that lies latent in everyone. In creating himself, he creates his own hero. He flouts isolation by flaunting his own lone self in its face.

But though life means one man alone with the darkness, in being a dandy I was never alone. Baudelaire, Rimbaud, Wilde, Byron, Tintin, Marc Bolan, Johnny Rotten, Quentin Crisp, Francis Bacon, the Dadaists : all dandies, roped together like mountaineers heading for the summit of beauty. I unabashedly declare my adoration of all of them. They have been the beacons in my night. I looked into all their mirrors and saw myself. You can

WRITING A BOOK IS, OF COURSE, A FORM OF failure. As a dandy I seek to be somebody rather than to do something. What I am matters more than what I produce. Why produce anything save my own carefully cultivated self? My greatest work is my personality. My life - and my death - are my art.

But art itself is worthless. It is material, earthly, impermanent. No matter how great, it still pales besides the transcending majesty of nature - or the simple beauty of my face. In his highest aspirations man is still mocked. No wonder that art and psychosis have been such tender lovers for so long; that the road

track me everywhere through their snow. I am a dandy. A dandy is a poet. But I do not create. God creates. I assemble. I am a professional plagiarist. I will steal from anyone and everyone and everywhere. Plagiarism is an art: the art of stealing from thieves. I put my hands in my pockets and find someone else's fingers and give them a friendly squeeze.

Of course, sometimes my life and art seem to me nothing but slops - a thin gruel with undigested lumps of Baudelaire, Byron, and Bolan. Of course, sometimes my art seems like nothing but mediocrity on stilts. Oh well, I shall stroke my mediocrity 'til it purrs, prod it 'til it springs yowling from my lap like crass vulgarity to stalk off round the world.

Being a dandy is a condition rather than a profession. It is a defence against suffering and a celebration of life. It is not fashion; it is not wealth; it is not learning; it is not beauty.

It is a shield and a sword and a crown - all pulled out of the dressing up box in the attic of the imagination. Of course life is nothing but a game of dressing up and make-believe. All dress is fancy dress except our natural skins. I know I am a pretend artist and a pretend writer. But I play with all my heart. Play transforms us, magically. Dandyism is a lie which reveals the truth, and the truth is that we are what we pretend to be.

Dandyism is a modern form of stoicism. It is a religion whose only sacrament is suicide. And so, like a suicide, I open my veins. I am here to bathe you in my little universe of melancholy. I am here to bleed for you. I may dress for Sebastian but I undress for everybody else. If I had not had to live I would never have had to let any of this out. Now, in writing *Dandy in the Underworld*, my only terror is the terror of being understood.

On alcohol:
Dignity is the only thing you can't preserve in alcohol.

On ambition:
When my school careers adviser asked me what I wanted to be when I grew up, I replied, without heartfelt irony, 'a woman'.

On Beau Brummell:
Prissily precise, Mr. Brummell was essentially a conformist. True dandyism is rebellious.

On the body:
The only function of my body was to carry my beautiful face around. It was merely a pedestal for my head.

On clothes:
The sense of being well dressed gives a feeling of inward tranquillity that psychotherapy is powerless to bestow.

On doing nothing:
The trouble with doing nothing is that you can never take any time off.

On friendship:
Friends are not necessarily the people you like best. They are just the ones that got there first.

On gentlemen:
A gentleman is someone who, however impoverished, will refuse on principle to do anything useful.

On money:
The outside world seemed populated with people so primitive that they did not know how to get money except by working for it.

On orgasms:
Women can fake orgasms, but men can fake entire relationships.

On rich women:
She had the kind of money that made you want to show up on her doorstep with adoption papers.

On sex:
I remember the first time I had real sex – I still have the receipt.

On theatre:
The stage gets stuck with anything too boring to be shown on television.

On therapy:
Therapy has a point. Simple people can feel satisfyingly complex for a moment or two.

This year sees Great Britain host the World Beard & Moustache Championships, most of which will probably be won by Germans with too much time and moustache wax on their hands. We asked the Rubbishmen of Soho to make their own assessment of some of the more interesting beards in their vicinity

This man has a sweet beard and face and a kind nature. We like the length. We think he once wrote a song about shaving one's face entitled "The First Cut is the Deepest." His style is reminiscent of songsmith and Oxfam shelf filler, Cat O'Stevens, but how canst be it so? His current look falls betwixt Pop Idol and Idle Prophet.

We enjoy this young man's full and firm facial rug. It would be a fine thing to cuddle up to in a dustbin with. A distinguished look that states boldly: "I've my own brand of snuff made at Smith's Charing Cross Road, I've been dead since 1975, and they still sell it, so put that in your pipe and smoke it!" A bit overly perfumed but highly recommended.

This is a fine gentleman with a fine beard, very influenced by Lenin's great face thingy ma jiggy. 'Tis a trustworthy beard that sets off his ears. The World Ear Hair Championships are to be upheld In The Year Of Our Lord Next Year, in the Antipodes. Unfortunately this character is exempt as he is an Antip-atron. The beard has artistic pretensions, but what is it saying? Toulouse La Trek or Take Hart?

This man looks nice and I love the confidence that he enjoys street drinking with. Not wishing to be distracted from the task at hand but it would appear that he hath sipped from a half bottle of Dr. Hillbuts Purly (Sic) Medicinal Gin. Not many of these left in the Grandiloquent Empire these days. Once upon time Soho was awash with chaps sporting the Street Drinking Beard. Now alas it crawls with scrawny street urchins below shaving age, but at least they have the decency to smoke pipes.

CHIN CHIN

A splendid example from the ne'er-do-well school. He may have the piercing gaze of the all-night tattoo parlourist, but at least some attention has been reserved for his shaving mirror. You are not supposed to judge the man behind the bearded mask, as it's against the handwritten rules, but this man looks like a very kind and sweet person with a very fine coloured beard. We used to meet his type in the now debunked'led Intrepid Fox of Wardour

Ladygentleboys always seem to slip into these competitions to confound and foil us. Not this time! No truly bearded would sport this tragic form of pogonotomy, since his cheeks are bald! Bring me the boy at 12 and I'll show you the beard of the man. He is probably a make-up strumpet at the Alhambra Leicester Square. A very practical beard, wethinks, for office wear, wooing and the alike.

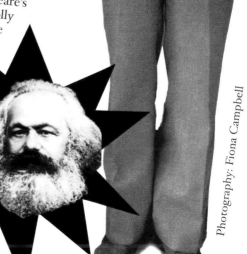

This beard is very handsome and looks in very good condition. We think we have seen this man at the single man's Pride Festival. It reminds us of our favourite merkin, used on many Shakespearian pro-ductions. And as we all know, young boys mysteriously played all of Shakespeare's ladies. Indeed there is a sense of folly here, but it is a fine example of The British Empire Lion.

This beard has to be the winner, by more than a whisker. It's bushy, has fine body and even tone colour-ing. And the comically dyed hair around the mouth gives one the impression of Al Jolson's lips, al-beit as a negative exposure. He also is the only contestant that comes from the Soho environs and can still be found living above Quo Vadis Burger house, fondling his face while reading large books. Mr. Groucho comes up Trumpers!

Photography: Fiona Campbell

AM I CHAP?

Readers are invited to send us their photographs for an
assessment of their Chappist credentials. Send your pictures to chap@thechap.net

STAR CHAP

Early signs of Chappism must be observed,
nurtured and rewarded. This young fellow
eschews the trappings of his generation, viz
computer consoles, kitchen knives and copies
of What Mobile?, choosing instead to reward
his intelligence with model aeroplanes, hand
grenades and a copy of The Chap.

This couple seem to be having fun and who are we
to put a stop to that? Well, if you insist: the hat is
an atrocious item that one might buy from a Third
World beach stall; the flower has been plucked too
early; the man too late.

Nice chaps, these. You could probably ask them directions to the nearest
branch of the Halifax and they would be extremely helpful. But ask them
where to find the nearest opium den and they wouldn't have a clue.
Nice, but not CHAPS.

These coves clearly take
themselves extremely seriously,
and for this reason we cannot.

Bridget was trying to use her new cordless Ladyshave in the yard when she became snagged in a fishing net. Oh well, that's life in a women's prison for you.

"Please find the enclosed picture for consideration," writes J. Thomas Grover, "of Mr. Daniel Lumbrezer, visiting professor of Sanskrit at the University of St. Christmas." Visiting professor of ill-fitting clothes, unimaginative velocipede and appalling valise, surely?

Sarah Allason strictly observes the new dress code for the Royal Enclosure at Ascot – namely no bare midriffs and no display of underwear, with a hemline not exceeding two inches above the knee – making her, au naturel, a Chapette.

"My name is George Allen and I live in Wiltshire. My interests are Polo, shooting and racing – I hope to have a career in bloodstock when I leave school." This photograph might win the heart of a Phillipino orphan girl, but not the approval of this department.

These young shavers seem to think that wearing their work clothes to drink all their mum's booze somehow makes them chaps. It does not. It merely makes them pissed.

Facial hair. Hairstyle. Spectacles. Nylon shirt. Poorly tied cravat. No cufflinks. No tobacco in pipe. The list could go on but there's really no point.

The Top Drawer

WHERE A GENTLEMAN RUMMAGES IN THE HOPE OF FINDING HIS FAVOURITE SILK HANKIE

FASHION FAUX PAS
Number 13: Boris Johnson

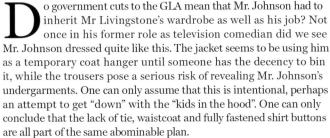

Do government cuts to the GLA mean that Mr. Johnson had to inherit Mr Livingstone's wardrobe as well as his job? Not once in his former role as television comedian did we see Mr. Johnson dressed quite like this. The jacket seems to be using him as a temporary coat hanger until someone has the decency to bin it, while the trousers pose a serious risk of revealing Mr. Johnson's undergarments. One can only assume that this is intentional, perhaps an attempt to get "down" with the "kids in the hood". One can only conclude that the lack of tie, waistcoat and fully fastened shirt buttons are all part of the same abominable plan.

But the kids don't go around trying to make expensive clothes look scruffy, as Mr Johnson has. They buy clothes that are expensive, but already scruffy. And as for their trousers – they wear those much further down their backsides than Boris.

BENJAMIN DISRAELI

One of Disraeli's outfits was described as "a black velvet coat lined with satin, purple trousers with a gold band running down the outside seam, a scarlet waistcoat, long lace ruffles and white gloves with several rings outside them". He rarely got up before midday, and all his adult life he was deeply in debt. He dealt with this by siphoning off money from the allowance that his mistress received from her husband.

Disraeli was an inveterate smoker of a hookah and a great admirer of "Turkish indolence, Turkish melancholy, and Turkish baths". Despite this, he was Prime Minister twice and Chancellor thrice, which is a lot more than Mr. Johnson has managed.

Jay-Z (a performance poet and board director), for his attempts to dress well without going too far (see below); never drinking anything but Moet & Chandon; and having the dignity to marry someone within his own social class.

UPSTAIRS

Bentley Fonzworth, for turning himself into a vulgar parody of a gentleman, to the extent of publishing an etiquette manual entitled, "How to be Posh and Ting" or some such.

Karl Lagerfeld, for terminating any lingering debate about whether he should be taken seriously, by producing the KL teddy bear.

Sebastian Flyte's teddy bear, Aloysius for surviving the appalling travesties committed in his name.

Eimer Ni Mhaoldomhnaigh, for designing this outfit for Ben Wishaw as Sebastian Flyte in the new film of *Brideshead Revisited*.

DOWNSTAIRS

Travelodge, for introducing "high-tech pyjamas" made of a fabric called DermaSilk, which "allows the skin to breathe, regulates body temperature and maintains the skin's moisture balance". The hotel chain had conducted a survey finding that two out of three guests complained of being "too hot or too cold". The hotel's proprietors are directed to our article on page 32, where they will learn how to keep one's temperature "just right".

Weaver & Wooff
by PG Woodlouse

I'M THINKING OF ATTENDING A BOOK LAUNCH, WEAVER - COULD YOU LAY OUT SOME APPROPRIATE ATTIRE?

THAT WILL DEPEND ON THE BOOK IN QUESTION, SIR....FOR LA NOUVELLE AMERICAINE I WOULD SUGGEST THE BOXBACK HOUNDSTOOTH WITH THE LEATHER GUNPATCHES...

IF IT'S A CONSTIPATED BLUESTOCKING SAGA OF THE DRABBLE VARIETY, THE OLD BLUE SERGE 3 PIECE, PERHAPS WITH PINCE-NEZ AND WHITE PLIMSOLLS A LA JAMES JOYCE...

MAY I ASK WHAT IS THE GENRE?

I BELIEVE IT'S A HARD-BOILED SEMI-PORNOGRAPHIC MENAGE-A-TROIS TWIXT A PLUG-UGLY LESBIAN SHIPPING HEIRESS, A SUICIDAL SOCIALITE AND A CONSUMPTIVE WRITER SET IN 1920S PARIS...

THEN I WOULDN'T BOTHER TURNING UP AT ALL SIR...

ATTERS' STIFF UPPER TIP

"Dear Atters, I was curious if you would know where one could order a moustache snood online. Thanks, Brian".

Well, Brian, I'm glad you asked. The moustache snood (or hammock) is a protective net which covers one's waxed whiskers. Essentially it prevents 'kinkage' and 'dribblage' while gambolling with the ladies and during slumber. Jauntily worn, a snood can also make one look quite dashing. We all love a lady in fishnets. Well, I'm no chauvinist, so let's give them a thrill too! One's lip sprouts coquettishly poking through fishnet gauze can only herald a night of spittle, tickle, snorts and erotica! In answer to Brian's query, one may purchase the item online via STERN, who can also furnish one with numerous other moustache accessories.

WWW.STERNHAAR.DE

HALL OF PLUMAGE

I have been informed by a reputable Hollywood source (Jude Law's private nanny) that the colonial actor allegedly has a very small "Dick Dastardly". Also, if Mr. Law insists on auditioning for the roles of both *Tank Top Girl* and Geoffrey from *Rainbow* then surely the clean shaved look would suffice. What's it all about, Alfalfa face?

AHH BISTO!

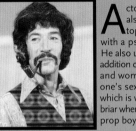

Actor Peter Wyngarde was also partial to colourful tank tops but coordinated them with a psychedelic set of whiskers. He also understood that, without the addition of a pipe, wearing long hair and women's clothes might cause one's sexuality to be questioned – which is why he always ditched the briar whenever a charming young prop boy walked on set.

THE WHISKERADE

A smorgasbord of moustachioed frolics and upper-lip erotica from Michael "Atters" Attree.

JUDGE MY SHRUB

Griffin Leach sent in these "candid" pictures of his friend Adam Libby, whom he claimed had "lost a bet made with a lady while on safari in Montreal, and, as a man of his word, had to remove his clothes". Personally I prefer the moustache with the clothes on, being partial to the ruffled shirt myself. However, when it comes to hirsute falsehoods, though I am not calling into question the veracity of Mr. Libby's upper-lip appendage, I cannot seriously condone a chest wig! Nevertheless, sir, your tache still wins a case of Spitfire, for being worthy of a spot of ack-ack from Jerry.

The man (or woman) whose photograph displays the most luxuriant plumage wins a whole case of Spitfire Ale. Send your entries to atters@ thechap.net or Judge My Shrub, PO Box 39216, London SE3 0XS.

COKED UP

Janet Taylor of Lock & Co. describes the origins of that most gentlemanly of titfers, the bowler, or Coke hat

L ock & Co., hatters, was commissioned in 1850 by William Coke to supply a new hat, designed to protect the heads of his gamekeepers while out riding from the hazards of low hanging branches and chance encounters with poachers. Their tall top hats were easily knocked off, damaged and in regular need of replacement.

A prototype of Mr. Coke's design was duly made, constructed from layers of muslin and stiffened with shellac – a varnish-like substance derived from an Indian beetle. The new hat was hard with a low, round crown, a small brim, covered in a rough and slightly hirsute finish felt. When Mr. Coke visited Lock & Co. to inspect the new hat, he took it outside onto the pavement and jumped up and down on it. The hat withstood the test and, in accordance with Lock & Co.'s tradition, it was christened the 'Coke' in his honour.

At Lock & Co. the hat continues to be called a Coke but it is more generally known as a 'Bowler', after hat makers the Bowler Bros. later manufactured their own version of it. In America it is referred to as the 'Derby' after the race meetings at which it was worn.

Lock & Co. is also renowned for its special hard hat-shaping device for the Coke and its taller crowned cousin, the top hat. Invented in the 1850s by an ingenious Frenchman M. Maillard, the conformateur head-measuring device is applied to the head, displacing the spokes of the machine and producing a card shape, or conform,

D'une élégance indiscutée...

CAPE
D. MORRETON
LA COIFFURE DE BON TON

D.MORRETON

which maps, the contours of the head at a sixth of life size. An adjustable wooden block is then made up around the conform to produce a block of the actual dimensions of the customer's head. Cards produced by the conformateur have established that American heads are slightly larger and longer than British ones, which have on average increased by at least three-eighths of an inch over the last fifty years.

Having started life in the country, the Coke rose from humble beginnings as an estate worker's hat and migrated to the city where it replaced the top hat. It became the badge of office for barristers, stockbrokers and civil servants until the 1980s. Today it is still the civilian hat of guard's officers, as displayed every year in the Combined Cavalry Old Comrades Association parade in Hyde Park, attended this year by Princes William and Prince Harry, both resplendent in their black cokes.

James Lock & Co. Ltd,
6 St James's Street
London SW1A 1EF
020 7930 8874
WWW.LOCKHATTERS.CO.UK

BOWLER BEARERS

A trawl through Lock & Co.'s ledgers turns up such illustrious Coke wearers as Sir Winston Churchill, Evelyn Waugh, the Duke of Windsor and Oscar Wilde. Sir Winston Churchill adopted a Cambridge – a flat-topped, square-crowned variation on the traditional Coke, named after the Duke of Cambridge, referring to it as his 'parliamentary' hat. Oscar Wilde's order for a Coke, meanwhile, sadly coincided with his detention at Reading Gaol. He was unable to settle his account and his name was entered into Lock's bad debt book for £3 and five shillings. Remarkably, on the day of the centenary of his death, his account was settled by one Royston Du Maurier, who felt that "some gesture must be made".

In The Avengers, Patrick McNee adopted various Cokes, among them a grey one with a distinctive tightly curled brim. The hat is so essential to his character that on the continent the series is known as Bowler Hat & Charm. When France's pre-eminent Avenger's fan club, the Steed Society, visited Lock & Co. they declared that it was indeed 'le temple du chapeau melon'. Despite the masculine origins of the hat, the Coke has also proved a hit for the ladies, particularly Liza Minelli in Cabaret. It is currently featured in Chanel's advertising campaign, where it is provocatively employed as the sole adornment of the young English actress Keira Knightley.

Other illustrious coke wearers include Terry-Thomas, Edwards VII and VIII, John Le Mesurier, Christopher Eubank, the Thompson Twins and Laurel and Hardy

THE TOP DRAWER

FASHION FAUX PAS
Number 15: Hollywood Actors

Brad Pitt is trying very hard to strike the debonair gentleman actor pose, with a nod back to the good old days of Tinseltown. He's put on a bespoke tuxedo, got someone to tie his bow tie and found a dumb brunette to stand near ... then he goes and ruins it all by borrowing David Soul's sunglasses.

Clark Gable, arriving at the Oscars in 1954, looks as if he threw his ensemble on between several stiff martinis. It adds to his natural swagger and makes it look as if Grace Kelly is trying to stand next to him.

He's Irish, he's half-crazy, he never shaves or has his hair cut, and his buttocks are probably covered in tattoos. Which is why **Colin Farrell** looks ridiculous in a suit. At least he's wearing a weskit, though it probably reeks of motorcycles and loose women.

Peter O'Toole also wears his Irish roots on his sleeve – but the sleeve was tailored on Savile Row. He is so genuinely louche that, even with his tie properly knotted and his pocket square in the right place, he looks like someone you wouldn't leave your grandmother with, let alone your daughter. His carnation probably smells of carnations.

Mickey Rourke thought that the dress code for the Oscars was to dress as an Oscar. Still, for a man aged 37-and-a-half, he looks in pretty good shape.

During the 1980s, Mickey Rourke was heralded as the new Brando, mumbling his way through cult films and picking fights with directors. His sartorial style was not remarkable, but he cut a noirish dash and won the hearts of numerous ladies. He is not related to the Mickey Rourke pictured left.

UPSTAIRS

Get Tweed. Wear Tweed. Drive

For setting off on an epic 3,000 voyage around the Indian Subcontinent in a tuk-tuk. Edd Rushton, James Kilkenny and Deniz Hasaan have filled their diminutive Oriental pleasure vehicle with nothing but bare essentials for the tropics: gin, a gramophone player, tea-making equipment and dinner suits. They are doing it for charity, and The Chap is behind them all the way to Bangladesh.

The Genuine Harris Tweed Company

For putting the crofters of the Outer Hebrides back into work. For the last few years, there have only been two ways of buying Harris Tweed: in ready made jackets (in only four different patterns) from one mill on the Isle of Harris, or in full 80-metre bolts from another. This prevented small tailors from buying any new tweed at all, ultimately leading to a dangerous dearth of this most exquisite fabric. The GHTC has reopened the channels between independent crofters, finishing mills and tailors so that the full range of patterns is once again available in any quantity.

HAND WOVEN
Harris Tweed
HARRIS TWEED
100% WOOL

BORVEMOR

DOWNSTAIRS

Indian Moustaches The effects of globalisation have had a catastrophic effect on Indian facial hair. Where once Indian gentlemen proudly bore vast moustaches and flowing beards, convinced they conferred virility, they are now buffing their chins in the belief that it will lead them to coveted jobs in the I.T. sector and pale wives with breast implants. The police force in India recently relaxed the rule requiring all officers to sport a bushy moustache, while the only profession where a moustache is still mandatory is among doormen of five-star hotels.

Tom Cruise

For barging his way into Germany to make Valkyrie with little more grace than Hitler's invasion of Poland in 1939. The film is clearly nothing more than an excuse for Mr. Cruise to prance about in SS uniform, while waving his Scientology badge in the faces of immigration officials.

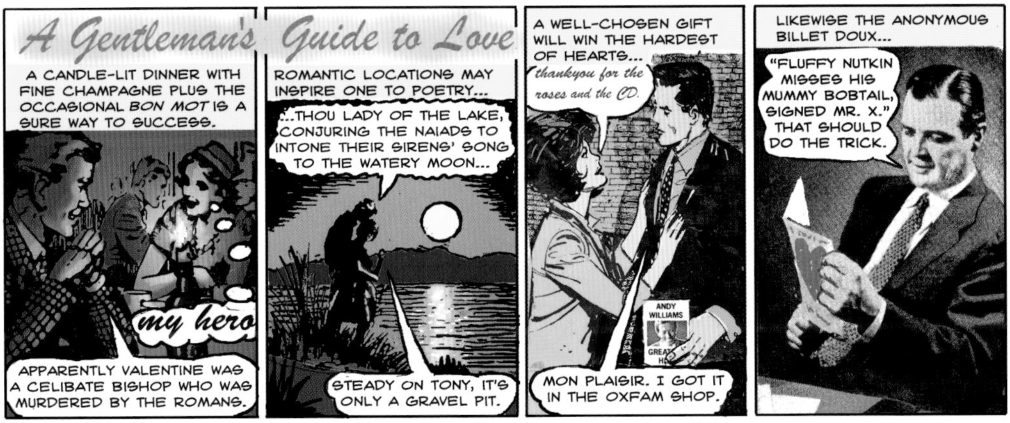
A Gentleman's Guide to Love
A CANDLE-LIT DINNER WITH FINE CHAMPAGNE PLUS THE OCCASIONAL BON MOT IS A SURE WAY TO SUCCESS.
my hero
APPARENTLY VALENTINE WAS A CELIBATE BISHOP WHO WAS MURDERED BY THE ROMANS.
ROMANTIC LOCATIONS MAY INSPIRE ONE TO POETRY...
...THOU LADY OF THE LAKE, CONJURING THE NAIADS TO INTONE THEIR SIRENS' SONG TO THE WATERY MOON...
STEADY ON TONY, IT'S ONLY A GRAVEL PIT.
A WELL-CHOSEN GIFT WILL WIN THE HARDEST OF HEARTS...
thankyou for the roses and the CD.
ANDY WILLIAMS
MON PLAISIR. I GOT IT IN THE OXFAM SHOP.
LIKEWISE THE ANONYMOUS BILLET DOUX...
"FLUFFY NUTKIN MISSES HIS MUMMY BOBTAIL, SIGNED MR. X." THAT SHOULD DO THE TRICK.

GRAND TOURING

JAGUAR E-TYPE 3.8 SERIES ONE ROADSTER

Veteran Motoring writer W de Forte recalls his first time behind the wheel of what many describe as the louchest automobile ever made

Some time in September, 1960, I had occasion to visit my chums at Jaguars, where a very special machine was waiting for appraisal. The prospect of a new model from Coventry was exciting, to put it mildly. It is difficult to imagine, after recent sorry events, but in those days the Cat people were riding the crest of a wave. Indeed, Sir William Lyons and his team seemingly could do no wrong (although the recent takeover of Daimler may not have been obviously beneficial!).

Swinging through the Browns Lane factory gates after an invigorating blast down from Shropshire along largely uninfested roads, I spotted a car-shaped dustsheet in the parking area, directly under Bill's lair. The contours were very low, very long and obviously of sporting intent. I'll admit that my nosiness overwhelmed my sense of propriety, causing me to sidle over and lift the corner of the cover. Alas, a tantalising glimpse of a rounded flank was all I managed before being rumbled:

"Stop right there, de Forte, or we'll have that old banger of yours towed away to the junkyard immediately!"

With the air of an apple-scrumping schoolboy caught in the act by the local bobby, I swivelled round to see the towering presence of service chief Lofty England marching towards me. The mock-martinet tone of his voice softened as he approached, his face dissolving into a smile. "Knew you wouldn't be able to resist having a shufti if we left it out here... the innate journalistic instinct, eh?"

After putting up with gentler joshing at the expense of my 'old banger' (how they'd have laughed on the other sides of their faces if they'd known that vintage Bentleys would be worth millions in the next century!), we adjourned to the office for tiffin. Somewhat inevitably, the rest of the boys gradually homed in to join us. And as the afternoon wore on, tea was replaced by a rather stronger libation, and we were all feeling distinctly merry by the time the main

workforce headed home. (Incidentally, the vast majority were on bicycles: wages were such in those far-off days that very few could imagine owning the fruits of their labours.)

Despite the absence of that fanciful modern concept, 'Global Warming', the evening air was still distinctly sultry when we eventually trooped outside to inspect the new arrival. The wraps came off with a flourish, and there it stood in all its glory: E-type, or XK-E, as our colonial cousins insisted it be known. Reposing in oblique sunshine, the car looked strikingly splendid. I was quite taken aback by its beauty. Some details were not finalised on this pre-production roadster, but who could have doubted that Jaguars had produced yet another winner?

The offer of a strictly off-the-record spin was eagerly accepted. Dropping into the snug cockpit, surrounded by leather and figured aluminium, I thumbed the starter and heard the big 3.8 litre six cylinder engine gurgle into life through its triple SU carburettors, a prod of throttle clearing its lungs with a satisfying rasp. Vvvrrrrmmmm. I couldn't help grinning as I felt the whole car rock sideways through torque reaction. "Exhaust's a bit throaty on this one – we'll quieten it down a touch for the great unwashed," said Lofty, anticipating my next question. He also admitted that the power output of this particular example may have been slightly in excess of the figure to be catalogued, which was similar to the outgoing XK150S's 265hp.

Ah, yes: *'Bliss was it that dawn to be alive, but to be young was very heaven'*. It is hard to believe that our dear friend William Wordsworth had not driven an XK-E when he wrote those lines. Threading gently out through the suburban contagions of Coventry, my *disco volante* felt entirely happy at 30-40mph in top gear, the revolution counter needle hardly stirring from its stop. Used thus, the E progressed with almost total silence save for a whoosh from the tyre treads. Even the exhaust contrived to stay subdued when dawdling.

Above all, though, I remember the car for its astonishingly compliant ride, courtesy of new independent suspension. While the model's predecessor, the XK150, betrayed its age and live rear axle by becoming wayward on occasions, the E's double-wishbone set-up, developed directly from racing experience, offered limousine-like comfort. Moreover, as I was shortly to discover, the chassis handled wonderfully at high speed. Truly, the best of both worlds, and this itself was a good enough reason not to christen the model 'XK160', as had been intended originally.

After skirting Lady Godiva's home city to the south, we picked up the old A45 coach road, the pace picking up as we plunged into glorious green countryside and traffic dispersed. A scintilla of extra throttle made the long bonnet rise with feline grace, the speedometer rushing past 60mph with contemptuous ease.

There was good reason to be heading this way. An early strand of Britain's much-delayed motorway network began near Dunchurch, about ten miles of largely empty dual-carriageway appended to the old A5 at Crick. Wily old Sir William liked to claim that Minister of Transport Ernest Marples had built this new superhighway expressly as a development facility for the Midlands car industry. A slightly dubious notion, perhaps,

'Bliss was it that dawn to be alive, but to be young was very heaven'. It is hard to believe that our old friend Willie Wordsworth had not driven an XK-E when he wrote those lines.

but there's little doubt that M45 was a handy place to test this motorcar's high-speed mettle!

A trace of mist was rolling in off the meadows as we crossed the unofficial 'start line'. After overtaking a dawdler who seemed alarmed by the novelty of a road with no junctions for so many miles, I was finally able to give the Jaguar its head. 5,500rpm in third launched us past the ton. Then into top (without much help from the dratted Moss gearbox, one of the car's less marvellous features), foot to the floor, and 110mph... 120mph... 130mph with a mellifluous trail of acoustic spume in our wake. And although I thought it prudent to straddle the central white line, she tracked straight and true at such elevated velocities.

Acceleration was waning now, but we had motorway to spare for an assault on the magic ton-fifty! A mile or so later, the needle on the big Smiths dial was still nudging higher, 150mph looming.

Speeding in an open car is truly exhilarating. Trapped in a screaming vortex, head buffeted, eyes streaming: I can only liken it to travel in an early aeroplane, or perhaps the first few moments of a parachute jump, before the canopy opens (the latter tends to follow the former, in my experience!).

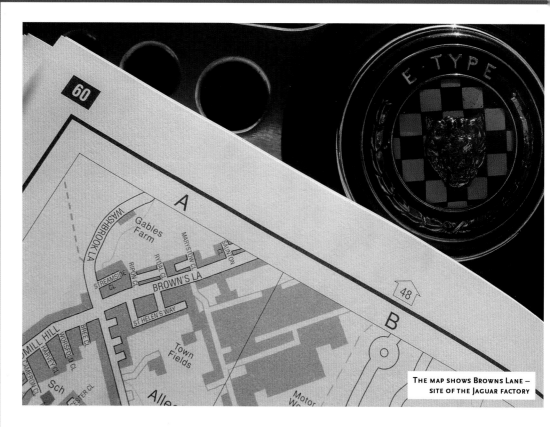

THE MAP SHOWS BROWNS LANE — SITE OF THE JAGUAR FACTORY

ROADSTERS, WHILE SLOWER THAN COUPES, STILL MANAGED 100MPH

THE WORLD SEEN THROUGH AN E-TYPE WIND-
SCREEN IS NOT WHAT IT WAS IN DE FORTE'S DAY

That too-distant day we clocked 152mph. Possibly the instrument exaggerated by a few percent, but I do know that we despatched eight miles of Tarmacadam in well under four minutes, in an era when most vehicles were lucky to do it in ten. Arriving back at Browns Lane, the return leg enlivened by a dice with a determined bod on a Triumph motorcycle, no doubt a tester from the nearby Meriden factory, I had never been more impressed by a car.

Reader, I bought one. As soon as RHD production examples became available, a red drop top became mine, making it the best £2,000 I ever spent.

Many E-types have passed through the de Forte stringbacks since. Apart from a ferrously challenged V12 automatic, I liked them all. But original is definitely best, as I re-discovered nearly half a century after my first drive, when the chance to sample an early 3.8 litre Series 1 arose.

A 1962 E-TYPE IN LOUCHE RED IS OFFERED FOR PURCHASE BY THE GENTLEMEN AT WWW.CLASSICANDSPORTSCAR.LTD.UK

Sadly, my aged bones dropped into the cockpit with less alacrity than in 1960, but once ensconced the cabin was as appealing as ever. Pressing the starter summoned the past in my mind, yet failed miserably to do the same in reality. Alas, the open roads we enjoyed then are now a seething morass of inhumanity.

And yet, pushing the loud pedal lightened my gloom. A bid to clock 150mph again would have no doubt resulted in a period of incarceration in one of HM's hotels, so I did my best to keep tight rein on the six cylinder beast. But my best fell short, and I must confess that I gave in to temptation a couple of times when goaded. Thus, an upstart in an Audi, of all things, learned that an old motor driven by an even older gent would not necessarily be driven at a molluscs' pace! Exiting a roundabout, the blighter pulled out to overtake. I waited until he was alongside, and then floored it in third. Soon he was a straining silver dot in my mirror.

A drag race is one thing, but it would be folly to presume that 1961's ultimate could match 21st century chassis technology. Fortunately, the road was straight. By current standards, the E has modest roadholding and will be embarrassed by whippersnapper hatchbacks in the twisties. No matter, because driving pleasure comes from a car's feel, sound and handling feedback, more so than ever now that speed is deemed to be so socially unacceptable.

The E-type is an automotive icon; of that there is no doubt. But is it suitable transport for chaps, one might wonder? Of course it is! While in the second half of the 1960s Jaguars attracted the wrong sort of clientele, and driving gloves and cravats were replaced by purple gauntlets and neckscarves – personified by that ghastly Simon Dee character – the marque later recovered its dignity, if not its profitability, and any fellow of taste should be proud to be seen in one now.

HOTEL
FOR SCOUNDRELS

Matthew Howard takes us on a guided tour of some of the key
locations in the film School for Scoundrels

In addition to spawning the memorable catch phrase "Hard cheese!" the tennis match in School For Scoundrels remains one of the most unforgettable sporting competitions committed to celluloid. Its appeal is universal – as evinced by a cursory glance at One's Tube, where countless versions of the match have been kindly and illegally uploaded by fans. Chaps, chapettes and the untweeded alike find something utterly compelling about the notion of a cad winning a game of tennis through sheer guile and cunning. Especially when the amours of a young lady named April are at stake. The fact is that the English love a bounder, and perhaps because we are so unsuccessful at sport on the international stage, the gentleman cheat has become a uniquely English archetype. One cannot imagine a Spanish or a Swedish scoundrel striding on to the court in a pair of white flannel trousers, and proceed, without the benefit of training, skill or indeed adequate equipment, to utterly thrash his opponent.

School for Scoundrels was entirely shot in and around Elstree Studios in Hertfordshire, and many of the locations are still intact. The railway station at which Palfrey alights on his way to Potter's College of Lifemanship, supposedly set in Yeovil, is actually that of Hertford East and pretty much unchanged today. The car showroom at which Messrs

The tennis court as it is today, with
the aura of a ruined coloseum
where great battles were fought

Matthew Howard (left) took the part of Henry Palfrey, while Atters was the obvious choice for Raymond Delaunay

Dunston and Dudley sell Palfry the Swiftmobile is located at 90-108 Pinner Road, Harrow. It now masquerades as a Hyundai dealership under the name "Colin Collins" (no hyphen). Finally, should you ever accidentally find yourself in Hendon, you might like to look up Palfrey's bachelor apartment, which can be found on the top floor of the virtually unchanged Thurlby Croft in Mulberry Close (off Parson Street) in Hendon, London NW4.

But the location most likely to quicken the pulse of any British film fan is the tennis club where Raymond Delauney thrashes Henry Palfrey under the watchful gaze of April Stevens. We are delighted to report that the court is still intact, though in a state of mild disrepair, within the grounds of what is now the Corus Hotel Elstree on Barnet Lane, London WD6. When The Chap visited to pay homage, the staff seemed blissfully unaware of hotel's crucial place in the cinematographic history of our sceptered isle, though the receptionist rather helpfully announced that she had studied School for Scandal for her A-Level.

What the staff do know is that the tennis court is scheduled for demolition in the near future, so we can only urge all T-T fans to make their pilgrimage there sooner rather than later.

The Chap made its own inspection of the site, inviting renowned tennis champions Matthew Howard and Michael Attree to recreate the legendary tennis match from School For Scoundrels. We need hardly report that the score was 6-0, 6-0 to Atters, with the third set unplayed.

Raymond Delaunay immediately sets himself an advantage by assisting April down the steps to the court

Delaunay: "I'll take this end. No need to change, is there? Would you like 15 to start or shall we play level?"

Henry Palfrey: "Aren't you standing rather close to the net?" Delaunay: "No, it's my game. I'll move back for the second serve."

"Hard cheese! Love-40. Sure you wouldn't like that handicap?"

Delaunay: "Ready?" Palfrey: "Not really."
Delaunay: "Ready now?"

April: "Nice shot, Henry".
Palfrey: "Thank you, April – oof!"

Palfrey: "Tricky spin you put on it."
Delaunay: "Not really. Court's a bit uneven."

Delaunay: "My game. And the set."

Thanks to: Rebecca Vincent, Liz Vincent, Pam Vincent. Special thanks to the staff at the Corus Hotel, Elstree www.corushotels.com/elstree Reservations 0844 736 8602

MOST EXCELLENT CANOPY

Alex Smythe-Smith huddles out of the April showers to look at the history of
that essential gentleman's accoutrement, the umbrella

Given the English climate, it is astonishing that it was the late 17th century before a waterproof umbrella made its debut on the streets of the capital. Although pre-restoration parasols had for some time been in abundance amongst the nobility, their role was to shade ladies' delicate heads from occasional but unforgiving sunshine. Yet squally conditions often forced the populace to remain indoors for fear of dampness infiltrating their bespoke garments. And so, eventually, parasols were reinvented to accommodate the inclement British weather, showers being more customary than sunshine.

However, umbrellas got off to a troubled beginning. Viewed as an effeminate appendage, they were initially only used by gentlewomen and, despite their undoubted benefits, it was a long time before rain umbrellas were accepted as suitable accessories for gentlemen. It took pioneering philanthropist Jonas Hanway to make them acceptable amongst male elements of London society. A busy chap dividing his time between The Marine Society, The Royal Navy and his governing duties at various hospitals, Hanway was forever hopping in and out of carriages and insisted on taking his umbrella with him to all appointments, in order to protect his fine attire from the elements.

His radical contraption was met with little enthusiasm from coachmen, however, who feared that its growing popularity might deny them business. For a while the rogues mercilessly heckled the avant-garde businessman whenever he strode by, brolly proudly swinging. But Hanway resisted such bullying tactics and, defying an outrageous rumour that he only used an umbrella because his income failed to cover the expenditure of carriages, continued to sport his somewhat cumbersome rain protector on a daily basis. His persistence paid off and eventually the idea of shielding oneself from a downpour blossomed, and the upper classes began to embrace this revolutionary accessory. Such was Jonas's reputation at this time that Londoners referred to all umbrellas as "Hanways".

As the notion of mobile shelter against a deluge became acceptable, coffee houses began popularising the umbrella, employing them to shelter customers as they dashed from their drained cups to waiting carriages.

But the early wooden crook handles with oiled silk canopies were difficult to operate and unacceptably heavy when wet, and genteel society breathed a sigh of relief when the first umbrella patent was registered in 1786 with ribs radiating from a central shaft holding up a circular coned canopy. The improved style opened the floodgates and inventors poured their innovative ideas into the Patent Office until the end of the 19th century.

In 1830 entrepreneur James Smith, sensing a budding market, found time between fathering nine children to establish the first umbrella shop in London. Politicians and local dignitaries, anticipating a soggy season, rushed to the premises to purchase top rate items, assured of a guaranteed repair service should any mishaps occur. But it took the Industrial Revolution to supply the masses and soon not only Great Britain but the whole of her Empire was awash with umbrellas. By now they were not only functional but had evolved into popular fashion objects. To meet the growing demand, a mass slaughter of whales was necessary to provide sufficient bone for the shafts, whilst mines from the colonies were plundered for decorative metals and jewels.

As the century dripped away, respected elements of society took to carrying their umbrellas with them, irrespective

Umbrellas were officially turned into sports equipment at the Chap Olympiad

Some gentlemen are so attached to their brollies that they even sleep under them

Seven singular facts concerning umbrellas and their bearers, by Torquil Arbuthnot

Mr. JS Duncan, in his 1801 work, Hints to the Bearers of Walking Sticks and Umbrellas, categorised umbrella bearers as "Shield-Bearers, Sky-Strikers, Mud-Scoopers, Inverters, Unicorns, and Self-Tormentors."

When David Dyce Sombre was adopted as the son and heir of the Begum of Sirdanah in Hindustan, he was permitted to take the royal umbrella (an indication of high rank in India) as part of his crest. Thus it featured on the coat of arms he used in Britain, where he was elected a Member of Parliament. He was ejected from his seat for bribery and certified insane, before dying in 1851.

Jane Austen noted that to be "equipped properly" for the spa town of Bath entailed the acquisition of an umbrella.

Evelyn Waugh recounted the following incident, glimpsed from a taxi in Paris in 1929: "He was a man of middle age and, to judge by his bowler hat and frock coat, of the official class, and his umbrella had caught alight. I saw him in the centre of a small crowd, grasping it still by the handle and holding it at arm's length so that the flames should not scorch him."

In 1936 a newspaper photographer snapped Edward VIII strolling along on a rainy afternoon under an umbrella. This photograph caused consternation among the Establishment: carrying a furled umbrella was one thing, but actually opening it was quite infra dig. A gentleman should keep his umbrella tightly furled at all times; at the sight of rain one may use one's umbrella to hail a taxicab.

The Bulgarian dissident Georgi Markov was murdered by the Bulgarian secret police in 1978 on Waterloo Bridge. A spy fired a poisoned pellet into Markov's thigh from an umbrella modified as an airgun.

The Golden Umbrella is a symbol of royalty in Burma, where the title of the ruler of Ava was "Lord of the Twenty-Four Umbrellas".

of the cumulus hovering overhead, ladies welcoming a spot of drizzle in order to display their latest design. Gentlemen showed a slightly more reserved style however, preferring to hold their accessory tightly rolled, in order for it to resemble the masculine walking stick. Even today, it is still not considered strictly appropriate for a gentleman to unfurl his brolly.

After the 1939-45 unpleasantness, an onslaught of technology resulted in telescopic umbrellas flooding the country. Whilst practical, they lacked the panache of their predecessors and high society continued to favour the more traditional full-length model. A decade later, oiled cotton canvases were replaced with nylon canopies. The forte of this new material lay in its strength, the fact that it failed to rot being an added bonus. An attempt was made during the decadent 1960s to market PVC umbrellas, but despite the transparency of the textile undoubtedly aiding pedestrians of these shores on our numerous dank days, early environmental anxieties dampened their allure, not to mention their sartorial unsuitability. The black umbrella remains the accessory of choice for gentlemen who wish to be taken seriously. Its metal tip, if properly sharpened, can also provide an impromptu weapon with which to fend of armed ruffians.

Sadly, vulgar golf umbrellas have since cascaded into the business world, their oversized canopies an ideal vehicle to exhibit coarse advertising. At the other end of the market, cheap, fold-up versions from the Far East are commonplace amongst the masses.

But for well-heeled chaps seeking traditional quality and service, James Smith and Sons are still thriving in New Oxford Street, London.

James Smith & Sons, Hazelwood House, 53 New Oxford Street, London, WC1A 1BL

FEAST OF
ST. STEPHEN

In a frank and erudite interview, Stephen Fry puts The Chap straight on precisely what the publication is and is not, as well as giving voice to some rather controversial but heartfelt views on the Panama hat

Ever since first appearing on *University Challenge*, *The Cellar Tapes* and *There's Nothing To Worry About* in the 1980s, Mr. Fry has been there to enunciate, entertain and educate our great nation. Picking a career highlight is tricky. There was his marvellous sketch show (co-written with Hugh Laurie) *A Bit Of Fry and Laurie*, his delightful role as General 'Melchy' in *Blackadder Goes Forth*, his acclaimed turn as Oscar Wilde in the 1997 film *Wilde* and, more recently, his role as learned host on *QI*.

And yet, for all his success, there has always been a hint of the antiestablishment about Mr. Fry. This is a man who spent three months in the rather Dickensian-sounding Pucklechurch Prison at the age of 17 for absconding from the Norfolk College of Arts and Technology with a purloined credit card. Far from emerging from the experience a ruffian however, Stephen Fry has gone on to become the country's foremost expert on just about everything except dancing.

> *"I hope these questions aren't designed to make a posing snob of me. I have no objection to others wearing quite as many flips and all the flops that fancy or need dictates"*

What, for you, epitomises the very essence of Englishness?
Lawks. So hard to say. Church bells pealing out a triple bob major, villagers clustered inside the tea tent at a rainy summer fête, The Archers Omnibus, swallows swooping and diving over a cricket field as the sun sets. These are all very middle class English images, of course. But then, as E. M. Forster observed, the English character is defined by the character of its middle classes. One might as easily suggest nylon sheets drying on a revolving clothes line in a garbage filled garden, drunken vomiting in the streets, sullen service in a fried chicken take-away and vicious playground bullying. But you probably do not want such pictures in your head. Which of us does?

What is your idea of absolute heaven?
Sitting in a box at Lord's cricket ground during an Ashes Test.

And your idea of a hell on earth?
Being at party where there is dance music or dancing of any kind. Having to dance. Not being able to talk because of the music at a party. Parties of any kind. Dancing of any kind. Having to watch dancing on television. Ballroom dancing is particularly inimical to me.

What three items of clothing would you rescue in the event of your wardrobe being invaded by a swarm of moths?
Two particular suits (one blue pin-stripe, the other dark blue) and my best dinner jacket. I should be unhappy to be pantless and sockless, however.

Are you happy with the way in which modern society is heading, or do you see room for improvement in any particular areas?
One must, as Gwendoline observed in *The Importance of Being Earnest*, always leave room for improvements. But there again I have no idea where modern society is heading. Nor do you. Nor does anyone else. Improvements? I hope you don't want to me to wank on about manners, respect, courtesy and suchlike drivel? You aren't the *Daily Mail*, for heaven's sake.

Have you ever pined for the services of a good tailor?
I'm not sure I ever have. One might pine for a good bookshop when stuck somewhere remote and in need of reading matter and I have certainly pined for an Apple Store, but to pine for a tailor would be strange and – dare one say it? – pretentious beyond permission.

"Airs of louche sophistication cannot be said, surely, to derive from exhibitions of virtue? It is hard to be louchely sophisticated while demonstrating impatience, anger or any outward affect that involves vanity, egoism or malevolent energy"

photograph: johnny boylan

Mr. Fry's choice of penny loafers to umpire local cricket matches shows a devil-may-care sartorial approach

What is your idea of a perfect English gentleman?
One who entertains no thought that he is any such thing. One who would more easily fly through the air than judge anyone else for being or not being a gentleman. One who would never use the word.

Can you name an example, living or deceased?
Martin Gilliat, now no longer with us. He was the Queen Mother's secretary for many years and came as close as anyone I have met. Not because of the caste into which he was born, but because of the kindliness, energy, sweetness of nature and eternal delight with which he met people and the radiant sense of bonhomie he propagated.

And his female counterpart?
I wonder what that might be? The word "lady" is almost impossible to utter without inducing nausea. "Gentlewoman" will hardly do… At any rate, amongst the most perfectly charming and excellent women I have met I would certainly count Phyllida Law, the actress.

Have you ever considered the wearing of sportswear for any activity other than sport?
Heavens yes. Who do you think I am, Sebastian Horsley (whom God preserve)? Not a shell suit, perhaps, but a rugby shirt or a cricket sweater are all unexceptionable about the house, surely? Fives gloves are ideal for gardening. Who has not flung on a badminton sock, racquetball shorts or hockey trousers when the need arises?

"Had you asked me in 1912 what type of facial hair I think is suitable for a gentleman, we should be agreed that only a hound of hell would go about clean-shaven"

Have you everfound it necessary or appropriate to wear a pair of flip-flops?
Often, but I have never done so, owing to an inability to find comfort in that class of footjoy. I don't have the toes for it. The rubber stem that is supposed to go between big toe and second toe will chafe and rub so. But I hope these questions aren't designed to make a posing snob of me. I have no objection to others wearing quite as many flips and all the flops that fancy or need dictates. They seem perfectly appropriate for beach, pool or light tropical terrain. They are the sandal of choice for two thirds of the world's poor, if not an even greater proportion. Waterproof, cheap, durable and available in a dizzying array of colourways. I have seen many children in poor villages in Africa, Madagascar, South America and South East Asia who own literally nothing other than shorts and flip-flops.

"My kingdom for a horse!" declared Richard III. What object have you ever craved with such intensity?
Any digital gadget a month or so before its due release. It is as if my whole being undergoes a need-a-pee-now experience. I am bent forward in urgent wanting, my face strained into a rictus of desperation and hope.

At the moment I am feeling this for Snow Leopard, the next Apple operating system, for the iPhone 3, the Palm Pre and the Nokia 97. Perhaps, such are the long lead times of magazines, these longings will have been fulfilled by the time this number of *The Chap* hits the news stands.

In a what-might-have-been moment for the Handlebar Club, Mr. Fry sported a magnificent (though fake) English moustache

"The tip of a vast edifice of research, the mouthpiece for all things interesting" – Stephen Fry

What item of clothing are you determined never to wear?
To be determined never to do something seems to be rather poor-spirited, bumptious and mulish, don't we feel? Was it not Arnold Bax who said that in this life one should try everything once, except incest and country dancing?

Which of the vices, if any, do you think can lend one an air of louche sophistication?
Most of them. Airs of louche sophistication cannot be said, surely, to derive from exhibitions of virtue? Perhaps it is hard to be louchely sophisticated while demonstrating impatience, anger or any outward affect that involves vanity, egoism or malevolent energy.

What type of facial hair do you think is suitable for a gentleman?
These are all issues of fashion and the moment. And therefore beneath one's notice. Had you asked me in 1912 we should be agreed that only a hound of hell would go about clean-shaven. Today things are a little different. Personally – and this is my preference only, not a prescriptive or proscriptive attempt at definition – I am all for scraping away the whiskery excrescences of nature and letting the skin shine free, but I have no objection to the growths that other men might sport.

How many different varieties of hat do you own, and which is your favourite?
Gracious heavens. How many varieties of hat, rather than instances of hat? Anyone who owns or wears a panama is asking to be thrashed, that much is clear. It's the kind of hat that unimaginative art directors dress sixty-year-olds in for TV advertisements that suggest a happy future for pensioners.

Midsomer Murders costume designers will, I'm afraid, commit the same sin – which they compound with Viyella shirts and shooting sticks and other such nonsense. I would place elastic-waisted trouserings, leather-buttoned cardigans and electric golf-carts above the vomit-inducing embarrassment of the panama. Yes, I truly would. At least your elastic-waisted trouser is honest. It isn't reaching for an effect it cannot understand, it isn't so blind to nuance, history and humanity as to be not a lapse, not an error but a mortal sin.

The panama is, let us not palter with the truth, exactly the kind of horror that is advertised in the back of the *Mail on Sunday* or the *Telegraph* magazines and fit only, therefore, for the most lost and hopeless cases of bourgeois embarrassment. As well to have tattooed on your forehead the words "I am a fatuous twat" as to wear a panama. Since the heyday of headwear, almost all styles and classes of hat have become loathsome, as a matter of fact; the panama is only the most extreme example.

A hat is now a self-conscious style statement that only the very few can get away wit h. Not only do you have to be socially and morally the kind of person who can get away with a hat, you also have to have the kind of head that a hat suits. A millimetre either way and you are no longer Wearing A Hat, you simply have An Object On Your Head – there is a great difference.

I have a top hat for weddings and absurd race meetings and that is about it. I don't ever wear hats when filming in the jungle, which I have been doing a lot of lately. They obscure the face with their shadows and annoy the cameraman. No, perhaps the best definition of a gentleman might be the kind of man who can wear a hat without looking pretentious, snobbish, self-satisfied or vain. Easier to find a virgin over sixteen, I would submit.

THE TOP DRAWER

FASHION FAUX PAS
Number 17: Tycoons

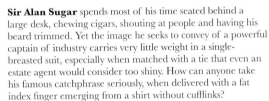

Sir Alan Sugar spends most of his time seated behind a large desk, chewing cigars, shouting at people and having his beard trimmed. Yet the image he seeks to convey of a powerful captain of industry carries very little weight in a single-breasted suit, especially when matched with a tie that even an estate agent would consider too shiny. How can anyone take his famous catchphrase seriously, when delivered with a fat index finger emerging from a shirt without cufflinks?

Baron Guy de Rothschild was in a double-breasted suit long before reaching Sir Alan's age. This was after fighting the Nazis in the Second World War and being evacuated from Dunkirk, being awarded the Croix de Guerre for his conduct on the beaches. It took him a year to join the Free French in London, and when he finally arrived there in March 1943, his cousin Jimmy welcomed him with a bottle of 1895 Château Lafite. "You're fired!" joked de Rothschild. He was wearing cufflinks.

Donald Trump has opted for the classic tycoon look: a hairstyle that resembles a wig, a trophy wife and a corset. They are all interconnected: the hair will collapse if the corset is unfastened, and the wife will disappear if the wallet is fastened.

Howard Hughes became a rather eccentric gentleman in his later years, but when young he was determined to be immaculately turned out at all times; sadly this later developed into obsessive compulsive disorder and a dislike of wearing any clothing at all.

What a gentleman is **Bernie Ecclestone**! Not only are his shoes buffed to a glorious sheen and his hair is neatly brushed, but he holds himself in a way that doesn't make his wife feel too self-conscious about her height. On the downside, he has neglected to don the jacket that matches his pantaloons de nîmes and is not wearing a waistcoat.

Sir Henry O'Neil de Hane Segrave was the first Briton to win a Grand Prix in a British car, winning the 1923 French Grand Prix and the 1924 San Sebastian Grand Prix in a Sunbeam automobile. He was a fighter pilot in the First World War but was invalided out. When he bragged that he would drive a car at over 200 miles per hour, it was generally thought that the war had made him mad. On 29 March 1927, he set a new land speed record in his 1000 HP Sunbeam Mystery at 203.79 mph. He never wore denim trousers.

UPSTAIRS

The Marksman Pub, for introducing beer as a form of currency. Dawn Kolpin, landlady of the pub in Shoreditch, London, got the idea after advertising on www.craigslist.co.uk, a local classified ads site, to swap a pub meal for "a small stack of CDs by anyone from Perry Como to The Pogues". The response to the ad prompted her to place a second advert with a list of items she was willing to exchange for a pint of beer. They included a screwdriver set, some wire cutters, serving trays and a party pack of fake moustaches. She will also accept services such as tuning the pub's piano, copywriting and photography. "It's amazing what you can buy for a pint of beer," said Ms Kolpin.

DOWNSTAIRS

Alexander Amosu, for designing the world's most expensive suit. Unveiled at a secret location, the suit had a price tag of £70,000. Described as a "luxury designer to the rich and famous", Amosu pushed the boundaries of fashion fatuousness by claiming "the economic crisis had not completely stopped the demand for designer fashion." The suit is made from a blend of vicuña, a South American animal that only produces enough wool for shearing every three years, qiviuk, the world's most expensive wool, and pashmina. The detailing includes 18-carat gold and diamond buttons. Mr. Amosu is trawling the world's maximum-security mental hospitals in search of a buyer.

The French, for reintroducing the beret as the national form of headwear. After years of decline, having been replaced by the ubiquitous baseball cap, our Gallic neighbours are adopting the beret as a symbol of a rural past, in a world of shopping malls, McDonalds and close-coupled lavatories.

Manufacturers around Orlon Sainte-Marie, once the beret making capital in the south-west, report sales doubling since the start of the recession. After facing closure less than a decade ago, the business is now producing around 300,000 berets a year. French milliner Stephane Jacquet said, "Most beret-wearers nowadays seem to be the *bourgeois-boheme* type. The beret is synonymous with France's rural past, where life was supposedly more rosy than today."

The French
For not inviting the Queen to the 65th anniversary of the D-Day landings in Normandy. As the only head of state to have seen service during the Second World War, the omission was more than a faux-pas. It may be easy to point the finger at the American-loving Nicholas Sarkozy, but to find the real culprit, one needs to look back to a speech made in 1944: "Paris – liberated by itself, liberated by its people, with the support of the armies of France, with the backing of the whole of France, of the true France, of eternal France."

General De Gaulle, speaking in August 1944.

AM I CHAP?

Readers are invited to send their photographs to chap@thechap.co.uk for an assessment of their Chappist credentials.

STAR CHAP

Clip-on braces, lack of neckwear, inconclusive moustaches, ill-fitting headwear, men marrying their daughters...this photograph can only have been sent from Australia.

Despite being a dead ringer for the comedian Michael MacIntyre (who is not a Chap) this Oriental fellow has found a uniquely individual way of expressing universal panache, which is of course what Chappism is all about.

"Are there any events, shops or places of interest for me, during my stay in London?" asks Brian J.C. Osborne, a property developer. Yes: the cutters at Huntsman have offered to horsewhip anyone who dares to walk along the Row in jeans. It would be a pleasure to see you there.

This photo came via email with the brief message: "A better one." One can only assume there were other photographs on the same roll of holes in the road or blocked lavatories.

Sir, your tie doesn't match your "blazer" (whose buttons you have fastened as poorly as a schoolboy's), you haven't shaved, and you clearly are trying to hide a physique more attuned to weight-lifting than the elegant sport of tennis. Nice racquet, though.

One can almost hear the crackle of unnatural fibres emanating from this "dressing" gown. Have they replaced those Groucho Marx spectacle and moustache sets with one to resemble an IT assistant who thinks he's a bit wacky? It will take considerably more than a bottle of cheap champagne to convince this poor young thing that it's bedtime.

Colour co-ordination betwixt one's tie and one's hookah is to be commended. Wearing a suit two sizes too large and a knot twice as large as is necessary suggests that one should attend to one's wardrobe BEFORE getting utterly zonked on hashish.

Roberto Vianello, an Architect and Interior Designer from Rome, writes: "I have a collection of more than 100 pipes. I smoked the wonderful Dunhill "Nightcap", but unfortunately it is now out of stock! So now I have to add pure Latakia to other mixtures to obtain a similar flavour, which is perfect with a glass of peat Single Malt Islay Scotch Whisky." If this man is not a Chap, the Pope is not a Catholic.

There is nothing to prevent midgets, dwarves and ladies, or all three combined, from being Chaps. There should, however, be rules prohibiting the drinking of pints of lager at weddings.

Take away the clothes, and you've got a couple of tramps arguing about which off-licence to visit. In fact, in the case of the fellow on the right, there is no need even to take away the clothes.

THE COLOUR OF RUSKIN

John Ruskin is frequently portrayed as a stuffy old curmudgeon who couldn't bear the sight of naked women, but the man's clothes belie a true revolutionary spirit, as Rev Michael Silver reveals

As a priest I am often asked why we had to endure BBC2's *Desperate Romantics*. My reply is that it was an attempt, perhaps, at cross-pollinating earlier crowd-pleasers *Up Pompeii* and *Tipping the Velvet*, for a Pre-Raphaelite palate. Most objectionable was its depiction of John Ruskin. The Beeb put on its most prurient lenses, giving us John the porn-gazing cuckold; a rather dull, avuncular figure set against a wild, revolutionary gang of painters and aesthetes. Yet Ruskin, it could be argued, was the true innovator – arguably the inventor of art history, public libraries and amateur road construction. One has only to consider his wardrobe for the evidence of his pioneering spirit.

The context for his crusade for colour is unexpected. We view Victorians as drab, in contrast to the luxuriant and vibrant age of George IV. Actually the move away from colour and towards a monochrome palette pre-dates the Victorian era and stems from around 1810, possibly reflecting the increasing influence

In an essay on watercolours, Ruskin extols the virtues of his bootmaker: "He is a man of dew. His sketches breathe of morning air, and his grass would wet your feet if you were to walk on it in Hoby's best."

of university life. Within the universities, 'subfusc' (black clothes, white tie) was the formal uniform. Professional men (clergy, academics, lawyers and medics) would be expected to wear their accepted dress during both the day and the evening.

In his undergraduate days, the boyish Ruskin contrived a subtle variation on subfusc for daywear. The lapels of his black swallowtail coat were embellished in red and gold. His neck-cloth was likewise black with a pattern in blue and red. James S. Dearden informs us in *Ruskin in Pictures* (1999) that, "until 1841, Ruskin's clothes all came from Owen, while Keene was his shirtmaker. The well known blue cravats came from Geohegan of 178 Regent Street." Later in life, Ruskin patronised Stultz & Co, the fashionable tailor of 10, Clifford Street, and in 1870 his boots came from Hoby & Co. of 20, Pall Mall. In an essay on the watercolourist Edward Clayton, Ruskin extols the virtues of his bootmaker: "He is a man of dew. His sketches breathe of morning air, and his grass would wet your feet if you were to walk on it in Hoby's best."

By his early twenties, Ruskin had begun to adopt the dark blue frock coat with a velvet collar with which he is most keenly identified. He wore this with a bright Oxford-blue stock, black trousers and patent slippers. This remained his mode of dress well into old age. Sidney Colvin describes the 40-year-old Ruskin as: "Elegant after the fashion of his time as well as impressive in a fashion all his own. There remains with me quite unfaded the image of his slender, slightly stooping figure clad in the invariable dark blue frock coat and bright blue necktie; of his small head with its strongly marked features, its sweep of thick brown hair and closely trimmed side-whiskers, above all the singular bittersweet expression of his mouth (due partly to the vestiges of a scar left on the upper lip by a dog's bite in boyhood)."

Nevertheless, Ruskin's colourful creed was responsible for other men's sartorial slip-ups. The folklorist Sabine Baring Gould, as a Cambridge undergraduate, subscribed to the new Ruskinian vision. Years later, he recounted the most embarrassing mishap that could ever befall a gentleman: dining in the wrong coloured tie:

"The youth of England had gone Ruskin-mad; and I was bitten as much as anyone. A young fellow of some private means and I were crazed alike. We did up his room in true Ruskinesque taste, and we both dressed aesthetically, in knee-breeches and stockings and brown or claret-coloured velvet coats frogged with braid. Also we wore ties according to the colour of the season… Old Squire

John Ruskin by Sir John Everett Millais, 1854

Blencowe insisted on carrying me off to dine. I had to pack my valise in great haste… On getting ready for dinner, to my dismay I discovered that [there was no white tie], so I had to go to dinner with a green tie, it being Trinity Season, and green the ecclesiastical colour. That finished my Ruskinism as far as dress was concerned."

In considering Ruskin himself, the double irony is that (a) He did not dress in exuberantly colourful clothes – the defining characteristic of Ruskin's wardrobe was its understatement, its cut and precision, and (b) The grounds upon which he so fervently promoted colour in life were not aesthetical but theological. In *Ruskin's Rainbow*, for example, he explains how aesthetics are the divine made visible:

"When it became the sign of the covenant of peace, the pure hues of divided light were sanctified to the human heart for ever; nor this, it would seem, by mere arbitrary appointment, but typical of the Divine nature itself. Not without meaning was the love of Israel to his chosen son expressed by the coat "of many colours"… We know it to have been by Divine command that the Israelite, rescued from servitude, veiled the tabernacle with its rain of purple and scarlet, while the under sunshine flashed through the fall of the colour from its tendons of gold."

Despite this pious approach, one fervent disciple was none other than Oscar Wilde.

From anyone else, surely, such religiosity would have filled the satirical Wilde with fervent disdain; from Ruskin's lips and pen, however, he took his sermons like a lamb.

Ruskin never passed over a chance to draw a moral message from colour. With a mixture of satire and solemnity, he asserts:

"At least half of that mental bias of young people, which sustains the wickedness of war among us at this day, is owing to the prettiness of military uniforms"

"Quite one of the chiefest art-mistakes and stupidities of men has been their tendency to dress soldiers in red clothes. At least half of that mental bias of young people, which sustains the wickedness of war among us at this day, is owing to the prettiness of uniforms…"

And what of Ruskin the revolutionary? Surely he was a chap of the deepest dye, since his youthful rebellion was not to rebel? His radicalism was to be groomed yet colourful, to be intensely romantic yet abjure sex, to question and renounce the strict Protestant faith of his youth, yet freely furnish scriptural references on every occasion. The man who faced down the art establishment to defend Turner and the Pre-Raphaelites may have looked studiedly formal, but his sartorial style gave a hint of the anarchic heart that beat beneath the frock coat.

Ruskin certainly lost faith in institutions, clergy and even love, but not (quite) in his circle of friends and not, it seems, in his wardrobe. Having settled on his individual style in his twenties, he stuck to it for the next sixty years. His wardrobe progressed from sartorial innovation to eccentric anachronism.

By 1878, when Ruskin was beginning to suffer from the mental illness that dogged his later life, Canon Scott Holland described Ruskin as resembling "something between an old-fashioned nobleman of the forties and an angel that had lost its way."

The man who faced down the art establishment to defend Turner and the Pre-Raphaelites may have looked studiedly formal, but his sartorial style gave a hint of the anarchic heart that beat beneath the frock coat.

Ruskin clearly cuts more of a dash here than Rossetti

Ruskin maintained his sartorial eccentricities right into old age

THE WHISKERADE

A smorgasbord of moustachioed frolics and upper-lip erotica from Michael "Atters" Attree

ATTERS' STIFF UPPER QUIP

It seems it's not just poor families who'll be tightening their braces this year – but our dear Royal Family too. The Whisker Groomer-in-Waiting announced that, due to austerity cuts, the planned distribution of Royal Wedding moustache mugs to every child in the land has now been cancelled. However, Prince William has delighted Royal watchers (and Desmond Tutu) by promising

his fashion icon bride a trendy Moustache Tattoo on her "topiary garden". The Royal Tattoo will also see the Queen awarding commemorative medals to her daughter-in-law's Royal hairs. The NUS are already planning lively street parties and The Banksy School of Art is being commissioned with a special mural to decorate the outside wall of the Palace.

HALL OF PLUMAGE

At over 80, Leslie Phillips knows how to keep his bounder's plumage in trim and places his acting success down to his pencil moustache making all his casting decisions. However (unlike that vulgar hedgehog Ron Jeremy, right) he always keeps his socks

on. Having been granted a private audience with the 'tached titan myself once, I shall forever revel in the fact that I stroked his lip weasel as he purred, "God I love your moustache…is it real?" The Chap eternally salutes you.

AHH BISTO!

According to porn star Ron "The Hedgehog" Jeremy: "No babe can resist me as a pizza delivery guy with this 'stache." Perhaps they are trying to keep him trim – it certainly looks as if Ron eats all the pizzas. He was once invited to address the Oxford Union on "Art House Cinema and the Porno Moustache." His bushy flicks include: One-Eyed Monster and Tales from the Crapper. Ron (retired) now provides moustache rides at LA's Sunny Side Up Care Home for elderly pornographers.

JUDGE MY SHRUB

Davey Evans proclaims: "I have the genetic class to have a gap within my front teeth and I intend to conduct myself rather like T-T!" You aim high, sir. However I'm not sure Terry-Thomas would clutter his lip-wand with an ill-advised "jazz spot" on his chin. Why most contemporary young bucks lack the chutzpah to grow solo I'll never know.
However, I admire your cheeky twinkle and pluck for modernity. More to the point, your fledgling barbette has good potential.

"Dear Atters," writes Barrington Buford, "enclosed is my charity effort grown for Movember. Your prestigious Handlebar Club informed me that removal of my beardlet would permit me membership." Although Barrington's whisker set mirrors Davey Evens', his roguish hair and bone structure project authenticity. This is rather easy to say when Barrington concludes: "PS: I must inform you that I am a rather big fan of yours." Bravo Barrington!
PPS: So am I!

A DECADE OF
ANARCHO-DANDYISM

Ten years ago, Torquil Arbuthnot and Nathaniel Slipper didn't exist.
Today they are highly respected authors of agit-fop. Here they look back at the humble
beginnings of the organ which now pays them enough to have their hair cut once a year,
as long as they take turns

1999

A chance meeting in the Portobello Road leads to
the founding of The Chap magazine, when penniless
artist Vic Darkwood chances upon boulevardier Gustav Temple's market stall. Temple is selling
"genuine" pieces of celebrity masonry, including
fragments of Cary Grant's rockery and Eva Peron's
ha-ha. While haggling over some Welsh slate from
Lloyd George's garden shed, Darkwood and Temple
notice the unimprovable perfection of each other's
tweeds and crisp boutonnières. After a few glasses
of porter in the nearby Lamb and Flag, the magazine is born. The first edition immediately wins the
Booker Prize.

2000

The Chap rents agreeable offices in Soho above
Mr. Paul Raymond's Revue Bar. Torquil Arbuthnot
and Nathaniel Slipper give up lucrative careers as
commodity brokers (specialising in bauxite, sisal
and cheese) to join the editorial board of the magazine; Arbuthnot as etiquette correspondent, Slipper
as head gardener. Their first article is the seminal
"Anatomy of Doffing", which identifies 73 different
ways of doffing one's hat. The Chap's influence on
headwear soon conquers the world and crooners

like Mr. Peterborough
Doherty and thespians
like Mr. Jonathan Dep-
pington rarely saunter
forth without sporting
a trilby or a fedora. In-
deed, Deppington once
attempted to trademark
his own doff, "the Pesky Wabbit", but it was ruled too
American by The Chap board.

2001

The Chap notices it is over 80 years since the last
Anglo-Afghan War and contacts the War Office.
The War Office agrees it is about time we had
another crack at Johnny Afghan and dispatches an
expeditionary force. Vic Darkwood resigns from The
Chap, saying he is taking the Queen's shilling and
off to give the Taleban a bloody nose. He is later discovered living in Stockwell under an assumed name,
running a 24-hour off-licence. Arbuthnot and Slipper
are sent to Afghanistan as war correspondents for
The Chap. They make it as far as the Lamb & Flag
in Dover, from whence they file their despatches,
which go on to win them the Pulitzer Prize for Conflict Journalism.

Civilise the city certainly confused tourists – who thought Britain was already civilised

The Chap Olympiad was the first sporting event that actually penalised any evidence of training

2002

Despairing ever more of the vulgarity of modern life The Chap decides to take to the streets. The first "Civilise the City" event takes place, when several dozen agreeable fellows saunter through the West End doffing their hats to all and sundry, assisting elderly ladyboys across the road and attempting to purchase pots of Lapsang Souchong in McDonald's. One chap gets a little over-excited and suggests they march on Parliament and take over the government in a bloodless anarcho-dandyist coup. He is told to have a nice cup of tea instead. The contingent repair to the New Piccadilly Café for a sharpener and a plate of ham and eggs.

2003

Mr. Stephen Fry presents a new noctovisual programme entitled QI. A member of the Chap's editorial staff lands a cushy job as researcher. Out of sheer idleness, he drops jokes and witty apercus straight from The Chap into the script for the programme. The ratings for QI soar and the show wins a sideboardful of awards. After a public outcry the staff

of The Chap all receive OBEs "for services to the Stephen Fry industry". Mr. Fry goes on to win Pipe Smoker of the Year and grants an interview to The Chap, in which he single-handedly destroys the Panama hat industry.

2004

The Chap notices that the summer Olympics are taking place in Athens. Rather than sprint around some Greek building sites in tight clothing, sweating and getting muddy knees, The Chap inaugurates the first Chap Olympiad in Regent's Park, claiming they actually began in 1894. The ceremony begins with the lighting of the Olympic pipe. Events include Freestyle Trouser Gymnastics, Synchronised Hat Doffing, Quill Throwing and Shouting at Foreigners. In a breathtaking act of plagiarism, London bids to stage the Summer Olympic Games in 2012. The I.O.C. offers to chip in on the marketing budget of the 2012 Chap Olympiad, in return for a few pointers on how to make their games "less boring".

2005

In the summer of 2005, the England cricket team had not won the Ashes since 1986-1987. Realising that in their current state they did not stand a chance against the fit, bronzed supermen of the Australian team, they called in The Chap for assistance. The team was set a specific fitness regime: each day began with a full English breakfast followed by a Woodbine; a gentle twenty minutes in the nets; then a five-course lunch followed by a bracing walk stopping at every public house on the way; a game of billiards and The Times crossword for the more energetic; a slap-up dinner followed by a trip to the theatre to see Chu Chin Chow; and finally to bed no later than 2 ack-emma.

10

TEN THINGS YOU DIDN'T KNOW ABOUT THE CHAP

1) The Chap is translated into 63 different languages, and then back into English, which explains all the typos and strange words.

2) Scotland Yard subscribe to The Chap because one of the regular writers hides clues to his nefarious crimes in his book reviews.

3) The 2012 issue of The Chap will feature a handy map of London, clearly showing St James's as "forbidden to foreign visitors".

4) Scientists have proved that if a man is so drunk that he cannot make any sense of simple children's stories, he is still able to read and fully understand The Chap.

5) Although it is not illegal to carry The Chap over the new bridge to Skye, rather than take it by sea, it is frowned upon.

6) In the next two years, it is thought that technology will become so advanced that future editions of The Chap will be in 3D.

7) When selling The Chap, a shopkeeper is more likely to pass the time of day in idle chit-chat than if one is buying a copy of Escort.

8) The Chap magazine is made from 100% recycled betting slips.

9) The most requested article by Chap readers is about Frances de la Tour's collection of 1977 Silver Jubilee memorabilia.

10) A copy of The Chap was once seen in a branch of W.H. Smith, but it turned out to have been left there by mistake.

CUTLERY · FAIR PLAY · MOTOR-LORRIES · PANACHE · CHEMICALS · BAR BILLIARDS

When the first Civilise the City took place, it was still legal to smoke a pipe outside a tobacconist

This punishing regime, together with the surprise tactic of being completely useless on the field, ensures a glorious victory.

2006

David Cameron becomes leader of the Conservative Party. In a vain attempt to suck up to the populace he tells them to "Call me Dave" and omits to wear either a tie or a pocket-square. He returns harrumphing letters from The Chap addressed to 'Dave the Dastard', writing 'not known at this address' on the envelope like the jackanapes he is. The Chap fears standards in the country have declined so far that the only civilised response is to climb a large piece of public sculpture. Miss Minna establishes a base camp/cocktail bar in the Turbine Hall of Tate Modern, while Messrs Temple, Attree and Arbuthnot conquer the summit of Miss Rachel Whiteread's pretentious pile of plastic boxes. They are escorted from the Tate with their heads held high and their feet even higher.

2007

The Chap decides to mount its largest ever agit-fop performance, influenced by the nihilist and absurdist ideas of Tzara and Picabia. A recently released inmate of Colney Hatch Lunatic Asylum is given the Dadaist made-up name of "Boris Johnson" and fitted with a crepe blond wig. With the agreement of the British Tourist Authority, "Boris Johnson" is allowed to stand as Mayor of London and, due to a computer

The north face of Whiteread – unconquered by man or beast until 2006

Despite freezing conditions near the summit, the chaps put on a brave face

error, is duly elected. Staff at The Chap continue to write his speeches using the "automatic writing" process pioneered by the surrealist André Breton.

2008

The recession hits Britain. In a move to earn some money, staff at the magazine while away their tea-breaks inventing a vaccine for the Ebola virus. The vaccine is an agreeable mixture of Gentleman's Relish, arrowroot, juniper berries, opium, tragacanth, Pimm's No. 3 Cup, Marmite, peyote and a pinch of turmeric. Michael "Atters" Attree hawks the vaccine round the pharmaceutical companies, and his negotiating skills ensure he signs over the rights for a crisp £20 note and Charlotte Rampling's telephone number.

2009

The magazine formally becomes a staple of British life when a copy appears in an episode of Midsomer Murders. Gustav Temple is awarded the Nobel Prize for Literature, but the prize is rescinded when his Interpol record comes to light. (An alternate winner is hastily chosen by sticking a pin in a list of the most unreadable contemporary Romanian poets.) Undaunted, Temple decides to ensure The Chap's economic future by staking the magazine's remaining funds on a "cast-iron plunger" in the 2.40 at Wincanton. Unfortunately the nag turns out to be a dud, but generous donations from readers ensure the magazine's survival, albeit in postcard format.

2010

During a night at the Lamb and Flag, Temple, Attree, Arbuthnot and Slipper decide to Chappify the Large Hadron Collider, by tipping into it sixteen gallons of the perfect vodka martini and a ton of Cavendish pipe tobacco. This magnificent attempt to further the wonder of science has disastrous consequences, as the world is ripped inside out, and the space-time continuum is flushed into a black hole, leaving only the editorial team of The Chap with severely blackened faces, puffing merrily on their pipes for all eternity.

DANDIES IN DECAY

Sebastian Horsley's definition of dandyism and his definitive list of its few proponents, among the living and the dead

Dandyism is a form of self-worship which dispenses with the need to find happiness from others – especially women. It is a condition rather than a profession. It is a defence against suffering and a celebration of life. It is not fashion; it is not wealth; it is not learning; it is not beauty. It is a shield and a sword and a crown – all pulled out of the dressing up box in the attic of the imagination.

Wilde and Brummell are usually held up as the progenitors of dandyism, but neither of these men was a dandy, in my not very humble opinion. Mr. Brummell was aspirational and no real dandy is aspirational. As for Wilde? What a phoney he was! And not even a real phoney! He bred for a start, and no dandy worth the name breeds. He must defeat the species role of his body at all costs.

This misrepresentation continues in modern times. The idea that David Beckham is a dandy is absurd. Dandyism is social, human and intellectual. It is not a suit of clothes walking about by itself. If Mr. Beckham's IQ had been two points lower he would be a tree.

Russell Brand is called a dandy. He practices Yoga, vegetarianism and other diseases of the soul. Worse, he recently took part in Earth Aid! This is unforgivable. The dandy remains deaf to the call of social justice. The depletion of his hairspray is more important to him than the depletion of the ozone layer. Convictions are for dullards, whose earnestness – the worst crime in the dandy's book – is there to be mocked.

Tracey Emin has been called a dandy! The idea that a woman can be a dandy is preposterous. There

Cartoon dandy:
Tintin

Gay dandy:
Quentin Crisp

Thin dandy:
Bunny Roger

Punk dandy:
John Lydon

Glam dandy:
Marc Bolan

More blandies than dandies: David Beckham, Russell Brand and Tracey Emin

are no female dandies for the same reason that there is no female Mozart or Jack the Ripper. The key attribute of dandyism – detachment – cannot come from someone with a womb.

So who are the real dandies? Charles Baudelaire, Quentin Crisp, Bunny Roger, Tintin, Marc Bolan, Johnny Rotten, Robin Dutt and me – not in order of importance. All these dandies are roped together like mountaineers heading for the summit of beauty. You see, my darlings, true dandyism is rebellious. The dandy is part warrior, part stargazer, part gambler, part crusader, part plunderer, part violator, part martyr. He is fit for the highest and the lowest society – and keeps out of both.

During the Second World War, Neil 'Bunny' Roger went to battle wearing a chiffon scarf and brandishing a copy of Vogue. When his sergeant asked him what should be done about the advancing enemy troops, Roger, who liked to wear rouge even with his khakis, replied, "When in doubt, powder heavily." When he ran into an old friend in the hellish, bombed-out city of Montecasino in Italy, he responded to his pal's incredulous "What on earth are you doing here?" with one word: "Shopping."

To be a dandy is to aspire to the sublime and isn't that just sublime! Dandyism isn't image encrusted with flourishes. It's a way of stripping yourself down to your true self. You can only judge the style by the content and you can only reach the content through the style.

Dandies are a brotherhood of higher types. The true princes of the world. The true priests of the world. Like precious stones, their personalities derive their value from their scarcity. Oh, I'm so clever! I wish I could sleep with myself!

DODGY DANDIES

Jarvis Cocker
Was a great dandy for about a year. And then was married, mortgaged and babied to life. Worse still, he grew a beard. Once you have completely lost your nerve you grow a beard.

Laurence Llewelyn-Bowen
The fop from a shop. You are not a dandy if you think you dress individually. He went to a fancy dress shop and asked for the King Charles Spaniel.

Vivienne Westwood
She is a peacock in everything but beauty. Women have but one task in dandysport: that of crowning the winner with garlands.

Henry Conway
Dandyism oscillates between narcissism and neurosis, vanity and insanity, Savile Row and Death Row. Conway doesn't have a mind to go out of. Too light even to make the badminton team.

Nick Foulkes
The dandy has no obligations, no attachments, no wife, no child, no occupation, no possessions, no obvious means of support, visible or invisible. Basically no use whatsoever. Mr. Foulkes has all of the above. I can make no more of him than a hedgehog. He is too dull to be ridiculous.

A SOUPCON OF BACHELORS

It is a truth universally acknowledged that ladies in search of husbands are bound to come across a multitude of bachelors. But which are the ones to avoid? Torquil Arbuthnot & Nathaniel Slipper provide a handy guide to finding a true chap for a husband

THE CAD

The Cad can be identified by his penchant for brocade waistcoats, suede shoes, cigarette holders and pencil moustaches. His most common utterance is, "And who is this glorious creature?" He frequents louche nightclubs, stage doors and ladies' finishing schools. He normally squires females from a narrow range of professions: artists' models, cigarette gals and ladies from the chorus line. If on his uppers he will concentrate on gauche heiresses who will pay for his upkeep. He is a "love 'em and leave 'em" character, although he dreams of marrying a busty blonde whose father owns a brewery near a racecourse. Inevitably he ends up running a pub in Godalming, wearing a monocle and calling himself "Major".

THE CONFIRMED BACHELOR

He wears cardigans with leather buttons, shoes shaped like Cornish pasties and keeps his change in a purse. He will have a slightly peculiar hobby, such as collecting bus tickets or building models of Tower Bridge out of toothpicks, or poisoning the neighbourhood cats. His other hobby is holding up Post Office and supermarket queues by complaining (erroneously) that he has been short-changed and/or been sold a dented packet of custard creams. He will work as a clerk or librarian, and will annoy his colleagues by buying his own tea-bags and keeping them locked in his desk. Although he believes women are only after his money, a mid-life crisis will see him buying a Ukrainian mail-order bride, being fleeced of his savings and left with a drink problem.

THE RUGGER BUGGER

On or off the playing field, and whether or not he actually plays the sport, he will be clad in a rugby/football/cricket shirt and a pair of trousers De Nimes. When he ventures out with the intention of "pulling" he will emulate his sartorial hero Mr. Jeremy Clarkson and wear a blazer over the ensemble. For important "dates" he will also wear a tie featuring one of Mr. Walt Disney's characters. It will always seem as if some element of his face is fake (the teeth might be too prominent, the nose too putty-like, the singular eyebrow too alive) but they are all genuine. His haunts are the changing room communal bath, the public house and the sports club bar. His idea of a romantic evening is to take a lady for a curry, and then to serenade her with all eighty-four verses of "Eskimo Nell" before passing out from a surfeit of chilled Continental lager. In later life he will marry his secretary or a rugger "groupie" and take up golf and being rude to waiters.

"The Rugger Buger's idea of a romantic evening is to take a lady for a curry, and then to serenade her with all eighty-four verses of "Eskimo Nell" before passing out from a surfeit of chilled Continental lager"

THE LATIN LOVER

Over-enamoured of brilliantine, the Latin Lover advertises his presence by overpowering aftershave, an open chemise and eye-wateringly tight trousers. His opening gambit to a young lady, delivered in an unplaceable Mediterranean accent, is: "I hate you! But... hate is so close to luuuurve..." He dances a little too well, breaks into husky song too often and pays for his own drinks seldom. He frequents discotheques, yacht basins and Eurotrash hotel bars. He can only flirt with the ladies where he finds them, as he cannot take them back to his pad, where he lives with his mother, his grandmother, two brothers and three sisters. In later life he will take to wearing a dubious toupee and lurking around "Glamorous Granny" competitions.

THE ELDERLY BOOKMAN

He wears a velvet smoking jacket, pince-nez and a scarf (as he has a perpetual sniffle). He is very fussy with his habits and professes not to own a noctovision set. If someone visits him in his agreeable flat in Bloomsbury he will spend all his time snapping, "Be careful with that netsuke/vase/folio, it was given to me by my very dear friend John Galsworthy/EM Forster/Sheridan Morley." He can be seen at the first nights of West End shows, prowling the bookshops of Cecil Court and holding forth in the saloon bar of his local pub, where he is considered "a character". He is scared of women as he believes they want to marry him so they can tidy his flat and get rid of all his "unhygienic" books.

THE MUMMY'S BOY

A lady can feel safe around this gentleman, as he is quiet, respectful of others and is unlikely to have six or seven paramours at the same time. Sadly he will not be very adventurous, what with having to be home by half past nine and only wearing clothes that his mother has purchased for him from Milletts. He is also somewhat over-reliant, expecting his tea and sandwiches to be prepared, clothes washed and ironed and special treats on his birthday. It should be remembered that most serial killers are retrospectively described as "a quiet sort who lived with his mother."

CHAP HUSBANDRY

A prospective husband should possess at least five of the following qualities

- A duelling scar obtained in Heidelberg
- A picturesque war-wound, but not a libido-threatening one
- The ability to hit a playing card at twenty paces with a Webley
- The ability to late cut between first and second slip
- A set in Albany
- A hint of danger
- A cruel set to the lips
- A goodish DSO or a decent MC
- A square jaw
- A poetic forehead
- A Himalayan peak named after him
- Fluent French and passable Arabic
- A mother who isn't a very good cook
- The talent to step into a play when an actor pulls out at the last minute and steal the show
- Sang-froid, savoir-faire and noblesse oblige
- Being able to drive and navigate at the same time
- Two Olympic gold medals
- A talent for the trombone
- Millions of pounds

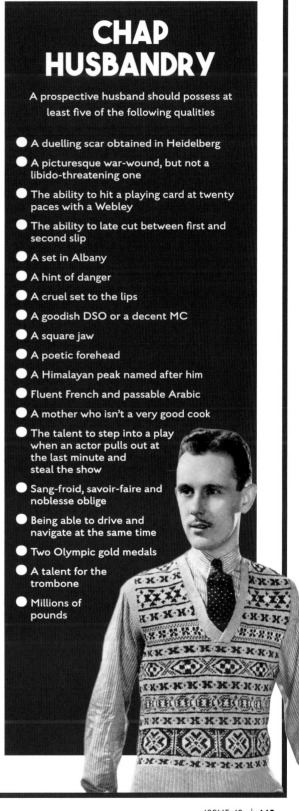

THE PERPETUAL STUDENT

Being a student is a splendid thing, with no responsibilities, four hours of learning a week and a student grant burning a hole in one's pocket. One can spend hours in the bar, before heading off to a nightclub with sticky floors where the disc Jockey ironically plays tracks by Wham! before staggering off home and leaving one's clothes in a messy pile on the floor (which can all be taken to the parents' house for cleaning). Clothes can be scruffy and thrown clumsily together, with pumps worn with suits and shirts not tucked in. While this is simply splendid between the ages of 18 and 21, by the time one hits 34 it is nothing more than tiresome, and exceedingly unlikely to attract the attention of the opposite sex, with the possible exception of elderly librarians.

THE PEACOCK THRONE

Edward VIII's impeccable sartorial reputation is based almost entirely on black-and-white photographs. Will Moul and Peter Cormie discovered that colour played as crucial a role in the King's wardrobe as cut and style.
Photographs courtesy of Sotheby's

When we think of sartorially influential men of the 1920s and 30s, actors and playboys like Fred Astaire, Cary Grant, Ronald Colman and Douglas Fairbanks Jr. come to mind. Yet arguably the most influential man of style of the Golden Era was not an actor nor a playboy, but a humble member of the royal family: Edward VIII, generally referred to as the Duke of Windsor due to his brief tenure on the throne.

The Duke's look became so iconic and influential that we now think of it as the look of the age. Plus fours in a ginger Harris Tweed, with slanted pockets, worn with harlequin socks and a Fair Isle sweater? Nobody had ever dressed like that on the golf course before the Duke of Windsor, and soon everyone from the local bank manager to Crown Prince Hirohito of Japan was doing the same.

Edward always carried with him a series of small boxes containing cloth samples, which he would use to compare the colours of what he was buying with what he already owned. He favoured Savile Row tailor Frederick Scholte for his coats, but often had the trousers (for the same suit) made at the American company of H. Harris. On one of his frequent visits to Scholte, Edward was greatly amused to see his equerry Fruity Metcalfe being turned away by the great tailor for requesting wider shoulders and a narrower waist on a coat.

The Duke is known for setting numerous trends, such as the short period during the 1950s when, thanks to the Duke's eye-catching red tartan suit pictured overleaf, tartan briefly came into vogue.

Unlike most men who gain weight and width with age, the Duke's frame and body shape went unchanged throughout his life, so his wardrobe, which was stored at his regular destinations around the world to minimise luggage, was full of classic pieces, both new and old, at the time of his death.

That is why, at the Duke's and Duchess' estate sale in September 1997 at Sotheby's, so many of his early suits still photographed well and sold for very high prices. Thanks to the Sotheby's catalogue, we are able to view just a small piece of the Duke's amazing wardrobe on the following pages.

Right

Double-breasted coat with softly padded shoulders by Scholte, London; matching trousers by H. Harris, New York, both 1950. The coat was made shortly before the vogue for rear vents and has no vents. The shirt is Hawes & Curtis, embroidered with the Duke's cipher.

Right

Hunting Lord of the Isles tartan evening suit. Double-breasted coat with wide lapels and side vents by Scholte dated 8.6.51, trousers by Harris, New York. Underneath is a green corduroy waistcoat by Scholte from 1947 and Hunting Lord of the Isles cummerbund.

Right

Grey and white ribbed suit with Royal Yacht Squadron buttons, 1938. The double-breasted coat is by Scholte, who later inserted side vents when the Duke decided to favour them again. Trousers by Forster & Son with front pleats and turn-ups.

Below

A rust and brown twill-woven Harris Tweed suit, 11.12.24. Coat by Scholte, trousers by Forster & Sons. The trousers are cut high in the waist and originally supported by an inner elasticated girdle, to maintain a looser hang.

Above

Pecan brown and beige wool Shepherd check suit, 1934. Jacket by Scholte, trousers/plus-fours by Forster & Sons. The Duke's own specification for plus fours fell a fraction lower than those worn by his grandfather, and he devised, with his tailor Forster, a looser-fitting version with cotton linings.

Left

Tropical safari suit, unknown English tailor, 1925. Jacket and shorts of medium-weight corded beige cotton. The shorts have deep buttoned cuffs so they can be lowered for extra leg protection. Tan leather Derby boots, probably by Peal & Co., and two sola topees by Edward Smith.

Right
Double-breasted navy wool blazer in light-weight navy worsted, with Grenadier Guards Officer buttons on the front and Welsh Guards Officer buttons on the sleeves. Coat by Scholte, dated 25.4.31, trousers by Forster & Sons. The Duke wore this on the 1936 Nahlin cruise.

Right
The morning coat and trousers Edward wore for his wedding to Wallis Warfield on 3rd June 1937. The morning coat by Scholte is a black cashmere herringbone weave and is marked H.M. The King, 25.1.36. The trousers are cut with an American style waist by Forster & Son and dated 9.6.32.

Left
Single-breasted Houndstooth coat with matching waistcoat by Scholte, dated 8.6.33, cut with shaped waist to wear with a kilt. The kilt is by Chalmers of Oban in Royal Stewart tartan, lined with cream silk satin.

Left
Rothesay Hunting tartan lounge suit, originally made for Edward's father, George V, in 1897, then altered to fit the Duke. Edward kept the original late-Victorian shawl collar but had the coat relined in green rayon satin.

Right
Dark green double-breasted corduroy shawl-collared dinner jacket with Beaufort Hunt buttons, by Scholte, dated 12.10.59, with green silk cross-grain on the lapels and side vents. Trousers by H. Harris, New York, in navy herringbone wool and cashmere, dated 1.2.56.

Right
Midnight blue worsted evening dress suit, 1937. The coat, probably Scholte, has lapels faced with black crossgrain, while the trousers are by Forster & Son, labelled 18.6.38. The white dress backless waistcoat is also by Scholte and the white bow tie is made of cotton.

VIV THE SPIV

Viv the Spiv is a full-time racketeer, impresario and import/export consultant. His services, much in demand for 1940s/50s social events, include the supply of top quality merchandise such as nylons, lipstick, nail varnish, knicker elastic, hair pins, chocolate and cigarettes (non-tipped). No coupons are required, and Viv assures his customers that none of it is nicked – it's just not paid for yet. All ladies' garments include a free fitting service and part-exchange can be arranged if the merchandise is suitable

What, for you, epitomises the very essence of Englishness?
Boiled beef & carrots with potatoes (tinned) washed down with a large Johnny Walker (Red Label).

What is your idea of absolute heaven?
Having a dead cert on the number 3 dog at White City, with a blonde on each arm.

And your idea of a hell on earth?
The paint coming off the number 3 dog at White City just as it hits the finish.

What three items of clothing would you rescue in the event of your wardrobe being invaded by a swarm of moths?
My special jacket with 18 hidden pockets, the socks that the local MP's wife bought me for helping her out when her old man was out campaigning, and my Tommy Trinder Trilby.

Where and when have you ever pined for the services of a good tailor?
I was in a wardrobe once with no clobber on, surrounded by French knickers & sweaters. Could have done with a tailor then, even a bad one!

Have you ever considered the wearing of sportswear for any activity other than sport?
I find them jockey shorts quite comfy, but they do tend to ride up.

What is your idea of a perfect English gentleman?
A bloke that says 'scuse me when he jam tarts.

Can you name an example, living or deceased?
Why, Mr. Churchill of course.

And his female counterpart?
Jane from the Daily Mirror. She's a bit of alright.

Have you ever found it necessary or appropriate to wear a pair of flip-flops?
Having two left feet, I much prefer a good pair of flop-flops.

"My kingdom for a horse!" declared Richard III. What have you ever craved with such intensity?
I've never craved horse, but I do like a bit of crackling now and again.

What item of clothing are you determined never to wear?
One of those prison suits with arrows on them.

Which of the vices, if any, do you think can lend one an air of louche sophistication?
Turkish cigarettes in holders (ivory of course).

How many different varieties of hat do you own, and which is your favourite?
A black trilby, a brown trilby and a navy blue trilby; all top bonce covers!

JOHN WATERS

Gustav Temple meets John Waters, the film director described as the "Pope of Trash" yet who shows a sensitive and, dare one say, intellectual side in Role Models, his new collection of essays on subjects ranging from Johnny Mathis to the Manson family

ow are you, Mr. Waters?
I'm well. I remember your magazine. You're lasting much longer than a lot of magazines in America (chortles).

When you write about moustaches and hats and little else, you've got more chance of longevity than if you follow the latest fads.
I wish I liked hats on me, but no man wears a hat worse than I.

In the book you mention wearing a hat for the Comme des Garcons show.
Well I had to, they made me. But I hate hats…even a skull cap looks stupid on me. I wish I did, and you have a whole magazine to them.

So let's talk about the book. The phrase "journalistic integrity" crops up several times. Does that mean you think of yourself as quite a serious journalist when you're doing these assignments, as opposed to a filmmaker?

Well, I'm serious about my career, but I hope I'm not too serious. There's a big list of source material at the back. I really wanted to make sure, especially when I'm writing about such outlandish things, that people realise that it is all true! I'm not making it up, I'm not exaggerating it for humour – these people already are already exaggerations, of something good or bad.

It's quite amusing, the idea of having journalistic integrity when you're interviewing a retired porn director in a house full of rats.
Being with Bobby was like being in Iraq. It took me a while to figure out that maybe his place was a squat, because there was a lot of space in there, although I didn't go in too deep, as it got dark and it was scary. There were critters under the roof and in the kitchen… and then when he told me the rats came at night, I started talking faster.

Rei Kawakubo (Comme des Garcons designer), gets a whole chapter in the book. I'm intrigued by your passion for her clothes.

"*I went to thrift shops when I was young, like every fashionable young person does. But now I pay too much money for clothes that others would have rejected in a thrift shop!*"

Did you come to them quite late in life?

No, I discovered them when they first opened their shop in New York, in the eighties or early nineties, when I couldn't afford it but I knew I wanted one of those handkerchiefs with holes in them. I like all the Japanese designers, Issey Miyake, Yushi Yamamoto, but I certainly don't think 20-year-olds should wear them. I went to thrift shops when I was young, like every fashionable young person does. But I can't find anything in them any more. So now I pay too much money for clothes that others would have rejected in a thrift shop!

I'm reminded of the Robert Crumb look, which is very "thrift store".

He always looks good, I've met him a few times. It's always such a shock to realise that he looks exactly like he does in his comic books. That's always disarming!

He wears hats quite well, doesn't he?

He does, yes, he does that William Burroughs look. A kind of subversive preppy, or a scary businessman.

Didn't Burroughs used to describe his clothes as a disguise, to hide the depraved nature of his life from the authorities?

He was also from a wealthy family who invented the adding machines, so maybe he was just dressing for his dad. My father used to hate coming round. "You bought that? They saw you coming." Some of them I just purposely didn't wear when I saw my parents, because I knew it was just asking for a fight.

But isn't it our job to outrage our parents, even into old age? Rather than letting them believe we're becoming just like them?

No, I disagree. I think when you're young, when you get your taste, then yes. Then later I think you reach a truce, where you know you can push each other's buttons and you choose your words with care. There's no need to descend into parent abuse.

"When we won a Tony award, we all got to wear ascots, which I'd worn in 7th grade and almost got beaten up for. I understand there's always a risk, when you're getting ready and you think, maybe I'll wear an ascot: you're asking for trouble"

There's a little thing we referred to in our last interview with you, which was David Lochary's character in Female Trouble, his flamboyant dress sense coupled with terrible cruelty and cutting wit. Is that something that appeals to you?

We always used to describe David Lochary as David Niven on a bad trip with criminal tendencies. When we won a Tony award, we all got to wear ascots. That was something I'd worn in 7th grade and almost got beaten up for. I understand there's always a risk, when you're getting ready and you think, maybe I'll wear an ascot: you're asking for trouble.

When you say ascot, do you mean what we call a cravat?

Yeah, like David Niven wore them. Only he could get away with it. And you can wear one in Gstaad if you're really rich; if it's your family's money, and not yours.

You mentioned in Role Models that attending the Manson murder trials almost inspired you to make Pink Flamingoes, and I wondered whether anything equally significant inspired Female Trouble?

Female Trouble was dedicated to Tex Watson (infamous Manson family member and murderer), which is something that, looking back, I might not do today, not that I wish him ill. I think the trials still had an influence on Female Trouble, because it's about someone being brainwashed to believe that "crime is beauty". So it was inspired by Manson and Genet together.

That's a lovely combination, isn't it?

Yeah, I still haven't got the Manson case out of my system, that's why I finally wrote about Leslie [Van Houten] in the book, even though I hadn't for 27 years, because she didn't want me to. Then I told her that I wasn't going to write about the crimes so much as about her getting better, but even for her to read [the case report] was very difficult. Because it's 40,000 words about one night, one terrible night in her life.

You seem to be fascinated by all the big American murder cases. What's wrong with our mass murderers?

I certainly agree that you have good true crimes books, everybody from the Krays to Killing for Company, to Myra Hindley and Mary Bell – who is the only person in London I'd really like to meet, but can't. Or to put it this way, you have really good writers about it, and cases that are bizarre and hideous enough. But I don't want to say that I'm for that ever happening – I'd rather none of them ever happened, but since they did, I like to read a good book about them.

And of course Jack the Ripper – surely the most famous mass murderer of them all?

Well yes, but it's hardly original to kill prostitutes. And it shows a great hatred of women and I'm a feminist, so I don't believe that any of those murderers can get better. The only ones that have fascinated me are the very few that show a possibility of getting better, despite doing something so terrible just once, that they would never do again. How you deal not only with the moral dilemma but the legal dilemma and society's dilemma.

You're obviously fascinated by lowbrow culture and highbrow culture in equal measure. I wondered how low you would go?

I've gone to demolition derbys. I've never gone to a blow roast. I drew the line at that. Once again, I'm a feminist, and I don't want to see bikers leading girls from table to table, giving blow jobs to men who've won a raffle while they're eating oysters and sandwiches.

I must admit I had never heard of a blow roast. But you are the man we turn to for information about such things.

Well I'm glad to provide it, I know that's my job. But I just have to know it's out there, I don't have to actually go.

What about the other end of the cultural spectrum. Do you go as high as Heidegger?

I think the art world is about as high culture as you can get. I'm very much against the idea of "art for the people". I like the elitism of the art world; I want more of that, actually. But I marvel at it just because

it's an extreme. There's nothing in my book that I'm making fun of; I really like all of it. But at the same time, I can respect things for just being extreme. As long as people really believe in something, I can respect their lunacy.

Was Baron Corvo, who gets a mention in your last book, Crackpot, one of those whose lunacy you respected?

He's a great writer. His real name was Frederick Rolfe and he was an angry Catholic who wanted to be pope and was pissed off that he wasn't. I love him. He was a homeless vagabond who wrote hate letters to everyone that ever wronged him in the church.
He was unfortunate in that he was deeply unhappy. You can't be an angry older man – and he was always angry. I wish he had been pope – think how horrible it would have been!

Role Models is published by Beautiful Books

The Whiskerade

A smorgasbord of moustachioed frolics and upper-lip erotica from Michael "Atters" Attree

Who could possibly forget that moving moment within Spinal Tap's rockumentary when Derek Smalls mauls a fan while tenderly announcing "This is Cindy's first moustache…" Yes, the union of music and moustache is a beautiful thing – but not, it seems, in Hamburg back in 1834. Baron von Ropp composed a song mocking fellow officer Baron von Trautmansdorf's thin and floppy whiskers (which smelt of herring). The ballad meandered around the regiment, and naturally the challenge to a duel was issued, revealing the exceptional standards of swordsmanship back then (both men were dead within minutes).

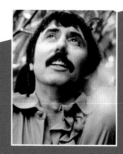

HALL OF PLUMAGE

American country & pop singer Lee Hazelwood. Lee was the originator of "Cowboy Psychedelia" (chaps and all) and the song *These Boots Are Made for Walkin'* spawned cover versions by Elvis Presley, Nancy Sinatra and ex fellow horseshoe-wearer Nick Cave. Lee claimed he grew his shrub ("way before the Beatles") to act as a microphone sock to soften his rock and roll hammered vocals. Lee also did a sterling impression of John Alderton (of TVs *Please Sir!* fame).

AHH BISTO

In 1980, "rock god" Freddie Mercury cut his hair and grew a horseshoe moustache (in just three hours). From that moment on, one could get pregnant merely by drunkenly slurring the lyrics to *Bohemian Rhapsody*. Even in rock Heaven, Freddie champions the fact that the Daily Mirror voted him Britain's Top 'Tache in 2009. Despite the accolades, it's a thumbs down from Atters. In my opinion, a comedy "porno" moustache *sans* ruffled shirt and hippy hair is like Col Gaddafi without his dolly female bodyguards.

JUDGE MY SHRUB

In an attempt to offset his overtly effeminate (yet satanic) demeanor, this furry familiar (named "Ooby") has decided to sport the more opulent and manly Dundrearies style of sideburns (also termed Piccadilly Weepers). Ooby works nights (as a nightmare) yet always insists on looking his bewhiskered best whilst instigating night-sweats. One's devotion to such grooming can only be applauded.

It appears this optimistic fellow (above, right) not only seeks to lap up some attention, but poor little Ooby too: "Dude, I got to show you the sweetest new dick tattoo I got," he announced via my bewildered Babbage portal. In a modest attempt to offset his cool cat demeanor, "Sweet Dude498" has plumped for a manly Pencil Tattooed moustache with matching cheeky Weepers (yes, I'd weep too). He still looks like a pussy to me. Ahh, Whiskas…

THE SAPEURS RISING

We sent our most intrepid reporter to the Republic of Congo to track down the local sartorial cult known as Les Sapeurs. Photographs by Baudouin Mouanda

By Nathaniel Adams

I arrived in Brazzaville armed with nothing but a white linen suit and a small French phrasebook. Having spent the autumn travelling in Europe, I'd wisely sent my linen beauty to Abu Dhabi with my mother. When I visited her, I picked it up and handed over the heavy wool collection, ready for my trip further toward the equator.

I had come to Brazzaville, capital of the Republic of Congo, to meet the Sapeurs: a group of dandies approaching the seriousness of a cult. The Republic of Congo is poor, like most Central-African nations, and still pockmarked on quite a few facades as evidence of its recent civil war. This is the reason the US State Department's profile of the country includes the delightful sentence "In March 2003, the government signed a peace accord with the Ninjas, and the country has remained stable and calm since the signing."

Like many people, the Republic of Congo only came to my attention via the Sapeurs. They are the members of an unofficial club called "Le SAPE," which, in French, stands for "The Society for the Advancement of Elegant Persons." Recent-

ly, a photo book called *Gentlemen of Bacongo* by the Italian photographer Daniele Tamagini was published to great acclaim. The cover is arresting: a black man in a bright pink suit with matching bowler hat and shoes, striding purposefully toward the camera down a dirt street with crumbling one-story buildings lining it, a cigar clamped tight in his theatrically scowling face. The pictures inside were astonishing: men in beautifully fitted suits in the kind of bright colours which can only be pulled off with conviction by people with the darkest complexions. And they were living amongst squalour. The moment I had some money in my pocket I knew that I had to go to Brazzaville.

I'd contacted Tamagini and he'd put me in touch with the President of a Sapeur association, a man named Destin Ndouri. It seems that the government, as well as the Sapeurs themselves, have recently realized that they're a cultural commodity. Mr. Ndouri has decided to capitalise on this. When I visited him at his clothing shop in the Bacongo neighbourhood, he was brusque and uncooperative at first. The first thing that struck me was that he was well dressed in a sense,

but not dressed up. He wore an olive-drab shirt and trousers, a white T-shirt, green striped socks and a pair of white Adidas sneakers. Around his neck hung a large gold cross. He looked like a rapper, if anything. We sat in his dark shop, the sweat thick and slick even under my light linen, surrounded by designer clothing, much that I recognized as knock-offs, but Ndouri seemed to be unaware of this fact and I certainly wasn't going to point it out.

When I told him, through my interpreter, that I'd like to speak to as many people as possible, he announced that it would cost me $100 per person. I was disappointed, not only because I'd come to Brazzaville at great cost, but also because it damaged my somewhat naïve preconception that the Sapeurs did this for the love of elegance alone. I explained that I don't pay for interviews and that I didn't need to see the Sapeur pageant he was now offering. I explained that I just wanted to speak with the Sapeurs and observe. Then I offered the classic journalistic proposition: "I'm going to write about you anyway, so I'll just have to write that you asked me for money." He agreed to speak and gave some answers that mainly consisted of boastful swaggering about him being the best-dressed man

> **HIS ANSWERS WERE MAINLY BOASTFUL SWAGGERING ABOUT HIM BEING THE BEST-DRESSED MAN IN BRAZZAVILLE, WHICH IS WHAT I'D HOPED TO HEAR**

in Brazzaville, which is what I'd hoped to hear from men who practice the Sapeur's form of sartorial one-upmanship.

I had better luck the following day, when local photographer Baudouin Mouanda introduced me to two off-duty Sapeurs. I was surprised to see that they dressed just like anybody else on the dusty Brazzaville streets. One owned a book stall and the other was a barber at a salon that advertised its affiliation with "Sapologie." Despite their casual dress, as we walked to the local beer garden they were hailed by passer-by and respectfully addressed by their Sapeur names: "The King of Colour" and the "Master of Colour." Honored to be in the company of such men of distinction, I bought beers and cola and they bought handfuls of peanuts from passing vendors and carpeted the dirt floor of the beer garden with the shells. They spoke about Sapologie and its importance to them: they saved their money and bought clothes so that on the weekend they could be heroes. They had difficult lives and this was their only outlet for expressing themselves and asserting a kind of dignity absent from their day-to-day existence. For 48 hours they could have elegance. That weekend I went to "La Main Bleue," one

of the Sapeurs' regular clubs. It is outdoors, on the banks of the Congo directly across from the hideous skyscrapers of Kinshasa. The courtyard consists of a perimeter of blue plastic patio tables and chairs with a wooden dance floor in the middle. We showed up at sunset and waited for the Sapeurs to arrive. They did not disappoint. Each strode in turn, erect and proud and splendidly turned-out in their most colorful and well-cut gear. Many had beautiful women on their arms. They took their seats around the dance floor, clearly sitting in areas of more prominence than the other patrons. They had come here to be seen by their friendly competitors and the mere mortals ringed round the edge of the yard. Many of them held the trademark Sapeur cigar between their fingers, never lighting it, presumably because they can't afford to smoke such a luxury item.

I suddenly realized that the Sapeur's obsession, living for their specific weekend clubs and working hard hours at menial jobs reminded me of another one of the rare examples of a kind of group-dandyism: London's original mods. As Pete Meaden has said of the mods, this was "clean living under difficult circumstances." Unlike the other clubs I'd

THE SAPEURS HAD DIFFICULT LIVES AND THIS WAS THEIR ONLY OUTLET FOR ASSERTING A DIGNITY ABSENT FROM THEIR DAY-TO-DAY EXISTENCE

visited in Brazzaville, this one played mostly local rumba for couples to dance to, rather than the rump-bumping "pongo," in which dancers, in what I suspect is a hangover from Colonial French vanity, face a mirror, holding their upper body forward and their bottom out.

As the night went on I spoke to a few Sapeurs and joined in a couple of dances with an attractive woman who bought me a beer and then turned out to be one of Brazzaville's more expensive prostitutes. I kindly declined her post-dance offers and spent the rest of the evening watching the Sapeurs. The DJ played their favorite songs, including many by Papa Wemba, a musician from DRC who is generally regarded by many to be the father of Le SAPE. When I left Brazzaville the next day, hangover in head and luggage in hand, braced for over 35-hours of flying time through 7 different airports, my impression was one of fortunate journalistic disappointment: I had met the Sapeurs, I had spoken and danced with them, and I'd learned that they weren't the fantasy of the photo books. But I'd also learned that potholes, peanut shells and a lamentable lack of affordable cigars can easily be overcome with a stubborn will to elegance.

ROSE-TINTED

Spectacle

Pandora Pitstop looks at the surprisingly sophisticated early life and career of the world's biggest-selling romantic novelist, Dame Barbara Cartland

B efore you ask, no, I have not read a Barbara Cartland romance novel, nor do I intend to. My interest in this lauded vision in pink was piqued by a very good review of a book she had written in 1971, recording her memories of the 1920s. *We Danced All Night* showed a side to Barbara Cartland that has been overshadowed by her more populist image, of a pink-clad nonagenarian writer of 723 novels of dubious literary merit.

Ms Cartland was born in 1901 into a family that, although not wealthy, was certainly well connected. She would learn to use these connections to her advantage in the 1920s, accessing many of the movers and shakers of the day who fell under the spell of her girlish charm and classic English rose looks. Her educational background is patchy at best, involving private tuition and finishing schools. She was a spiritual child seeing angels, reading fairytales and revelling in the romantic writing of Elinor Glyn.

Barbara was a product of her time, when good girls did not read newspapers, wear face powder or lip rouge and only prostitutes were believed to be capable of feeling passion towards a man. She claimed to have been proposed to 49 times, only accepting the 50th. She was skilled at surrounding herself with titled and/or wealthy men who became role models for her novels'

heroes. She could manipulate with the best of them. She got what she wanted and discovered that the secret to social climbing towards a peerage was through charity work. But how did she get started on the social ladder?

Barbara's mother Polly moved her children to Belgravia, London after the Great War. Polly was by now a war widow and a sentimental Edwardian. Barbara was a young debutante who loved to dance. Her recollections of this period of her life show her to be a supreme socialite cleverly infiltrating the Bright Young People and the Mayfair Merry-go-round set in secondhand designer clothes (what a Chapette!); her flirtatious manner masking her ability to glean information and then secretly feed it to gossip columns. By 1923, she was a social diarist in her own right for *The Daily Express* and at this time she penned her first novel, *Jigsaw*, a tale of an innocent girl in wicked Mayfair. It earned her £250.00 and very mixed reviews.

Cartland's career in journalism was furthered through her friendship with the 44-year-old Lord 'Max' Beaverbrook (she was 22). He took a personal interest in her and edited her work himself, thus improving her skills, one of which was saying 'no'. He introduced her to his influential circle of powerful men like Winston Churchill, Lord Birkenhead, F.E. Smith and millionaire Sir James Dunn. Like ripples created in

Glamour Girls in the Fast Lane

One of the regular female racing drivers at Brooklands in Cartland's time was Eirane Naismith, better know as "Paddie". Actress, air hostess for the British Air Navigation Company, pilot and racing driver, she was also occasionally chauffeur to the Prime Minister, Ramsay MacDonald, who had a particular liking for Austins.

Paddie firmly believed that cars only had one speed – flat out. She won a demonstration race in 1931 at Brooklands, organised by Barbara Cartland in response to an article in the Daily Express entitled 'Do women drive motor-cars with as much skill as men?' It is worth noting that fellow female racing driver Fay Taylour's fastest lap at Brooklands was second only to Whitney Straight's Mountain Course record, which already showed that the girls were more than capable of competing with the men.

Paddie mostly raced a supercharged Salmson belonging to fellow actor and flyer Sir Derwent Hall-Caine. In 1932 she won the Ladies' Outer Circuit Handicap in the Salmson, with Fay Taylour second and a Mrs. Gripper in her husband's Frazer-Nash in third. She competed in the RAC Rally driving a Standard, a car which she also used to enter in Concours d'Elegance with one of her four sisters, Miss Jill Naismith. One of the features of this car was that it was fitted with a radio. She also had a 13hp Ballot, from which she used to dispense drinks from its inbuilt cocktail bar.

At the Whitsun BARC Meeting at Brooklands in 1934, Paddie finished third in the First Long handicap, but blotted her copybook at the Autumn Meeting when, after finishing third to R. F. Oats' Amilcar and Arthur Dobson's Bugatti, she was hauled before the stewards, fined £2 and excluded from the results for consistently ignoring the safety lines painted on the road at the fork.

As well as working as an air hostess at Heston Airport (now Heathrow), flying between London and Le Touquet, Paddie also entered the Centenary Air Race from Mildenhall in the UK to Melbourne, Australia, with her sister Jill, in a Leopard Moth.

a mill pond, Barbara's own circle of friends spread ever outwards. She dated flying Ace George Henderson, got to know Amy Johnson and was enamoured with the Bentley Boys (particularly Glen Kidston). She was often seen at Brooklands, the ascot of its day, known for 'all the right crowd and no crowding'. She was also a keen dancer – they all were – and was never short of an escort to all of the fashionable clubs like The Kit Kat, The Embassy, The Cafe de Paris and Quaglino's – anywhere the Price of Wales could be found.

Along with the other Bright Young Things, Cartland enjoyed the new motorised version of the paper chase – the treasure hunt. She could be found with her chums at 2am, racing away from Horse Guards Parade, dashing about London at night in search of clues and ending up at dawn in a Park Lane residence for breakfast and a dance band. There were fancy dress parties and 'pyjama and bottle' parties where one brings a bottle (any bottle would do, from India ink to vintage Bollinger) and the (then) all-new murder mystery party. After night clubs, the theatre was Barbara's second home and she was encouraged by her friends Noel Coward and Tallulah Bankhead to write a play. Her effort was *Blood Money* in 1926, deemed a bit racy and banned – but only because she had used the name of a real Indian prince.

In 1927 Barbara met Alexander McCorquodale, the son of a wealthy printing baron. He was an 'outdoors' man and driving enthusiast and, in her eyes, the embodiment of a romantic ideal. He was also proposer number 50. They honeymoon was a grand tour of Europe in a new Rolls Royce, complete with chauffeur and ladies' maid in the front seat. They mounted up £17,000 in debt in their first year, as Barbara launched herself as a society host-

Barbara Cartland's roguish chums try to break her new glider while she poses for a photograph beside it in 1931

The Barbara Cartland Reading Room at Brooklands Museum is available for children's parties

ess and charity fund raiser, soon earning herself the monicker of a "self-pulicising juggernaught".

One of her most famous promotions was a Ladies' Race at Brooklands in 1931. The competitors were drawn from society beauties and female racing drivers, staged for the papers to promote women as good drivers. The race consisted of one lap around the track, with the contestants perched behind the wheel of a supercharged MG. In commemoration of this event, the Ladies' Reading Room in the Brooklands club house is still tinted pink today and is named in her honour. On the 'must do' list of any socialite in the 1920s and 30s, motorsport was at the top, but a close second was anything to do with aeroplanes. In 1931 Barbara met Flying Officers E.L. Mole & E.C. Wanliss, who discussed with her their interest in the aerotowing of multiple gliders from one plane for long-distance flights. Single 'hand launched' gliders were popular in Germany, where restrictions imposed by the Versailles Treaty made them a necessity.

The idea put forward was to tow several gliders from one plane and, once at 10,000 feet, they could be released and glide to their required location, thus saving fuel. Even Barbara saw the commercial advantage in such flights crossing the Channel or delivering post. She heartily supported the idea and arranged to have her own glider built at a personal cost of £150.00. The 'Barbara Cartland' glider, piloted by Flying Officer Mole, took part in many air rallies and even won races against express trains. The glider successfully delivered goods and post over distances of between 100 and 200 miles, proving it was

THE AIR MINISTRY DID NOT TAKE UP BARBARA CARTLAND'S IDEA OF USING GLIDERS IN THE WAR, BUT THE GERMANS DID AND WE SOON FOLLOWED SUIT

a viable option. Barbara herself occasionally was a passenger in a 2-seater model. The Air Ministry did not, however take up the idea; it was deemed to dangerous, but Germany did and went on to use gliders it in its invasion of Crete during the Second World War. The Allies were then spurred into production of military gliders as troop carriers under the guidance of Officer Mole (now Group-Captain) and used hundreds of them on D-Day. Barbara would later be recognised for her contribution to their development.

After her marriage to Alexander ended in divorce in 1933, Barbara married his cousin Hugh in 1936, whom she claims fell madly in love with her upon meeting her on the day of her wedding to Alexander. Barbara became Countess Spencer in 1976 and stepmother to Lady Diana. With the birth of her three children, Barbara gave up the social columns and embarked on a career as a self appointed 'expert', writing on love and marriage, child rearing, social and political issues of the day and women's health issues. She was a regular contributor to *The Mail*, *The Mirror* and social diarist for *The Sunday Observer* and *Tatler*.

From the late 1930s, Cartland was a prolific writer of best-selling romantic novels, until her death at the age of 98 in 2000. She was, according to the *Guinness Book of World Records* in 1983, the top selling novelist in the world, with 350,000,000 copies sold, and holder of the most novels written in one year. 23, to be exact.

So, whether Barbara Cartland's literary oeuvre is to one's taste or not, it merely forms the tip of a very large iceberg. A pink one.

Sir Roger Moore

Age: 83
Occupation: Actor
Birthplace: Stockwell, London
Education: Battersea Grammar School, RADA
Early Career: Modelling: Knitting Patterns;
Television: Ivanhoe, The Saint, The Persuaders;
Film: seven James Bond films, The Wild Geese etc
Other interests: Goodwill Ambassador for
UNICEF; campaigns on behalf of PETA.

What, for you, epitomises the very essence of Englishness?
Good manners, audible pronounced language and
baked beans on toast.

What is your idea of a perfect English gentleman?
A well-mannered, courteous and kind man who
always offers to buy his actor friends dinner.

Can you name an example, living or deceased?
David Niven.

And his female counterpart?
My wife Kristina, who puts everyone else before
herself.

What is your idea of absolute heaven?
Spending the day with my wife Kristina, enjoying
a nice lunch, watching a DVD, having a little
snooze and a nice dinner.

And your idea of a hell on earth?
Press interviews.

*What three items of clothing would you rescue in the event
of your wardrobe being invaded by a swarm of moths?*
One of my blazers – whichever my fluctuating
waistline allows me to fit into that day; my grey
flannel trousers and one of my lovely, crisp,
white Eton shirts. Meaning I could at least be
presentable as I swat the moths.

*Are you happy with the way in which modern society
is heading, or do you see room for improvement in any
particular areas?*
There is always room for improvement. Good
manners cost nothing.

*Where and when have you ever pined for the services of a
good tailor?*
When I realise that too many good lunches mean
I can't fit into anything in my wardrobe!

*Have you ever considered the wearing of sportswear for any
activity other than sport?*
Not really. I had to wear trainers for a while earlier
this year after spraining my ankle badly and was
unable to get my shoes on. Didn't like them.

*Have you ever found it necessary or appropriate to wear a
pair of flip-flops?*
Never!

*"My kingdom for a horse!" declared Richard III. Which
object have you ever craved with such intensity?*
A pork pie, with a little tomato ketchup.

What item of clothing are you determined never to wear?
Jeans.

*Which of the vices, if any, do you think can lend one an
air of louche sophistication?*
Drinking fine wines.

*What type of facial hair do you think is suitable for a
gentleman?*
A moustache or full beard. Not a silly in between
one or stubble.

NOCTOVISION REVIEWS

By Robert Chilcott

THE PERSUADERS!

40TH ANNIVERSARY EDITION BLU-RAY
Network £79.99

Two playboys arrive at Nice airport: Danny Wilde (Tony Curtis) in a private jet, sipping champagne with a harem of air hostesses in white knee boots, and Lord Brett Sinclair (Roger Moore) with an Aston Martin full of smooching dollies. The pair first lock horns at a set of traffic lights, revving up, teetering on the verge of popping their corks. The viewer is treated to a split screen spectacle of a wholly irresponsible car chase along the coast to Monte Carlo, to the jingle strains of a Tony Hatch/Jackie Trent composition, *Gotta Get Away*. As they narrowly miss an oncoming stunt car, Roger Moore comments on the DVD how nice it was not to have to wear seatbelts back then.

The formula is set up immediately. In the hotel, Sinclair instructs the barman how to mix his Creole Scream: "A jigger of white rum, a dash of bitters, chilled vermouth (*chilled*, not iced) and a measure of grenadine, then mix. Stir in some crushed ice, shake, strain and pour. Top it off with one olive." Wilde interjects that it should be made with two olives, "so that they can bounce up against each other". Sinclair is so incensed – "I'm afraid the spectacle of two olives bouncing up against each other is a pleasure I shall forgo" – that he removes his bow tie for a punch up, and the venue is comically trashed just before the gendarmes turn

up and cart the pair off in the back of their van.

A retired judge has engineered their meeting. He's been keeping a dossier on the two millionaire playboys, Sinclair, a titled Englishman and Wilde, a stockbroker from the Bronx. He gives them a drink and a stern talking to, forcing them to examine their carefree lifestyles: "You can speak seven languages but all you do is order a drink with them". He offers them a deal: three months in jail for the damages or do a job for him: find the sister of a Mafioso. Realising their lives are shallow, they become international do-gooders, with the judge their spymaster.

Initially there's a tension between the two, but obviously this can't be sustained. Their buddy relationship is tested in an early episode, in which a childhood friend of Wilde turns out to be a hitman

that the judge has sent them after. Wilde realises his allegiance is now with Sinclair and the present. They can't go on fighting in each episode, so very quickly they become pals, though certainly devoid of any homoerotic subtext. In a later episode, Sinclair's attempts at amour with his English rose Juliet Harmer are forever thwarted by his duty to protect Wilde from an assassination attempt. Sinclair reveals occasional moments of awareness, explaining his motives and the sense of purpose his new role gives him.

The format had been road tested in a late episode of *The Saint* by producer Bob Baker, where Roger Moore had joined forces with a brash Texan oil baron, played by *The Champions'* Stuart Damon. Baker took the idea to Lew Grade, who had just won an award for service to industry. After seven years as Simon Templar, Moore had the itch and was reluctant to do any further television, having stretched his acting chops in the psychological horror *The Man Who Haunted Himself*, but after that film flopped he discovered Grade had presold him in this new series. When Moore protested, Grade stuck a cigar into his mouth and appealed to his honour: "The country needs the money. Think of the Queen". After original choices Rock Hudson and Glenn Ford turned down the American

WHEN MOORE PROTESTED, GRADE OFFERED HIM A CIGAR AND APPEALED TO HIS HONOUR: 'THE COUNTRY NEEDS THE MONEY; THINK OF THE QUEEN'

role, Curtis was next on the list. Arriving at Heathrow to begin production, he was busted at the airport for possession of a pistol and some dope "What's this?" they asked. "It's marijuana", said Curtis. "In our country we call it cannabis resin," sneer the officials, and Curtis was promptly fined £50 by the local magistrate.

The Persuaders follows the usual ABC recipe from Grade's stable yard – slapstick and sartorial excesses, second-hand plots and back projected locations to pad out the set pieces of banter, camaraderie and playboy ephemera, though admittedly given a huge boost by the interplay of Curtis and Moore, the latter's laissez-faire retorts a perfect counter to the former's more earthy wisecracks and kvetching. Being a British production, though, it is usually Moore's comments that get the upper hand: "Daniel you really do give fresh meaning to the word 'peasant'".

And there's a more than generous delight of damsel eye candy, including all the usual suspects: Kate O' Mara, Annette Andre, Anoushka Hempel, Madeline Smith, and, naturally, Valerie Leon as a soap salesgirl dressed as a space queen driving a moon buggy around the streets of NW6. Other guest stars range from Lionel Blair as the instructor of a troupe of gogo dancers, to Terry-Thomas as Sinclair's bounder

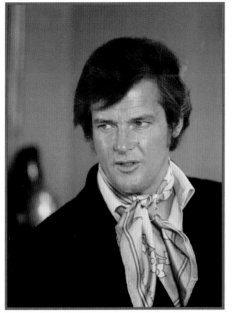

of an uncle, though even the scriptwriters are all too aware of his persona, giving Curtis the remark: "He looks like how an Englishman is supposed to look when they want him to look like that in the movies".

Leisurewear fetishists will revel in the striped cravats sported by Moore – perhaps his effortless good nature granted him permission to carry off such flamboyance without jumping the shark. Moore had extolled the virtues of Yorkshire cloth while working on *The Saint*, so much so that he had now become a co-director of menswear manufacturer Pearson and Foster. Curtis also had a hand in his own wardrobe, rubbing up the producers with a penchant for driving gloves and chunky ties always askew (perhaps modelled on the Italian playboy Gianni Agnelli, The Rake of the Riviera, who dressed with deliberate errors to give the impression that he didn't care).

Every tiny detail is visible on this Blu-Ray transfer, though the modern high definition pixel spectrum struggles with the unique colour balance of Moore's turquoise/opal shade of shirt – the digital age does not comprehend such garish palettes. Amidst the familiar extras of mute outtakes, clapper boards and foreign advertisements, the best value special feature is a TV spot of Curtis on Russell Harty, where the actor talks about

> THERE IS A TENDER REUNION BETWEEN CURTIS AND MOORE ON THE ALAN TITCHMARSH SHOW, WITH GENUINE WARMTH AND AFFECTION BETWEEN THE PAIR

happiness and existentialism, extolling the spontaneity of humanity: "Life is like dropping a stone into a pond and seeing the waves ripple – it'll pay off somewhere along the way." Curtis thinks to plan is fatal, foreseeing a day when we've expired all the world's resources and will have run out of toothpaste and toilet paper, and bonds with Harty: "Pal, I'm right in there with you". Why was television allowed to be so good back then?

There's also a tender reunion between Curtis and Moore on the Alan Titchmarsh Show from a few years ago, with genuine warmth, affection and humour between the pair. The series was very big in Germany, though this is attributed to a radical redubbing, virtually a new script of in-jokes and pro-American sentiment. The last hurrah of the ITC action adventure series (*The Protectors* and the *Jason King* spin off had proved far less durable), *The Persuaders* alas only survived a one-series 24-episode run. While popular in Europe, it failed the US market and got canned immediately. This proved fortuitous for Moore, as it allowed him to trim his Byronic flop and go far out as Commander Bond; though he had to lose a few pounds off the waistline, after a year of drinking, not the usual actors' substituted ginger ale, but the real champagne that the production had afforded.

Adam Ant

Amid the stylish vintage décor of Time For Tea in Shoreditch, Michael "Atters" Attree meets erstwhile dandy highwayman Adam Ant, to discuss dandyism, New Romanticism and Terence Stamp over several tequila-laced lager beers, kindly provided by Johnny Vercoutre

re you experimental with facial hair?
I am now. I have attempted to in the past, but now I've gone for a Lord Cardigan cherry-bun style.

Do you use any facial hair accoutrements?
I dye it. I use mascara.

Mascara? Really? Damn. I thought that trick was a secret of my own. Do you admire anyone with facial hair?
I like D.H. Lawrence's beard, with a roll neck. I like Royal Navy beards. I tried a Robert De Niro *Deer Hunter* style for a short time, but only when I was having a few days off.

Do you find the ladies like Adam's whiskers?
Some girls do; some girls hate it and they complain about a rash.

Did you make the 80s or did the 80s make you?
I think in retrospect I was given the New Romantic label; recently the V&A did a pop culture exhibition and

labelled me as a New Romantic. I think it's the worst tag I could have. In the history books I'm blocked into this whole thing. Some of the guys I knew, like Spandau Ballet, were alright, but I never set foot in the Blitz club.

What do you think of the latest 1980s revival?
It's not really a revival; I think it's more kids liking a period of history and getting their version of it, like we do. When punk came around, people forget that Malcolm and Vivienne were in their shop SEX and Let It Rock before that. They had a jukebox and were doing Teddy Boy clothes, T-shirts with Jerry Lee Lewis on, so even then it was retrospective – they were looking back at rock 'n' roll even then. Rock and roll came out of America, but America came from England.

What do you think of the current 1940s revival?
One of my favourite groups when I was growing up was the Bonzo Dog Doo Dah Band and Vivian Stanshall; I know the words of many of his works by heart. I came from an art school background. That was really

Photograph: Michael Attree

A new royal family, a wild nobility ...

my thing; *Eleven Moustachioed Daughters* and *Sir Henry at Rawlinson End*. I know it all off by heart and I bloody love it. My definition of style is that certain styles and fashions are so good you can't get rid of them, no matter how hard you try. There'll always be an undercurrent of that style. I think it's getting bigger now and people are ready for a bit of individuality.

What would you say were your Chappish qualities?

I like to dress up on occasions, but the main thing is to shave in the morning. The toilette, as women would say. Getting a good shave and not cutting your throat and being clean and ready to go. Anything you put on, if you're clean, is going to hang well, and I think that's the main thing that leads into sartorial correctness. I go down to Jermyn Street and I get a shave – it's quite a process.

How would you personally describe or interpret Chappism yourself?

When he walks into a room, you wouldn't notice him at first, but eventually you'll notice something, like a

pair of shoes. One article would be out of place. No matter how limited the budget, they've always got the best. If he wears Levis, it'll be 501s. Also, its 'look but don't touch'. A courageous stance, where you walk into a room and you're wearing make-up and everyone else is in Fred Perrys. There are 60 of them and one of you and you have to stand your ground. Invariably they all just shut up, especially as you're the one with the girl, not them.

Is there any Dandyism in popular music these days?

Unfortunately not; I think it's got lazy. It's turning into a sort of horrible Fred Perry funeral, with guys wearing casuals. Posing like hooligans, with football terrace chic, which makes me sick to my stomach. I think punk was the last great effort where things were really turned upside down. A T-shirt with a swastika and a Jesus upside down, or the Cambridge rapist on it, or two 14-year-old boys smoking cigarettes. And to wear them you had to be a part of something, you were actually saying f**k off or leave me alone, or that I don't give a s**t. The last

> ANYTHING YOU PUT ON, IF YOU'RE CLEAN, IS GOING TO HANG WELL, AND I THINK THAT'S THE MAIN THING THAT LEADS INTO SARTORIAL CORRECTNESS

effort was Sigue Sigue Sputnik. Everyone hated them, but they tried something – they were like the New York Dolls. They had a go, and they had a bit of glory there. And maybe Suede, when they were wearing flares. Blur were doing well, then they started being sort of, you know, jolly lads. It led into the Gallaghers. Paul Weller I don't mind. He's a sort of a mod dandy. He's a bit safe.

How should a true Dandy conduct himself?

A dandy should be a gentleman, opening doors, being courteous. The aesthetic of it is to be an arrogant, wealthy wastrel who squanders his inheritance, but if you read about Beau Brummell, for example, he wasn't rich. He had to use his wit and style. He invented the suit. He had the Prince Regent kissing his arse, and eventually he crossed a line and said "Who's your fat friend?" I met Quentin Crisp a few times, he was a dandy but was the nicest man you'll ever meet. He'd be out with 700 mad kids running around him; he'd be sitting there smoking a cigarette and having a drink and nobody would touch him.

His room was a bit dusty, I believe. Was the man himself clean?

He used to say "after a year, the dust doesn't get any worse". Francis Bacon – his studio was like a nest. I think there's something interesting about the cleanliness of the artist; they like to get really messed up and then get all cleaned up again and go out gambling.

Did or do you ever drink at their (and my) favourite Soho waterhole, The French House?

No, I never drank alcohol until about six years ago. No drink, no smoking, no drugs. I don't like drugs at all. [He takes a sip of his tequila-based beverage and florally takes a puff of his Turkish cigarette.]

When it comes to women, would you consider yourself a cad, bounder or gentleman?

[Without any hesitation] Gentleman. Honestly, hand on heart, there's nothing as beautiful as a woman. They can give you more pleasure than anything and so I see no reason to treat them with anything other than respect. I've never hit a woman in my life. When I was little, my granddad held his fist up – he'd been a sailor in the First World War – and said, if I ever see you hit

Photograph: Hanson Leatherby

a woman I'll give you that. [Adam holds his persuasive be-ringed knuckleduster-like fist up to my face] And if you ever see a man hit a woman, give him that.

And how should an English gentleman conduct himself?

The thing about the whole Chap ideal is that there are a lot of kids who aren't from the background that that comes from. The Duke of Windsor, he was the man. He was this guy who just had natural style even though he was a small guy. I met Fred Astaire once and he was just... [Shakes his head admiringly]. If you look at pictures of Fred Astaire, instead of a belt, he'd have a tie wrapped round his waist when he was rehearsing. These guys, they weren't particularly handsome, but they were well suited and booted. You learn a lot from just looking at them. The first guy that I ever approached to help me with advice, who became a distant mentor, was Terence Stamp. I went to Fortnum and Mason and met him, because I was interested in taking up a bit of acting. I was at Number One in the charts at the time, in 1980, and I went in there in my pirate outfit and he had his moustache and all these girls were looking, and he came in wearing a three-piece suit and all the girls just went crazy. He sat there with a lapsang souchong and he's just got it.

He gave me a very good education; he was quite brutal. I think a lot of the military influence came from looking at *Billy Budd* and *Far from the Madding Crowd*. He really did learn to use the sabre; he'd done a lot of drugs, so there was quite a weird element to what he said. He was also a great writer, as was Dirk Bogarde, who is another of my heroes. When you find out that at home he was drinking a pint of Guinness in his dressing gown, but when he stepped out that door, it was like the song, *It's Your Duty to be Beautiful* and if you're an entertainer, that's part of the job, and a lot of them think it isn't. And yet they'll still go to the Groucho, knowing there's a load of paps outside and you'll get that [masks his face with his hands] And that's laziness. It's the worst enemy. I can't bear that. No one can style me and no-one can dress me, so when I do a photo session I get all the stylists phoning me up: "Hello, what do you want?" "I'm a stylist." "Who for? Not me."

Any other men of sartorial style you admire?
Brian Setzer from the Stray Cats – I think he's a dandy, with his hair piled high, pompadour-y. People like Little Richard and early Elvis. No-one taught him to dress like that. Who else? I think the 60s did turn out some really dangerous fashionistas. Brian Jones, the early Stones – they looked fantastic. Dirk Bogarde underlined. Terence Stamp doubly underlined. Marcello Mastroianni.

What's your opinion on Mark Ronson's style?
I met Mark Ronson, I spent an afternoon with him, and he's a very intelligent, gracious young man and I think he is very talented and will have a very long career. He's a gentleman. He's got the right idea. I can't judge anyone until I meet them, with the exception of the Gallaghers. I don't have to meet Liam Gallagher; I mean, you can just smell him. But I think Mark Ronson's a bit of a chap. He's picked up on this John F Kennedy-era style; he's got this sort of Staypress thing. He does it well. Pete Doherty thinks he's Rimbaud – which is a shame, because he's a talented young man

... We are Family

Photograph: Michael Attree

but soon he's going to be dead. He'll lose his teeth and then his looks; he'll lose his girlfriend and then lose his life. He's going to die and it's a terrible thing.

Is it? You may have gathered that popular music's not my forte so I shall deviate here. Everyone is frightened of dying itself but are you frightened of death?
Erm...not...er...no. I'm not frightened but I'd hate to lose interest in everything. But I've experienced that, by being put on antidepressants for many years against my will, without actually being dead. I've been sort of dead for many years.

Did you ever twig you were dearly departed at the time?
You don't realise it, but you do when you come out of it. It may be coincidental but I didn't write a song or pick up a guitar for several years. When you can't wait for the next Jeremy Kyle show or the next pie or just how long it's going to take to get from the bed to the settee, you are a dead person. So I'm not scared of death....they talk about old people, like only 'they are' like old, but we are all old, we're going to get old. And I've got a lot of respect for old people. I don't think there's enough shown to them. I love their stories.

Part Two of this interview (the slightly darker part) may be read at www.thechap.net/archive

For a list of Adam Ant's forthcoming tour dates, visit www.adam-ant.net

the LIP Weasel

Michael "Atters" Attree with his round-up of all things hirsute and occult

PRODUCT REVIEW
Haiku

Truefitt & Hill "ultimate comfort" pre-shave oil.
£16.50 (60ml)
Compact and bijou
The zesty scent is a treat
I drank mine with gin

If you'd like a haiku review of your grooming product, please send to: Atters, The Chap, 2 Mount Place, Lewes, East Sussex BN7 1YH

THE HIRSUTE HALL OF INFAMY

Here Be Beauty

I feared this was some desperado heading for battle, but New Zealand's Ged Maybury (sporting an admirable imperial partial beard) was merely heading for a steampunk powder room.

There's a something pleasingly defiant about the way Mr. Hill displays his liberally waxed "English" handlebar here. And who can blame him? Since the public smoking ban, I too stare furiously at my absent Hamlet cigar.

Spotted during a "Look Away" themed party, this steampunk has either mastered the art of follicular chaos or glued a Benedictine monk's scalp to his chin. Either way, his image powerfully imbues that sense of hirsute phantasmagorical Mesmer.

Here Be Monsters

Steam KerPlunk? Our brave (and rightly anonymous) knight sports what is known as the "Bingo Wings" moustache. Should he confront a monster of old, he'd no doubt cry "Thou shalt not pass!" Well, sir, you haven't.

If this estate agent were described by, say, an estate agent, he'd be "hugely desirable, with south facing whiskers and modernised hair, with a newly decorated shirt, matching neckwear and adjoining 'roomy' cardigan."

Had "Bwana Ian" been snapped wielding that machete in the tropics (or a Big Brother household) then he might have justified his costume. Show me leech welts or, better still, some decent facial topiary!

THE PENTAGRAM OF ATTERS

Many years ago, I sold a batch of bygone pictures to an oily costermonger in London's Crouch End. During the transaction, eccentric Bonzo legend Vivian Stanshall sauntered up and promptly purchased one of the pictures I had just sold. The work was a reproduction of the 1950s "Crying Boy" by kitsch Spanish artist Bruno Amadio.

Legend chillingly declares that any home displaying this "cursed gypsy boy" painting shall be hexed by fire. A few months later (from my Mount View Road garret window) I watched in horror as black smoke billowed from Vivian's Muswell Hill rooftop. In unison, a newsreader on TV announced, "A coincidental twist to Mr. Stanshall's untimely death is that, exactly 100 years ago today, the real Sir Henry Rawlinson, Victorian Army officer and Orientalist, died, on 5th March 1895."

Eerie postscript: our editor has noted the date that, unwittingly, I submitted my grisly tale to The Chap: 5th March, 2012

DRESSING DOWN

LAPSE OF PANACHE
Abercrombie & Fitch

On the morning of St George's Day, April 23rd, swathes of immaculately dressed chaps and chapettes gathered outside No. 3 Savile Row to demonstrate peacefully – but firmly – against Abercrombie & Fitch's proposed plans to open a children's store there. At 10:15am, our chumrades-in-arms marched around the corner to Abercrombie's flagship store on Burlington Gardens, stabbing the air defiantly with placards declaring "Give Three-Piece a Chance". On the very steps of enemy HQ, Mr. B The Gentleman Rhymer led the troops in song, chanting "All we are saying is, give three-piece a chance" adapted from John Lennon's original. Once pitched outside A&F's flagship store, demonstrators were greeted by hordes of press, both local and international, accumulated on the opposite pavement. Also in attendance was the Chief inspector of Savile Row Constabulary, who commented to one of the protestors: "In all honesty, this is the best-dressed demonstration I have ever seen." We hope the Chief Inspector will add his signature to our petition and help keep riff-raff off the Row.

BOND OFF THE SAUCE

As a bastion of many refined vices including smoking, infuriating one's tailor and of course the well-made Martini, James Bond has, for decades, been a guiding sartorial beacon for numerous readers of this publication. However, news has recently reached us that the previously stylish, urbane Bond, now thuggishly portrayed by Daniel Craig, is to be seen swigging from a bottle of Dutch lager in the new film, *Skyfall*, due for release later this year. The film's producers have come to a $45 million arrangement with Heineken that will see the Bond character taking part in a series of adverts promoting the insipid lager beer. Sam Goldsworthy, owner of London dry gin distillery, Sipsmith, recently remarked "This is the most maddening piece of news I've heard in a while. Ian Fleming would be turning in his grave."

However, Daniel Craig has hit out at critics, claiming that this kind of sponsorship is, in the current financial climate, a necessary evil. "This movie costs a lot of money to make, it costs nearly as much again if not more to promote, so we go where we can. The great thing is that Bond is a drinker, it's part of who he is, rightly or wrongly; you can make your own judgement about it. Having a beer is no bad thing – in the movie it just happens to be Heineken."

The Chap wonders whether this lackadaisical attitude might lead future films in the James Bond canon to even darker places, including the introduction of expensive hoodies to Bond's wardrobe or perhaps, horror of horrors, a car chase with Bond at the wheel of a Renault Clio.

WILLIAM WALKER'S DREAM TROUSERS (PATENT PENDING)

Do you suffer from inside leg chafing? Are you a martyr to fly dyspepsia? Or do you sometimes simply feel far too wistful to match your tweed jacket with one of the pairs of trousers hanging in your wardrobe? Fear not, my dear man. What you need is a pair of William Walker's Dream Trousers (Patent pending).

These new and wondrous items of legwear are a marvel to wear and an inspiration (literally) to own. A cross between one's favourite pair of well-broken-in corduroys and the Emperor's New

Clothes, these fictitious strides are available in any fabric and style one would care to imagine. Say farewell to 'breech brace' and turn-up trouble, by purchasing a pair of your very own, imagined-to-measure, fully pre-envisioned William Walker Phantom Pants.

Viv the Spiv's JOKE CORNER

I jumped on a bus at Marble Arch and asked the conductor for a 2d ticket to the West End and he says, "We don't go to the West End!" I says to him, "Well it says so on the front of the bus!" So he says to me, "It says Persil on the back, but we don't take in washing!"

"In my local, I asked for a pint of Best Bitter. As the barman placed it on the bar, he said to me, "Looks like rain again." To which I promptly replied, "Yes it does, but you still charge three quid a Pint for it, don't ya?"

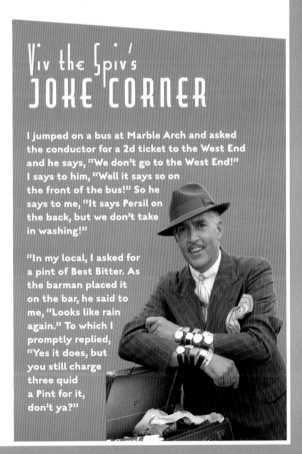

CHRIS EUBANK

Gustav Temple meets Christopher Eubank, the former pugilisit who retired in 1998 with a creditable 45 wins, two draws and five losses under his belt, to discuss dandyism, gentlemanliness and declining standards in sport

Have you noticed a decline in standards in sport in recent years?

It is what it is at the time. Like the seasons of the year, there are always changes, sometimes not so good and sometimes amazing. The decline is not necessarily a bad thing, because when the amazing inevitably does come around, there is so much more wow, e.g. Tyson, Bolt…

What is your opinion of the poor social antics of some of today's well-known sportsmen?

I should remind them that they are custodians of their father's surnames, and that they have a responsibility to upholding what they are only caretakers of. It is incomprehensible to me that they should slap the very face of their future legacies. The phenomenon of modern-day cannibalism. Girls without virtue and men without code.

Should sportsmen conduct themselves in any particular way outside of their sporting arena, or should they have licence to behave as they wish?

I refer to the above.

> IT TOOK THE SAME COURAGE TO WALK ON TO A TV SET CARRYING A CANE AS IT TAKES TO VAULT THE ROPES AND THEN ENGAGE IN A PROFESSIONAL FIGHT

You are often described as "eccentric". Are you happy with this description?

I am not an eccentric, however, I heard that if three different people on different occasions call you a horse, you should go and buy yourself a saddle.

Would you consider yourself to be a dandy?

I simply am what I am.

You retired from boxing in 1998. How have you amused yourself since then?

I have struggled hard, but with dignity.

Have you ever been interested in English country sports such as hunting, shooting or fishing?

I used to have catch men, so those three pursuits are a little out of my league.

Does the dandy exist in modern society?

Yes, however, he or she is usually recognized as an eccentric. They want to make anyone who wants to be charismatic feel awkward, so that one backs up into conformity.

Where do you think the best-dressed people may be found today?

As I do not base style on either cloth or expense, and do so on charisma, I would have to say Jamaica.

THE FIRST TIME I USED A CANE ON A TV SHOW, IT TOOK THE SAME COURAGE AS IT TAKES TO VAULT THE ROPES INTO A PROFESSIONAL FIGHT

What for you is the definition of a gentleman?

A gentleman is a person who is considerate in almost all situations and usually cloaked in dignity.

Can you name an example of a perfect English gentleman, living or deceased?

Leslie Phillips.

And his female counterpart?

Helen Mirren.

Have you ever considered the wearing of sportswear for any activity other than sport?

If you go through archive photos you will find a picture of me going to a world movie premier in boxing boots, shorts and T-shirt and Tour de France cap (orange).

Are you happy with the way in which modern society is heading, or do you see room for improvement in any particular areas?

Duh.

How should a true gentleman conduct himself?

I refer to the first question.

Erroll Flynn took the role of Gentleman Jim in a biopic about the great boxer. Who would you like to play you in a film about your life?

This is not my field of excellence; I would seek the counsel of Guy Richie or Martin Scorsese, as they seem to understand how to portray the grit in a man.

You are officially Lord of the Manor of Brighton and spent over £1M of your own money on flats for the homeless. Do you think of yourself as a modern-day philanthropist in the 19th century style?

If I was that, then it is not something that I should second.

Does your dress code reflect the position you hold in society, or do you think anyone can dress like an English gentleman, regardless of his position?

Anyone can wear what they choose, however, it should be noted that frocks do not suit men. One should never try to be what one isn't. If one is comfortable in a suit of clothes, then the majority will pay it no mind, but if one is not comfortable and at ease with himself, then the public will smell the stench.

What advice would you give to our younger readers, who would like to become proper English dandies?

If you want to be one, then you already are; all you have to do now is intellectualise and realize your balls of steel. The first time I used a cane on a TV show was terrifying. I walked out to the set, which had a studio audience, and it took the same courage as it takes to strut, vault the ropes and then engage in a professional fight. It's not easy being a dandy, at least not to start with. Once initiated, it is truly a badge worth wearing.

What item of clothing would you advise any man never to wear?

A frock.

What three items of clothing do you think should form the basis of every gentleman's wardrobe?

Jeffery West shoes, Cad & The Dandy tweed jackets and I would like to make swagger one of the items of clothes, but it must be with a sense of dignity.

Do you obey the traditional gentlemanly dress codes such as never wearing brown shoes in the city etc?

That I would certainly obey; old school can never be out schooled.

Would you ever visit a horse-racing track, and if so, how would you dress for it?

Appropriately.

AM I CHAP?

READERS ARE GIVEN A THOROUGH AND UNCOMPROMISING ASSESSMENT OF THEIR CHAPPISHNESS. SEND YOUR PHOTOGRAPHS TO CHAP@THECHAP.NET

Svenn Jakobsen declares himself "Certainly no Lumberjack, but quite OK!" whatever that means in his peculiar language. In our language, he is without qualification a Chap. He is billed as "Kreativ Leder" of "Teknopilot", which is probably a very boring job indeed, but sounds exotic and mysterious to us.

Whereas Peter Jeucken, who hails from the less exotic Netherlands, could possibly have a fascinating job, such as head of televisual murders at the constabulary. A pity then that he is wearing such an incredibly boring outfit that makes him look like the new boy at school. Sometimes tweed is not ok, and sometimes chestnut brogues simply cry out to be christened by a spattering of mud.

"Greetings from Germany," writes Strick Poet. "Am I Chap? ;o)" Greetings from England, good sir, where gentlemen wear shirts, trousers with pockets in the right places and are more decisive about their facial hair. And also use punctuation marks to punctuate rather than draw pictures.

"Is my brother Glen a chap?" writes Jackie Bessant. "Here he is preparing for the Chap Olympiad and, yes, the Penny Farthing is a permanent fixture in his house!" Please tell your brother that plus fours are freely available on the open market, and there is no need to fashion pretend ones out of an old pair of chinos. Neither is there any need for trompe l'oeil Penny Farthings.

"My name is Gilbert Ruegg. I live in Switzerland. The foto was taken at a retro-vintage-event in Switzerland last year, where people from the 40s dominated. I took it as a cover for my last CD." Did you really? And what form of music was on the CD – Reggae, Classical, Death Metal? It's just that the clothes don't give any indication.

"My name is Edward Richard Mumby, and I wore this little number while being inducted into the Sixth Form. Apologies for sideways orientation." Congratulations for turning up to school in a pin stripe suit and pipe. Presumably they sent you home on account of your hair? Or was it the lack of footwear?

How extraordinary. Karl Hagen looks like Edward Mumby (see left) 20 years into the future. Whatever "sideways orientation" was, it ended up with motorcycles in the living room and strangely pointed shoes. This is what the future has in store for us. And this is why we are not looking forward to it.

"These photos were taken at the Chap Olympiad," writes Claire Banton. "I'd travelled down from Teesside to take my father Ian Banton along. On the walk from Goodge Street station we were approached by a local down-and-out, who asked my Father the location of his penthouse – so can we assume (despite the fact he was wearing a duvet as a cape) that our attire met the required standards?" Madam, we are confused – is this a photo of you with the down-and-out or your father?

Colin Shaddick is reading, publicly, from a book entitled "Isn't Sex Noisy?", doubtless from his own quill. He is wearing some sort of undershirt which is not tucked in; has a spectacles case as a pocket square and a hamster dangling from his chin. How eccentric (he probably thinks he is). His badge shows membership of the Eccentric Club, so he clearly isn't.

"I took my prom as an opportunity to show my fellow teenagers how it should be done," writes Connor Potts of Basingstoke. "One apologises for the lack of facial hair, pipe and properly fitting attire; however, time, youth and funding were severe limitations." Colin Shaddick, please note. This slip of a youth is already far more eccentric than you, and his acknowledgement of his own shortcomings means they may be entirely overlooked.

═ GASTROMONY DOMINE ═

Cai Ross argues that Keith Floyd's seminal cookery programme, Floyd on France, set the standards for all TV cookery programmes that followed

I f, as is claimed by many music fans, Bob Dylan's *Highway 61 Revisited* marked the moment when pop music transcended the genre and became a serious art form, then I believe that *Floyd on France*, broadcast in 1987, was one of the great evolutionary touchstones of TV cookery. There are now whole television channels that owe a significant debt to the two-headed genius of Keith Floyd and David Pritchard. It is a revolutionary and curiously unheralded fork in the road of British television. This wasn't just the next Darwinian step in the development of gastronomic TV, it was the peak: still unmatched a quarter of a century later.

Like Keith Floyd's TV career itself, the magnificence of *Floyd on France* (or FOF) is largely fluked. There is a guerrilla-style quality to the series, owing to the manner in which Pritchard and his production team "begged, borrowed and conned" their way into various French kitchens, domestic and professional. This required a front man that could react with spontaneity and charm to the most unexpected upsets. And upset, he seemed to be, a great deal of the time: harassed by the increasing demands of his director and hamstrung

> FLOYD DISMISSES HIS OWN PIPERADE, BEFORE TAKING MIMI BY THE HIPS AND SUGGESTING THAT "WE SHOULD GO OFF TOGETHER SOMEWHERE"

by circumstance. For example, the day when he had to cook Coq au Vin with Gevrey Chambertin for 35 grape pickers in a kitchen small enough to fit into a widower's bedsit.

This irascibility, always fun to watch, was evenly tempered with Floyd's delightful, smoky, public school charm. As a French friend called Monique leans into shot to help stir the Soupe de Poisson, he coos, "To make this soup you need a beautiful lady with blue eyes."

However, his beguiling manner also came in handy when dealing with adversaries as well as friends, and there was no greater nemesis (perhaps in TV cookery history) than Madame Mimi from Biarritz - she of the infamous Piperade incident.

As Floyd gamely tries to cook up this Basque egg and pepper classic, terrifying Mimi tuts and hisses her disapproval at every turn of the spoon. A cooking instructor herself, she provides a commentary of relentless criticism, culminating in an unwillingness to even sample the final product on the grounds of predictable disappointment. Floyd translates her eventual review thus: "The peppers are raw. There's not enough salt. There's not enough pepper. In brief, it's absolute rub-

bish." In a flash, Mimi has taken over and cooks up her own Piperade as Floyd looks on. He compares the two dishes by dismissing his own efforts as "lumpy, nasty British Rail style scrambled eggs with a tin of old ratatouille stuffed into it," before taking Mimi by the hips and suggesting that "We should go off together somewhere."

I am struggling to think of a modern TV chef who would allow him or herself to be so completely upstaged, or who would allow their culinary skills to be so exposed to such justifiable criticism. Yet it is Floyd's willingness occasionally to appear the second-cleverest person in the room that gives him a winning vulnerability. Reunited with an old mentor, Claude Arnaud in Provence, Floyd assists him with the puppyish enthusiasm of a Home Economics student trying to win a star from his teacher. It was the twin ingredients of quiet subservience and a hand grenade temper, which gave *Floyd on France* its heart and soul. The balance wouldn't last throughout the entire Floyd canon.

During a cooking sketch in Bergerac, Floyd reveals another aspect of the enduring quality of FOF: "They can't afford the film to show the cooking of a meal from beginning to end," he deadpans while plating up Escalope de Veau au Moutarde Dijon (an absolute cinch to make and glorious with a crisp green salad and wild rice). Film! It's all on film. Where later Floyds followed the rest of the TV industry into using video cameras with ubiquity, his first few series were shot on honest-to-goodness celluloid. It might seem a trifling matter, but it is a lynchpin in FOF's claim to greatness. While video gave cameramen greater flexibility and gave the producers a licence to rein in the budget, the sterile effect it had upon its subject invited a note of disposability to the fray.

Floyd on France is a classic vinyl album of a show. Not that Floyd seemed to care. "Sorry about this," he groans over some glorious footage of fishermen lolling on the Dordogne. "This is where Clive tries to win a few prizes for really evocative photography." Such distraction was Floyd's bête noire, but thanks to Clive's efforts, the series features footage that has you searching for a travel agent's website as you watch, even 25 years later.

It isn't easy to create a world into which one desperately seeks to immerse oneself. Hugh Fearnley Whittingstall took a similar leaf out of Floyd's recipe book with the first *River Cottage* programmes which, delightful though they were, were essentially a

"I'd like to see Madame Mimi from Biarritz have a crack at something like this"

bucolic fantasy with a Robinson Crusoe narrative, masquerading as a food programme.

Watching the show for the first time as a 12-year-old boy, Keith Floyd presented a sort of hero figure. He was the same age as my parents but still retained the arrested naughtiness of an untamed schoolboy. Fresh out of shorts, I was already shopping around for influences, building up the ideal of the man I wanted to grow up to be. Revisiting the programme now, that irresistible spirit of mischief is still very much the star of the show. Floyd and Pritchard appear to be grown up alumni from Willans and Searle's Molesworth books: expelled from St. Custards and inveigled somehow into the BBC. Still smoking and drinking because of the naughtiness factor, yet always able to draw upon a suitable Latin quote if the moment demanded. Apparently, other children my age wanted to grow up to be Nick Faldo. Deus avertat!

The use of voice-over in the series was in itself an art form, robbing the device of its innate pomposity with a precise irreverence. In one episode, they comment on a truculent French chef silently creating a beautiful dish of chicken with freshwater crayfish. "The atmosphere was so tense," explains the Floyd voice-over. "The director didn't like the cook very much. The cook resented the film crew being in

there…" Pritchard joins in: "He really was very miserable wasn't he? The lighting man nearly bopped him. I'm really glad this sequence is coming to an end. It's really gone on a bit, hasn't it?" The warmth of good-natured camaraderie is enough to brown toast.

It didn't last. Various stories have emerged through the years about the deterioration of the Floyd/Pritchard relationship. Floyd made his claims in his semi-posthumous and surprisingly nasty autobiography, Stirred Not Shaken. Pritchard offered a counter-version in his far more enjoyable reminiscence, Shooting The Cook.

Probably the true nature of making these shows, the endless travel, the boring hotels, the loneliness and estrangement, as well as the constant monkey-performances of contractual obligation, eventually became utterly unbearable for Keith Floyd. In contrast to the bouncing Toad, "Poop-poop"ing his way through his cooking sketches in the first half of the Floyd oeuvre, later shows present a somnolent, weary fellow, his infectious enthusiasm cast adrift in a bottle somewhere like a suicide note. At one point in *Floyd Around The Med*, he pads around a restaurant kitchen, silently preparing something or other. Finally, he croaks, "That's cooking, baby" with such dead-eyed disdain that you half expect him to crawl awkwardly into the oven and padlock the door from the inside.

Keith Allen made a programme about Keith Floyd in 2009. It was like having the memory of your favourite uncle desecrated, finding out how much he hated your dad and fancied your mum, and now he needs to borrow some money to buy his teeth back from the pawnbrokers. It was unbearable to watch and I had to turn it off before the end. Perhaps Floyd agreed. He died while he was watching it.

If there is a single moment from *Floyd in France* to treasure above all, it is of the chef, shirtless, leaning back in his chair against a tree, glass of wine cradled in his lap, gazing up into the beautiful French sky with a look of serene contentment on his face. Britain's first rock star chef, in the middle of filming his own *Exile on Main Street*, privately aware that he was creating the greatest cookery programme ever made.

On the night he died, I slipped Keith Floyd's theme song, *Waltzinblack* by The Stranglers on to the stereo in my restaurant. When it began, the chatter in the room slowly died down and, for a moment, everyone smiled warmly. Then they returned to their walnut tart with Armagnac icing (*Floyd on France*).

Barry Humphries

Age: 78
Profession: Comedian, Dadaist, author, bon vivant
Education: Camberwell Grammar School, University of Melbourne
Early Career: Philip Street Review Theatre, various dada pranks, Dame Edna Everage
Other interests: Bibliomania, avant-garde music, collecting art, not drinking

What, for you, epitomises the very essence of Englishness?
Tweed. A Devonshire tea. A felt hat.

What is your idea of absolute heaven?
My answer would be too impolite for this magazine but would involve several members of the opposite sex.

And your idea of a hell on earth?
Loud music in a restaurant.

What three items of clothing would you rescue in the event of your wardrobe being invaded by a swarm of moths?
A purple cashmere sweater, a pair of bespoke silk pyjamas and my favourite collection of ties.

Are you happy with the way in which modern society is heading, or do you see room for improvement in any particular areas?
I do not like modern life, I prefer to live in the past – it is more dependable.

Where and when have you ever pined for the services of a good tailor?
I enjoy the services of a good tailor but I have longed for members of my audiences in Australia and America to share them. If theatre audiences buy good clothes, when do they wear them?

What is your idea of a perfect English gentleman?
A well-educated, amusing man who removes his hat in lifts and wears clothes that are so good, you don't notice them.

Can you name an example, living or deceased?
The late Mark Burleigh, creator of Annabel's nightclub.

And his female counterpart?
A girl who wears hats and gloves (but little else).

Have you ever found it necessary or appropriate to wear a pair of flip-flops?
I wear flip-flops a lot but they are minimalist, made of leather and made for me.

"My kingdom for a horse!" declared Richard III. What object have you ever craved with such intensity?
A painting by the Edwardian artist Charles Conder.

What items of clothing are you determined never to wear?
A tracksuit and crocs.

How many different varieties of hat do you own, and which is your favourite?
I own hats in every style and my favourite is a Fedora, made in Paris of dark green velours.

Dressing DOWN

= CHAP AGAINST CHUMP =

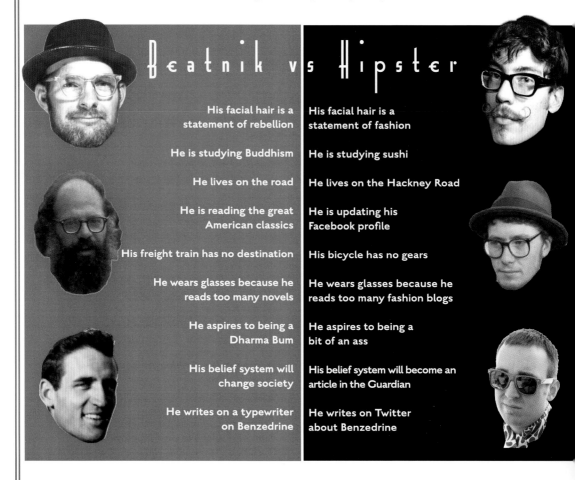

Beatnik vs Hipster

His facial hair is a statement of rebellion	His facial hair is a statement of fashion
He is studying Buddhism	He is studying sushi
He lives on the road	He lives on the Hackney Road
He is reading the great American classics	He is updating his Facebook profile
His freight train has no destination	His bicycle has no gears
He wears glasses because he reads too many novels	He wears glasses because he reads too many fashion blogs
He aspires to being a Dharma Bum	He aspires to being a bit of an ass
His belief system will change society	His belief system will become an article in the Guardian
He writes on a typewriter on Benzedrine	He writes on Twitter about Benzedrine

THE FOURTH GRAND ANARCHO-DANDYIST BALL

This year's decadent soiree sees the Chaps return to 2010's elegant venue, the Grade-2 listed Bloomsbury Ballroom. The theme of the Ball is "eccentric", with the Gonzo Dog-do Bar Band headlining – Britain's only tribute act to Vivian Stanshall's surrealist 60s dada music-hall electro psychedelic outfit. Other acts will include a real live flea circus, tap dancing ladies, one-armed jugglers, birdsong impersonators and more. In the cocktail bar, the Flirtinis will teach you how to flirt, Viv the Spiv will teach you how to smoke contraband chocolate and our bartenders will teach you how to drink 1930s cocktails. The dress code is eccentric, eclectic, electric, esoteric.

The Bloomsbury Ballroom
Bloomsbury Square
London WCIB 4DA
Saturday 1st December 2012
Tickets: 0207 724 1617
www.nightof1000waistcoats.com

BOOK OF STRANGE ODDITIES

QUEER FACTS

WHY A "BROWN STUDY"?

WHEN A PERSON IS DEEP IN GLOOMY THOUGHT HE IS SAID TO BE IN A "BROWN STUDY" BECAUSE EVER SINCE OLDEN TIMES THE COLOUR BROWN HAS BEEN THE SYMBOL OF ANYTHING MOROSE OR MELANCHOLY. THE ARMY EXPRESSION "BROWNED OFF" IS ANOTHER EXAMPLE OF THIS COLOUR AS A SYMBOL OF GLOOM.

No.2

WRITTEN AND ILLUSTRATED BY GLYN PROTHEROE

Viv the Spiv's JOKE CORNER

Out in the garden having a spit & a draw, I peeped over my fence to see young Mary next door, digging a hole in the flowerbed. Being curious, as always, I asked what she was doing. "I'm burying my Goldfish, Mr. The Spiv," came her tearful reply. "Oh, I am sorry," I said, then mentioned that it was rather a large hole for such a small fish. "No it isn't," she replied. "Because it's in your cat."

Coming out of my local Fish 'n' Chip shop the other day, I was getting my gnashers stuck into a piping hot Kate & Sydney (Steak & Kidney) pie, when an old Oil Lamp (Tramp) sitting on the ground looked up at me and said, "I ain't eaten for three days Guv'nor."
"Well," I replied, I wish I had your willpower!"

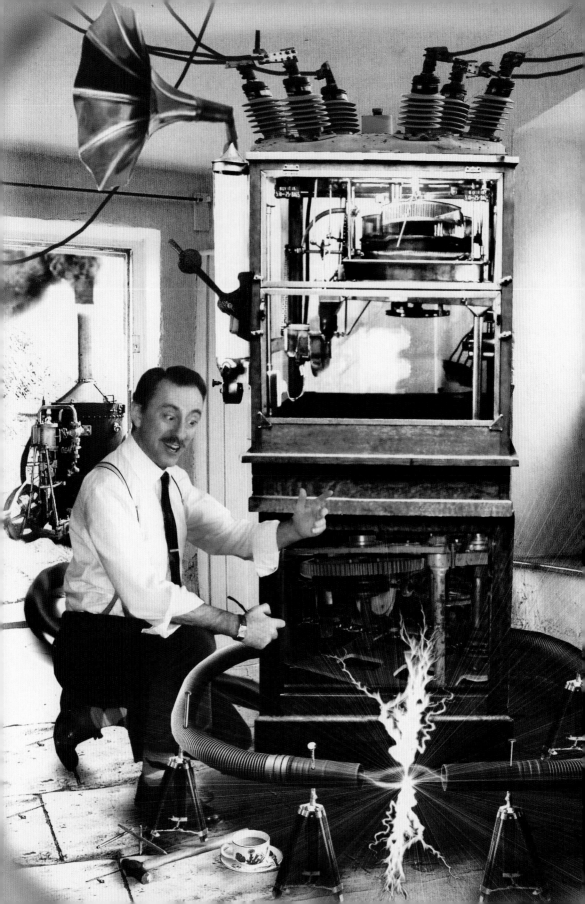

THE
Gentleman's
MEDIUM-SIZED HADRON COLLIDER

How to build a device that will answer some of the big
questions of the Universe in your garden shed or garage

by William Walker

Gentlemen! At something of a loose end now the cricket season is over? Washed the car and manicured the lawn to within an inch of its life, and now find you've nothing to occupy the old grey matter this weekend? And to top it all off, the good lady wife is away visiting her Mother in Hull, and there's no-one about to cook your lunch!

Well, how about answering some of the big questions of the universe? What about seeing how matter behaved a tiny fraction of a second after the Big Bang? Not too bothered? Thought not ... but then again, what about firing up the old steam boiler and smashing a few lead nuclei together? Now, that's more like it, now isn't it, sir!

If you've ever put up a shelf or two, making your own Hadron Collider couldn't be simpler, with these easy-to-follow, step-by-step instructions. Right then, strip off the old tweed jacket, roll up the shirtsleeves, square that knot in your tie, and let's get started!

YOU WILL NEED:

One (1) steam engine.
One (1) cwt. nutty slack – for the burning of.
One (1) small tin of hadrons; or, failing that; two (2) 2H lead pencils (not graphite) – for the colliding of.
Pipes (4) bent billiard, churchwarden etc., – for the contemplation with.
Four (4) various tins of tobacco (2oz) – for the relishment of.
One (1) pint bottle of Wainwright's – the whistle, for the wetting of.
One (1) ball of hairy string – for the tying with.
Three (3) rolls of sticky (or Sello) tape.
Length of hose from vacuum cleaner.
One (1) Stapler + staples.
Two (2) grease guns, sans grease.
One (1) large hammer.
One (1) pound of six-inch nails.
One (1) flat-head screwdriver (just in case).

SAFETY EQUIPMENT:

One (1) medium-sized tie clip.

STEP ONE
Stoke the boiler and get it, and your pipe, lit and fuming. While you are at it, put the kettle on.

STEP TWO
You should already have several parts of an old steam locomotive in the back garden, so nip out and bring in two pressure release cylinders, the bigger the better.

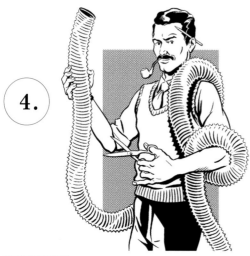

STEP FOUR
Into each of the grease guns, sans grease, insert a modicum of hadrons. Fresh out of hadrons (and who isn't?) and pushed for time (and who isn't?) Then do as I do and substitute the lead of a 2H pencil (not graphite). Well, there are surely some lead nuclei in a lead pencil, aren't there?

Cut the vacuum cleaner hose in two (later to be invisibly repaired with sticky tape, to ensure the trouble-and-strife is none the wiser).

With the stapler, affix one half of the hose on to each grease gun. Seal with tape.

STEP FIVE
Arrange the sections of vacuum cleaner hose in a circle, so the open ends are opposite each other and approximately six inches apart. Nail them to the floor.

Move on to pipe number three (possibly a bent briar and a wad of Brown Study).

While the tea is brewing, contrive to connect your steam boiler to the two cylinders with the hairy string and sticky tape, taking care that the joints are sound.

STEP THREE

Remove ends from grease guns.
Nail the grease guns, sans grease, one on to each of the pressure release cylinders.
Move purposefully back into the house for your second pipe of the day (possibly the churchwarden and the Erinmore Mixture). Brew tea. Consume with digestive biscuit and gusto.

Open the bottle of Wainwright's beer, pour, allow to settle, drink in one. Position oneself approx. six inches from the hose ends. Don't worry, it's quite safe. If you're concerned about safety, simply squint your eyes; this should help in the event of flying detritus.

STEP SIX

Throw the pressure release lever and send the lead pencils hurtling towards each other.
Look on and gasp, as the very heart of 'matter' is revealed. You may even catch a glimpse of the Higgs Boson, in which case you have made scientific history. Lean back and reward yourself for a good day's work, by packing your fourth pipe of the day with a goodly wad of Old English Curve Cut. Well done, old Chap!

STALAG FIXTURES

Steve Pittard on the lengths taken by prisoners of war in camps such as Colditz to ensure their games of cricket were uninterrupted

T he lack of games facilities in an all-British camp is a disgrace," bemoaned Charles 'Lucky' Lockett on first entering Colditz. He spent much of his leisure time in the attic with the Colditz Cock (the legendary glider), though his right to play cricket should have been covered by the Geneva Convention. Captors were duty bound to 'encourage as much as possible the organisation of intellectual and sporting pursuits'.

British officers at Oflag 4C, Colditz, in 1941

PoW camps received a standard Red Cross sports parcel, which contained numerous soccer and rugger paraphernalia but only two cricket balls (often composite). Sometimes the string proved more useful than the contents. At Stalag VIIIB in Lamsdorf it was used to fashion cricket nets. Cricket balls soon became damaged or irretrievable and some individuals became adept at winding string around a pebble and then applying varnish to produce a serviceable cricket ball. Stumps and bats would be included in later Red Cross sets. With Linseed in short supply, bats became brittle, though at a push oil from sardine cans acted as a substitute. Annoyingly, some bats became further weakened by well-meaning M19 boffins who inserted covert screwdrivers as escape aids into the handles. Pads and boxes were also scarce but cable knit sweaters abounded. Such items were practically de riguer among British airmen, whether engaged in playing cricket or not.

Chaps incarcerated in Spangenberg Castle (Oflag IX A/H) found it virtually impossible to find a suitable spot to pitch wickets, but remained undaunted. The only viable area appeared to be a curved section within the dry sunken moat, about 40 feet wide. Though littered with rubble, tin cans and debris, Major-General Fortune soon organised the levelling of the undulating surface and topped it off with three inches of soil. Having pounded the pitch into shape with croquet mallets, to keep it in good order, a by-law made it verboten for players to wear anything other than rubber-soled shoes. The wicket consisted of plywood boards trimmed to meet MCC specifications

A standard issue WWII Red Cross cricket ball

Nets fashioned from unwound cricket balls at Stalag VIIIB in Lamsdorf, Germany

and propped up by stones. Tennis balls were used but needed fine tuning because of their steepling bounce. In overt ball tampering shenanigans worthy of a Pakistan Test bowler, Elastoplast patches were sewn on either side to provide a better weight. This refinement also aided spin and offered some protection against the rough-hewn stone walls.

A couple of Old Harrovians, familiar with the confines of house-yard cricket, adapted the rules to accommodate the idiosyncratic playing arena. On one side, a 4-foot high grassy bank sloped up to the 30-foot high curved castle wall and any rebounds remained in play. The unpredictable angle of the ricochets often made monkeys out of the fielders. Third man region contained a flowerbed. It was designated a boundary, though awarded only one run, to discourage hits there. Another allotment received similar dispensation, after an irate Colonel protested that reckless off drives played havoc with his tomato crop.

Matches consisted of two innings each, limited to fifteen overs, and took place between two and four o'clock. Thus nobody need bolt their lunch or be late for tea. Batsmen retired once they'd reached 20, though some bounders deliberately nudged singles when nearing this landmark. Then on 19 they would attempt to slog a six and depart with a score of 25. With all the rules finally ironed out, a team tally of 50 was considered par. No side exceeded 100, with the Highland Brigade capitulating to all out 0.

Officers bagged the pitch on Sundays for encounters against NCOs. Also rival huts challenged each other and 'club' fixtures took place between Gunners, Greenjackets, Commandos, etc. Though a terribly unreliable team player – he kept escaping – Terence Prittie sent a detailed account to Blighty documenting the queer cricketing arrangements. German censors intercepted the report and, thinking it must contain a secret message, spent days trying to crack the hidden code. Completely stumped, they resorted to sending it to Lord Haw-Haw, whose department concluded that the text contained a perfectly ordinary explanation of a most irregular cricket game.

Many PoW cricket rules anticipated modern one-day regulations. At Spangenberg, any delivery passing even a whisker outside leg stump was signalled 'wide'. Lamsdorf introduced neutral umpires, resplendent in hospital white coats. This extremely well-organised camp hosted a triangular 'Test' tournament in 1943 between England, Australia and New Zealand, which often attracted an audience, admittedly captive, of 2,500. England failed to reach the final, leading to the selectors being sacked. For the following summer's competition, South Africa replaced the Kiwis and boasted 'Billy' Wade, a Test wicketkeeper, on the team.

Pitch invasions sometimes marred proceedings. Germans failed to respect boundary lines – notably the Polish border – and one goon trespassed on the outfield with his bicycle and German shepherd in tow. Another jackbooted Kraut received a volley of abuse and demanded to know the exact meaning of 'stupid bastard'. He was assured the English expression referred to 'a person who walks across cricket pitches instead of around them'. Sir Francis Lacey, a former MCC secretary, blamed the war on Europeans not playing cricket: "Had Hitler and Mussolini been cricketers, I do not think we should have had all this trouble that is going on in Europe today". Hitler did toy with cricket but considered the sport insufficiently violent for the tastes of German Fascists. To make it more appealing/ sadistic, he advocated the removal of pads.

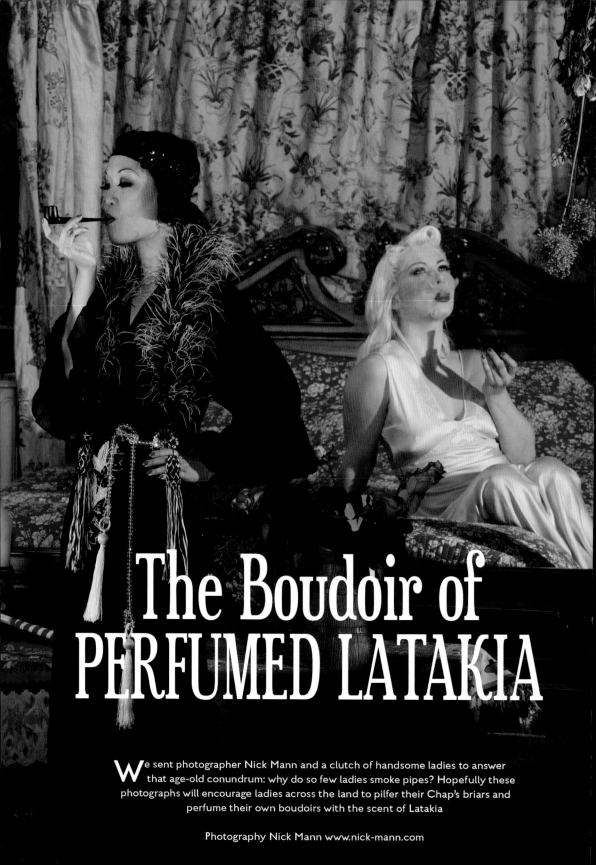

The Boudoir of
PERFUMED LATAKIA

We sent photographer Nick Mann and a clutch of handsome ladies to answer that age-old conundrum: why do so few ladies smoke pipes? Hopefully these photographs will encourage ladies across the land to pilfer their Chap's briars and perfume their own boudoirs with the scent of Latakia

Photography Nick Mann www.nick-mann.com

cent Binks. Pipe: Meerschaum

Model: Annette Bette Kellow. Pipe: Clay pipe

Model: Banbury Cross. Pipe: Straight Falcon

Model: Marianne Cheesecake. Pipe: Clay Pipe

It's just not CRICKET!

Steve Pittard on the illustrious career of cricket obsessive supporting film characters Charters and Caldicott

Charters and Caldicott, two cricket obsessed English gents, stole the show in Hitchcock's *The Lady Vanishes*. Cinema audiences chortled at the whimsical badinage between the bluff heavy-set Basil Radford (Charters) and dapper mild-mannered Naunton Wayne (Caldicott). Their marvellous rapport owed to inspired casting, as the chaps had only met once before, appropriately during a theatrical cricket match. Wayne's background was light entertainment, in musicals such as *Going Gay*, while Radford was predominantly a straight actor.

At the start of *The Lady Vanishes*, set in 1938, an avalanche sees Charters and Caldicott holed up in a Balkans hotel. They talk earnestly of England being on the brink, and the awfulness of their communications cut off in a time of crisis. However, they aren't referring to the storm clouds gathering over Europe but of the unfolding Manchester Test. Frustrated at being kept in the dark, Charters intercepts a guest's phone call from Blighty. However the caller hasn't the foggiest idea about the state of play, as an aghast Charters – "You can't be in England and not know the Test score!" – slams down the receiver in disgust…"the fellow's an ignoramus."

Later, when aboard a transcontinental train, a young socialite Iris Henderson (Margaret Lockwood) is kicking up the devil of a fuss trying to convince fellow passengers that an elderly spinster, Miss Froy, has mysteriously disappeared. Charters and Caldicott are quizzed but dead bat any suggestions of noticing Miss Froy in the dining car, as they were deeply engrossed in a cricket discussion. Iris protests, "I don't see how a thing like cricket can make you forget seeing people," as an indignant Charters counters, "Oh don't you. Well if that's your attitude there's obviously nothing more to be said! Come Caldicott!…a thing like cricket!"

However, they did know Miss Froy… all too well. Her request for the sugar bowl had scuppered Charters' demonstration – the scattered sugar lumps representing fielding positions – of how Wally Hammond fell victim to an umpiring howler. They are loath to lend any credence to Iris's story, as the merest whiff of foul play would mean a delay, thereby missing the Basle connection and moreover the last day of the match. After an eventful journey, involving a shoot out with dastardly Krauts, they arrive home in good time but are dashed when alighting from the train to spot a billboard: TEST MATCH ABANDONED – FLOODS.

Their comical cameos went down a storm and the chums reprised their double act in *Night Train to Munich*

(1940). Caldicott is taken aback to see his old Oxford pal Dicky Randall (Rex Harrison) swanning around as a monocled Gestapo officer. Charters muses whether Randall might be a traitor but Caldicott pooh poohs such an idea, noting that Randall once played for the Gentlemen. Discovering that the leg-break bowler's cover has been blown, they tip him off by tampering with a waiter's tray. Caldicott, remembering Randall always had doughnuts sent up to his room for afternoon tea, hides a note under said confection warning him he's "batting on a sticky wicket". It turns out Randall's penchant was for rock cakes but, no matter, he makes good his getaway despite Charters, posing as his German chauffeur, driving on the left.

Crook's Tour (1941) sees the cricket loving coves take centre stage with another ill-timed sojourn, during a West Indies visit. Bungling from Bagdad to Bulgaria, the intrepid Englishmen once more unwittingly get mixed up in espionage and somehow foil a plot to wreck a British oilfield.

The actors appeared together in many other films. For copyright reasons they were not always called Charters and Caldicott but were unmistakably the same characters; overgrown public schoolboys, permanently baffled by foreigners, women, and the working classes. They viewed life through the prism of cricket. Playing a bachelor boffin, Wayne's character summed up a lawyer acquaintance (and former Surrey cricketer) as a "Nice chap" though "too inclined to nibble at the loose ball I always thought" *It's not Cricket* (1949) sees them play a couple of ex military men, Major Bright and Captain Early, now turned private dicks. The priceless pair are at the crease when an old Nazi adversary, Otto Fisch (Maurice Denham), pretends to be a fielder and purloins the ball, taking off in a jalopy. The outraged Englishmen commandeer a tractor and are forced to take extreme action – driving across the pitch and flattening the stumps - in order to get their ball back, which on closer inspection unscrews to reveal a stolen diamond within.

Basil Radford and Naunton Wayne were now national treasures, as inseparable "as mild and bitter or mustard and cress". In 1952 their inimitable partnership was broken when Basil was clean bowled by a heart attack while reaching for a beer in a Mayfair restaurant. Naunton's innings ended in 1970, but their screen personas lived on. A 1979 remake of *The Lady Vanishes* featured Arthur Lowe as Charters alongside Ian Carmichael. The crass production did them few favours. The American scriptwriter didn't know the first thing about cricket, and in his initial draft had Len Hutton referred to as a bowler! Luckily Carmichael, an MCC member, put matters right.

In Keith Waterhouse's agreeable 1985 serial *Charters and Caldicott*, the eponymous duo are now retired… that's assuming they ever worked. Robin Bailey, who had previously played the crusty Brigadier in *Tales from a Long Room* was first-rate as Charters with the impeccably mannered Michael Aldridge the perfect foil. During one of their monthly lunches at the Pall Mall club the old buffers have a difference of opinion concerning a batting statistic in a *Times* obituary and repair to Caldicott's apartment to consult the relevant Wisden. There they discover a dead girl's body and, equally shocking, an error in Wisden, which they conclude must contain a coded secret message. They investigate the rum business with the denouement taking place during a real Old Trafford Test. There, Charters and Caldicott have to contend with such disgraceful behaviour as a blackguard brandishing a revolver and ladies entering the members enclosure.

EDITH WITH ATTITUDE

Hip-hop was invented by languid 1920s socialite Edith Sitwell, argues Mr. B the Gentleman Rhymer

Hip-Hop, that much maligned and derided of cultural phenomena, officially turned 40 years old last summer. In August 1973, a chap called Clive played some records at a party in a recreation room on Sedgewick Avenue in the Bronx, to raise some money for his younger sister to buy a school uniform. It seems an awfully long trek from those altruistic beginnings to the hedge-funded, greed-and-lust-fuelled behemoth that hip-hop appears to be today.

In the beginning, the disc jockey was king. Clive, or to give him his *nom des disques*, DJ Kool Herc, would isolate the part of each carefully selected ditty that he observed would create a frenzy of dancing and, using two copies of said gramophone disc, loop said section to create a continuous piece, thusforth keeping the audience on their toes and generally having a splendid do of it.

After a time, disc jockeys would invite their chums along to M.C. at these events. These masters of ceremonies would generally have been rambunc-

tious types, who would invite the party-goers to join in singalongs or occasionally raise a toast to guests and generally keep the spirits up.

The M.C.s rapidly became the focal point of said soirees, often to the chagrin of the disc jockeys. The natural conclusion of this was The Sugarhill Gang's *Rapper's Delight*, the first ever 'rap' 45 single, which is understood by some to have left old Clive in something of a miff, being of the opinion that hip-hop was the realm of the DJ rather than the rapper. Whether this was true or not, *Rapper's Delight* was a huge hit and commercial hip-hop was born.

So there's a little potted history of the birth of rap. Over the 40 years hence, scholars have pontificated upon its influences and where it all sprang up from. The obvious and most widely held beliefs are that its furthest back influences were African tribal rhythms and chants, then later the early jazz-era scat singing of Cab Calloway and Slim Gaillaird. The 1960s brought James Brown and his staccato funk howlings, shortly followed by the more righteous beat poetry of the Last Poets and Gil Scott-Heron.

I would like to propose an alternative hypothesis: Hip-Hop was invented by Dame Edith Sitwell. At a recent dinner, her Grandson, William Sitwell, who currently edits *Waitrose Kitchen*, a rag extolling the finer points of cooking from tins, declared as much and told fellow diners that his granny was "better that 50 Cent".

Edith, who along with her brothers Osbert and Sachaverell formed a literary and artistic group around themselves in the early 20th century, wrote *Façade-An Entertainment* in 1918. A series of poems to be recited over music written by William Walton, a friend and protégée of hers, it was first performed in 1923 at a recital arranged and promoted by this group of siblings.

The performance proved a controversial one, as many critics of the day saw it as something of a 'highbrow jape' and considered the Sitwells to be nothing but attention seekers. This use of poetry, performed rhythmically over music, was seen as too radical for many, as did much early (and indeed later) rap.

Upon listening to the piece, be it the BBC's 1930 recording featuring Constant Lambert and Sitwell in the M.I.C as it were, or the (now considered 'definitive') performance from 1951 featuring Peter Pears, the staccato rhymes and time signatures of the 'readings' are unmistakably hip-hop-esque. The words within, although seemingly nonsensical, appeared to allude to Dame Edith's unhappy childhood. Although brought up within an aristocratic family (her mother, the former Lady Ida Emily Augusta Denison, claimed descent from the Plantagenets and her father was the 4th Baronet of Renishaw Hall, in the splendidly northern sounding Eckington, Derbyshire), or perhaps because of it, she had little time for her parents, largely due to their having locked her into an iron frame to 'help' her apparent spinal deformity. When asked by her parents what she wanted to be when she grew up, she replied simply 'a genius'. She was banished to her room without any supper.

The similarity with rap didn't end with the cadence of her rhymes and the controversies of her performances. Sitwell was an unusual dresser, wearing velvet or brocade gowns, often topped off with a turban. She was also an early advocate of what would become known as 'bling', adorned with large amounts of jewellery, with a particular penchant for wearing many rings. She was also, like her modern hip-hop peers, not averse to the odd 'beef'. Being

a woman who both thought and dressed in an unusual manner, at a time when women were rather strenuously encouraged to toe the line, attracted its share of detractors, most of whom she was more than happy to engage in a bout of sniping with. One of these was Noel Coward who, after deriding Edith and her brothers in a skit, was not spoken to again by Sitwell until her 70th birthday.

Coward is, of course another of whom it could be said was a precursor to hip-hop. His half-spoken, half-sung songs such as *Mad Dogs And Englishmen* display a similar joie-de-vivre to early B-boys the Funky Four Plus One or The Jonzun Crew.

In 1948, the Sitwell siblings had toured America, two years before Dylan Thomas arrived in New York and staked his own claim in rap's unwritten history, making recordings of his poetry at the same time as the first be-bop records were being made and living in a style befitting a be-bopper. His recitals were unpredictable affairs, his audience unsure in which state of inebriation the speaker would appear, much in the same way that audiences fifty years later would wonder how many members of the Wu Tang Clan might arrive at any given show and how long they might bother playing for.

These recordings had none of the rhythmical zeal of Sitwell's *Façade* though. At the time of her death, her name was said to have been associated with 'snobbery, self promotion and literary feuds'. What could be more hip-hop than that?

To view the entire recital of Façade, visit YouTube/users/thechapmagazine

Dressing Down

== CHAP AGAINST CHUMP ==

Oscar Wilde Vs Graham Norton

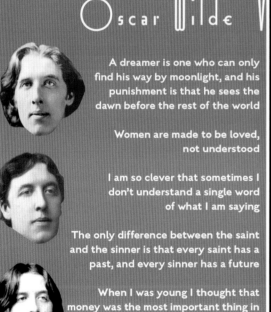

Oscar Wilde	Graham Norton
A dreamer is one who can only find his way by moonlight, and his punishment is that he sees the dawn before the rest of the world	Forty freaked me out. I didn't see it coming. I was moving jobs and moving house and it just hit me like a ton of bricks
Women are made to be loved, not understood	I loved Lucille Ball growing up
I am so clever that sometimes I don't understand a single word of what I am saying	I think the word is so adult!
The only difference between the saint and the sinner is that every saint has a past, and every sinner has a future	My mobile rang one day and it was George Michael. He wanted to come on the show on Friday. We were like, "Okay, if that's what you want"
When I was young I thought that money was the most important thing in life; now that I am old I know that it is	Those years between drama school and getting onto the stand-up circuit were pretty lean
Morality is simply the attitude we adopt towards people whom we personally dislike	I don't think you should have to try to be nice, I think most people are nice
I have the simplest tastes. I am always satisfied with the best	I don't think I've got bad taste. I've got no taste

THE ARTS OF THE GENTLEMAN:
= CLUBS =

Tom Cutler on the art of belonging to a suitable club,
i.e. a club that no-one has ever heard of

D inner parties are strange affairs – not that I'm often invited to one, mind you, either because I'm rather unsociable or maybe because they've gone out of style. But it was at one of these rare dos a while back that I found myself seated near a fat lady in pearls who loudly enquired of a chap on the other side of the table, 'Gerald, are you a homosexual?' Later, between the poached sole and the grilled pears, she leaned across to me to announce, apropos nothing and in a voice reminiscent of Edith Evans, 'Giving birth is like extruding a house – with the windows open.' There was a gasp, before a tweedy lady smoking a cigar, and improbably called Frank, was seized by a wave of hysterical laughter, and every-one relaxed.

I find these occasions a bit of a strain, even without excitements of this sort, though that wom-an might have had a point about childbearing. I recall my wife once indulging in a mammoth labour of some 33 hours in a seaside hospital where the gas-and-air flowed like water. This extravagance culminated in the birth of my son, and as soon as he'd been checked over they attached a plastic bracelet to his wrist bearing the legend, 'Male. Unnamed'. Actually, we had settled on a first name but there was still some horse-trading going on over the suitability of a couple of my suggestions for middle names. Having got 'Jedediah' through as his main one (after a character in *Citizen Kane*), I was obliged to drop the proposed 'Horatio' so as to get a Sherlock in there. I've always been a fan of Mr. Holmes and I was planning on calling any subsequent son 'Mycroft', that being the name of Sherlock's brother. But it never happened.

Mycroft Holmes was an interesting man. Sherlock describes him to Dr. Watson as very stout and very clever but lacking in ambition and practicality. His life is slow and routine, and though he especially dislikes company, he is nonetheless a member of a gentleman's club. 'There are many men in London, you know', explains Sherlock in *The Adventure of the Greek Interpreter*, 'who, some from shyness, some from misanthropy, have no wish for the company of their fellows. Yet they are not averse to comfortable chairs and the latest periodicals. It is for the convenience of these that the Diogenes Club was started, and it now contains the most unsociable and unclubbable men in town. No member is permitted to take the least notice of any other one. Save in the Strangers Room, no talking is, under any circumstances, allowed, and three offences, if brought to the notice of the committee, render the talker liable to expulsion.'

As I've said, I am rather unsociable myself, though not unclubbable. Indeed, over the years I have become a member of several clubs, most of them in London. The societies to which I belong are not the smoke-filled gentleman's clubs of yesteryear, so disdained by the eccentric members of the Diogenes. Rather they are associations of aficionados as peculiar and sometimes as socially wary as myself.

The first club I joined, and of which I am still a member thirty-something years later, was the Magic Circle. This society is as hard to get into as many of the most exclusive establishments in St James's. Membership is by invitation only and subject to a rigorous and terrifying examination, consisting of a performance in front of an audience of professional magicians who take no prisoners. Still, I squeaked through.

The chief delight of Monday Nights at the Magic Circle is sitting in the clubroom surrounded by cabinets full of old posters and magic props, discussing tricks and swapping secrets with my long-standing magician friends, and gossiping magical gossip. There is a terrific library, a nice bar, and a superb little theatre where you can

watch visiting performers do their stuff or stumble through your own rubbish knowing, as you drop the cards for the umpteenth time, that you have never been so well lit.

The Circle, as it is known to its members, has always represented a cross-section of male society. Over the years I've met deaf, blind, and crippled magicians. We've got accountants, dustmen, teachers, policemen, Anglican priests, Rabbis, broadcasters, and barrow boys. Several London cabbies have been members; there are lawyers aplenty, a few writers, some well-known politicians of both sides, and, of course, several famous magicians. I know of two transsexuals, two professional stuntmen, a one-armed fellow, a rapist and a paedophile. The latter pair are, I should say, no longer members.

There was a successful push a few years back to allow women in, but they remain very few and far between. Every religion, race, and colour is represented: black, white, brown, Muslim, Jew, Hindu, Christian, and atheist. There are even

some Americans. What holds this unlikely mix together is a shared love of the art of magic.

Another London association to which I belong is the Handlebar Club. This most convivial society was formed in 1947 in the dressing room of comic actor Jimmy Edwards. It meets on the first Friday of every month at the Windsor Castle pub in Marylebone. To be a full member you must have, 'a hirsute appendage of the upper lip with graspable extremities'. You also need to be able to drink a fair amount of beer. Beards are not allowed, but only in the sense that a pigeon fanciers' club forbids rabbits, on the ground that they are not pigeons. There are always plenty of wives, girlfriends, and pretty

female moustache lovers at our gatherings, which means that you don't have to stare at a lot of blokes all evening – one disadvantage of the traditional gentleman's club.

A few years ago I had to go to New York on business. While deciding where I might be able to get a proper drink and put my feet up in some style I stumbled upon the Corduroy Appreciation Club, founded by 'Thane of Corduroy' Miles Rohan. I dropped Miles a line, mentioning my fondness for the whistling cloth, and we spent a bleary corduroy-clad evening in the Rum House, near Times Square, discussing, amongst other things, 'corduroy's' etymology and scoffing at the popular notion

that it comes from the French *corde du roi*, meaning, 'the king's cord'. Actually, the French call the material *velours à côtes* and the word 'corduroy' probably comes from 'cord' plus 'duroy', an obsolete type of coarse English fabric.

Anyway, Miles made me a member of his club and asked me to address their next meeting, at which everyone would be obliged, as usual, to wear at least two items of corduroy. But I had to go home. A year or so later, the club celebrated the 11th of November 2011 as the date most closely resembling corduroy: 11/11/11. Straight after this Miles wound the club up, on the grounds that enough was as good as a feast.

Along with the Muff Diving Club (muffdivingclub.ie), one of my favourite societies is the Ancient Order of Froth Blowers (1924–1931), who aimed 'to foster the noble art and gentle and healthy pastime of froth blowing amongst gentlemen of leisure and ex-soldiers'. This quintessentially English institution embodied that element of earnest silliness which no other nation can match.

The Pipe Club of London is another fraternity that has always appealed to me but of which I have never been a member. Meeting regularly in St James's, the PCL's activities include pipe smoking and visits to pipe factories, so there's nothing too athletic about it.

I suppose the ultimate low-hustle club must be UKRAS, the UK Roundabout Appreciation Society, who get together to discuss, yes, roundabouts and, now and again, the wildlife that live on some of the larger junctions. At the most energetic end of the spectrum is the Ejection Tie Club. To be a member you must have been fired from a military plane in your ejection seat and survived. The sole benefit of membership is the tie, the purpose of which, rather like a Mason's handshake, is to identify members to each other when they are in mufti.

Although British clubs have traditionally been exclusively male, one of the finest forbids men altogether. Not far from the village of Messing-cum-Inworth in Essex lies the hamlet of Ugley. It appears in the Domesday Book as Ugghelea, the ancient name meaning 'woodland clearing of a man named Ugga'. Today it boasts one of the country's most deliciously named groups: the Ugley Women's Institute. I once heard a lady from The Ugley Women's Institute (it may have been the Ugley secretary) complain that they were fed up with announcing themselves at WI conferences with, 'Hello, we're Ugley.' I'm told they grew so tired of jokers shouting out at fêtes, 'You lot are Ugley, aren't you?' that a decision was made to change their name to the Women's Institute: Ugley Branch. I'm not sure it's much of an improvement. ✒

129 DE GRACY

129. E. DALTON

CROOKS LIKE US

Peter Cormie on a time when criminals dressed better than most people on the right side of the law do today

Dr Peter Doyle's books *City of Shadows: Sydney Police Photographs 1912-1948* (2005) and *Crooks Like Us* (2009) draw upon a remarkable hoard of photographs of the New South Wales police force, discovered and saved from a flooded Australian warehouse in the 1980s by the Historic Houses Trust. In *City of Shadows*, we are treated to an overview of the collection, from crime scene photographs – vehicle crashes, gruesome murder victims, and suicides – street scenes, views of the city and mug shots. Whether your interest is long-gone architecture, crime voyeurism,

fashion and social history, this book and *Crooks Like Us* offers something for everyone.

The shift in focus in *Crooks Like Us* to the portrait section of the archive is in keeping with the persistent public fascination with the larrikin, the small-time transgressor who refuses to comply with society's rules and impositions. Mostly represented here are the underclass of their day, from hardened criminals to 'chavs' on their way to joining them; whores, their customers and madams; thieves and their fences; robbers and rapists and sub-Pavlovian recidivists; a rag tag bunch of petty and not-so-petty

criminals. Doyle's detailed research to identify those pictured, and their crimes, affords humanity to the often haunted, tired eyes that stare out down the years. One cannot help but be moved by the people pictured and their stories.

In Jeremy Bentham's view of the perfect prison, the Panopticon, the dual roles of the criminal justice system – discipline and punish – were brought together in a single building. The prisoners knew not when they were being observed and would behave themselves, just in case, in order to avoid punishment. The mug shots here, some originally published for police use as a supplement to the NSW Police Gazette and later as a stand-alone publication, The NSW Criminal Register, and no doubt known to the criminals pictured, performed the same disciplinary function, one of the coercive methods of control that so fascinated Michel Foucault.

For the vintage fashion collector/wearer, this kind of resource is an invaluable guide to who wore the clothes we find, and how they wore them. The second volume, focused on mug shots, is an astonishing resource for the looks that many in the vintage com-munity try to establish or emulate. From Dapper Dan to Desperate Dan, most of early 20th century male society is represented. Some of the tailoring on display is clearly of the highest order. But mostly these are poor men, down-at-heel working class Orwellian chaps with tieless neckline, stained coats and trousers threadbare at elbows and knees, ill cared-for hats holey from handling, though jauntily tilted. These are the men for whom patience and pity persist, the small time crooks and swindlers, "There but for the grace of God".

Crooks Like Us is available from the Books department of The Chap Recommends at www.thechapmagazine.com

LACE UP YOUR
PAMPOOTIES

**Liam Jefferies on the history, practical usage
and purchase possibilities of the brogue**

A s with the Breton Jumper in the previous issue, this article aims to provide a paradigm for the gent looking to source a pair of brogues suited to his taste, budget, and traditionalist loyalty. Let us begin, as ever, with a look on the attributes of the shoe.

The brogue is a low-heeled boot or shoe, composed of a multiple-piece upper in sturdy leather with serrated edges and "broguing" perforations. There are five styles of standard brogues, based on the toe-cap styles which define such; these are full brogues, half-brogues, quarter-brogues, longwings, and the Ghillie brogue.

The full brogue (bottom left) is characterised by the perforated extensions from the toecap that run along the sides of the shoe and up the centre, resembling a letter "W", or a bird with wings splayed, earning full brogues the moniker of "wing tips" to our American cousins.

The Co-respondent shoe (in the US Spectator, below) is a full brogue with contrasting panels. It is often wrongly assumed that the full brogue is the most formal version of the shoe, when quite the opposite is true. The same is evident in the Ghillie brogue, which features no tongue and has laces which tie up to the calf. Worn nowadays primarily at formal social occasions, the functional features belie the Ghillie brogue's humble beginnings as the footwear

of their namesake, the land managers of a Scottish estate.

Half-brogues (above), introduced by John Lobb in 1937, have the same broguing and perforations as the former, though with a straight toe cap, while quarter-brogues are the same but sans 'medallion' (the perforations on the toe cap). The Longwing brogue (below) has extensions that fully encompass the length

of the shoe, meeting at the seam of the heel. These are known in the US as 'English Brogues' and vice versa. There is also a form of broguing that originated with Gieves and Hawkes of Savile Row, a random pattern of perforations different on each shoe, supposedly originally conceived by firing a shotgun at a pair of shoes, resulting in the Buck-shot brogue (above, right).

Other definitions of the brogue are the single brogue, which consists of a sole and an upper and the double brogue, which features a welt, an added strip of leather between the two. This is the only characteristic that defines whether a shoe is in fact a brogue. Be it an Oxford or Derby closure, Monk strap or even slip-on; if it has broguing, it is a brogue.

The brogue can be traced back to 18th Century Ireland, and the untanned hide shoes farmers would don to tend to the sodden fields. The shoes could be turned upside down to allow water out of the holes punctured throughout the top. The name derives from the Old Irish term bróg, which itself is derived from the Old Norse word brók, which translates as

"leg covering". Other names which have been used to describe the style include, but are doubtless not limited to: Brogan, Curan, Revilins, and, to the folk of the Aran Islands, Pampooties.

As time progressed, the working class shoe was picked up by the land owning squirearchy for stalking game and treading countryside bogs. It was this preference which determined the shoe's more developed style regarding placement of the punctuation and the addition of a heel. The style continued to creep towards more formal wear, with the loss of the full perforation and the application of tallow wax for waterproofing. This "English Style" brogue went on to considerable success with the gentry, and was given a surefire boost towards popularity and away from rugged workwear in the 1930s, when it was favoured by none other than the Prince of Wales, in suede, paired with a grey lounge suit. The two-tone co-respondent model was favoured by Jazz purists throughout the 1940s and 50s, and the brogue was subsequently copied by the masses when favoured by screen stars such as Fred Astaire and Gene Kelly.

WHERE TO BUY

AUTHENTIC INVESTOR

As with many staples of footwear, it is hard to define the authentic originator of the style, no less to attribute any certain aspect of the design to one company. Luckily, however, the finest footwear in the world is made in Northampton, England, so go there and you cannot go wrong. This Bourton Derby Full Brogue from Trickers (right) is as good a place to start as any (£375). Other reputable Northampton brands are Church's, Grenson, Barker, Cheaney and Crockett & Jones.

CONTEMPORARY MODERNIST

For the chap in pursuit of something offering a sideline gander at the classic brogue, yet retaining Northampton quality and Goodyear welts, look no further than Jeffery-West. This brand has taken brogues into the darkest corners of the earth and returned with blood in the holes. Their Dexter 'Kill' Punch Gibson Cardenal Antick (left) is a perfect example, retailing at £245.

GENTLEMAN ECONOMIST

Loake offers reasonably priced, classic country brogues, made in their factory in Northampton. Their Fearnley Brogue (right) retails at £160. Naturally one may visit the second hand market for shoes, but always ensure they are Goodyear-welted, for this is the gold standard in shoemaking and, what's more, can be easily replaced and made like new again.

For a visual companion to this series, follow @SartorialChap on Instagram.

STEED STANDS THERE

This summer the sky went dark when it was announced that Patrick Macnee had died at the age of 93. Sunday Swift recalls his iconic dandy character as John Steed in The Avengers

John Steed is one of the first images to spring to mind when one thinks of 1960s TV series *The Avengers*. He is the constant figure that links the noir style of the first series, the dream-like cartoon of the final series and everything in between. *The Avengers* created a surreal world where nothing was normal and aesthetics were paramount. It was a world where one goes in for an eye-exam and, instead of identifying letters of the alphabet, one must recognise the differences between men's hat styles. Seeing is not enough: one must be discerning and dedicated to the gentlemanly aesthetic.

It comes as no shock, then, in a world so focused on style, that a dandy character like Steed would develop. Arguably, given the more serious and noir-like tone of the programme before Macnee debuted in the episode *Hot Snow*, one could even suggest that it was Macnee's flair that transformed the programme into the techni-coloured and highly stylised programme we remember today.

Even if you don't remember all the episodes, you'll remember that man in a bowler hat, Chelsea boots and tailored suit. Piers D. Britton and Simon J. Barker even suggest that Steed's image "even more than Cathy Gale's and Emma Peel's leather boots, became the visual essence of *The Avengers*." Curiously, though, despite becoming one of the most iconic images to represent the programme, Steed was originally a stereotypical, mysterious man in a trench coat and a trilby with a cigarette hanging out of his mouth, lurking in the shadows to whisper secret information to David Keel (Ian Hendry).

"CRAVATS WERE IN THERE FIRST. TIES ARE SYMBOLS OF CONFORMITY. CRAVATS HAVE FLAIR, MASCULINITY. YOU WON'T FIND A TIE IN MY WARDROBE."
PATRICK MACNEE

Macnee wrote in his autobiography, *The Avengers: The Inside Story*: "Nobody told me how I should play Steed, or relate to people. I never, ever got a brief. It was never written down. The script for *Hot Snow*, the first episode in December 1960, said: 'Keel is about to push the bell button when the door is flung open. Steed stands there.' Just that, nothing else. No description. Nothing. So I just made him up. The added threat of instant dismissal three weeks later enabled me to create him myself, very quickly. [...] He was never a character in literature like Bulldog Drummond, Simon Templar or James Bond, or a personality somebody else had first created in another medium. Steed was never written down."

Through Macnee, Steed was transformed – and in doing so, Macnee transformed the programme itself. He infused Steed with very specific, iconic vestimentary images to create a sartorial soufflé: the playful theatrics of Sir Percy in *The Scarlett Pimpernel*; the British understatement and wit of Major Hammond in *Q-Planes*, the precision and correctness of the great Beau Brummell himself, and the Edwardian dandyism of Patrick's own father 'Shrimp', were all integrated into Steed's identity. Macnee wrote in *Blind in One Ear*,

"The only difference between Macnee and Steed was one between a silk topper and a bowler."

In addition to all of these influences, there was also an intentional move on Macnee's part to distance Steed from James Bond. Creator Sydney Newman had originally been inspired by *Casino Royale* for Steed's character. Macnee writes, however, that "In this book were scenes of the most unbelievable sadism, horror and beastliness, and graphic descriptions of the villain hitting Bond's testicles with a carpet beater – terrible, ghastly stuff. To my thinking, this seemed to be the opposite of what I was interested in. Bond used women like battering rams and seemed intent on drinking and smoking himself to death."

Macnee showed himself something of a forward thinker in his attitude toward women in particular – not only did he reject the violent, womanising action figure of Bond, but he also fought against the studio when they complained Steed was not 'masculine' enough against his partner Emma Peel. But the audience, like Macnee, understood what the studio did not. One of the greatest attractions of *The Avengers* was the fluidity of gender: the gentleman dandy in the bowler who could talk himself out of a crisis, and his mod female dandy partner could kick her way out.

But it wasn't just the change in aesthetics that made *The Avengers* such a success – anyone can put on a nice suit. What mattered most was how well he wore it. Macnee gave Steed panache and style, and very specific expectations about the correctness of a gentleman's appearance. In interviews during *The Avengers*' original run, Macnee stated that clothes and accessories "should reflect personality. Steed's things are light and flibbertigibbet. I use the Edwardian look – it's different. I have a number of peculiar likes and dislikes. They mean a lot but I can't give reasons for them. I've chosen my clothes on my own instinct completely."

His instincts proved in good taste – in 1963, Macnee was voted one of the Ten Best Dressed Men in the World. In fact, Steed's wardrobe was so striking that Pierre Cardin and Hardy Amies invited Macnee to help design a line of men's apparel based on Steed's own wardrobe – an offer he later regretted turning down.

It was his concern with the precise details that made Steed unique – Macnee proved knowledgeable about men's fashions, and how to use them to make statements about one's persona. Both Macnee and Steed proved to have a flair for iconoclasm, and used clothes to protest against what they saw as a mundane society. In an interview in 1967, for example, Macnee stated, "I want to outlaw ties. Useless garments. Nasty, dangly, stringy things. Serve no purpose at all. I wear them as little as possible. And I hope the men of Great Britain will follow my example. Cravats were in there first, you know. Wasn't until 1840 that a few traitorous eccentrics abandoned 'em for those dreadful ties. Ties are simply symbols of conformity. Cravats have flair, masculinity. You won't find a tie in my wardrobe."

Macnee also loved "exceptionally wide cuffs. No good reason – except that I can wear enormous cuff-flinks" and embraced the pin-stripe suit despite (or, perhaps, like his affection for the cravat, because of) the fact that it had gone out of fashion. His famous umbrella? "Nothing special about that – except that it must have a knobbly handle. I detest smooth handles. That's terribly important." The fashions change considerably throughout the show, but once that whangee-handled gamp is introduced, Steed is rarely seen without it. Macnee explained that, as a war veteran, he chose the brolly because "I prefer umbrellas to guns".

And that famous bowler hat that came in co-ordinating colours to his tailored blazers? "A devil to iron," Macnee explained. "No common bowler. One flat-irons it on the side."

The fashions might have gone a long way to securing Steed's popularity, but one must never forget that Macnee's comic timing had the power completely to change a scene. That Old Etonian charm came with a mischievous glint in his eye, which told you to take nothing seriously – because neither Steed nor Macnee seemed to be. He met the mundane with slightly surprised, widened eyes and raised eyebrows, but the dastardly villains with ridiculous plans were usually met with a subtle smile and a waggish riposte.

In announcing Macnee's passing on his website, his family wrote, "Macnee was an ambassador for the tradition of the British gentleman, with his special brand of congeniality, humour and intelligence, his remarkable physical agility, and his unfailing good manners, sense of decency, and fair play. His comments and responses to questions were laced with a tongue-in-cheek, somewhat subversive sense of irony, along with a lightning-fast wit". Patrick Macnee was, of course, much more than the character of John Steed; and yet, in creating a figure of such legacy, part of Macnee will endure as that man in the bowler hat, Chelsea boots and tailored suit. The "ambassador for the tradition of the British gentleman" will live on.

Am I Chap?

THE CHAP GIVES ITS READERS AN UNCOMPROMISING SARTORIAL ASSESSMENT.
PLEASE SEND YOUR PHOTOGRAPHS TO CHAP@THECHAP.NET

Dr. John Ward (left), British archaeologist in Luxor, Egypt and Scotty Roberts (right), American Historian.
Had you not told us which was which, we would secretly have hoped that the fellow in the foreground was the American one – and he is! Apart from the fact that Dr. Ward is wearing all the correct items of apparel, he has thrown them together in a way that perhaps only an Englishman abroad can. His hat is also the right size for his head.

"Waiting for a lift to a wedding at which I was an usher," writes Charles Miller. "Had to get a pair of trews and was fitted out with this pair from Huntsman of Savile Row – best of all was the 1956 owner's label for Lord Reith."
We can only assume that his lordship insisted on all BBC radio broadcasters being dressed in a similar way. If only Auntie had kept that up, as well as Reith's "Inform, educate, entertain" mantra.

"Am I chap?" writes George Packe Drury-Lowe. "I'm the one on the right." The right of the photo or the viewer? If the former, then our compliments, madam. It must have been very difficult to find a pair of shoes to match that bag, but you managed it. If the latter, your trousers have too much break and your umbrella seems to be made of plastic. Everything else in your outfit seems to be coordinated with that.

Kieran Whitman also got hitched, but not in morning dress. We think he just about pulled it off, and getting the hotel to lay a tweed carpet for him was a nice touch.

"After spending a most delightful Sunday at the Glyndebourne Opera Festival," writes Oliver Dütsch, who is of Teutonic origin, "I wondered if my 'picknick outfit' might meet your requirements and qualify myself for the highly coveted denotation as Chap." Sir, it does, but on this side of the Maginot line we normally keep our shoes on for dinner.

It is hard to tell exactly what is going on here, but presumably the coach driver is on his pipe break, while the passengers are given a plastic glass of bubbly to keep them quiet. Black shoes with a light grey suit? Fine for a coach driver, one supposes.

"I have sent you a couple of examples," writes Matt Weallans, "that might put me in the bracket of being a chap."
Sir, there was no need for the extra information; we are quite capable of making a sartorial assessment without the presentation of a urine sample.

Walter Binney sent us this pithy message with his photograph: "Working class chap, but still chap." Indeed. Perhaps if you were middle or upper class you'd be able to afford some sleeves for your jacket.

"I attach the following image for your hilarity," writes Jonathan Ratty. "My rowing companion, Trevor (at the front) and I formed one of the honour guard flotilla for Her Majesty's barge, Gloriana, when she recently attended the Magna Carta 800 celebrations at Runnymede." Hilarity? I don't think so. Misery, ennui, weltchmertz, perhaps.

Mr. Sparrow, BSc (Hons), MBA, there is a stain on your carpet. And one on your reputation too, for wearing a dress shirt with wing collar and a cravat.

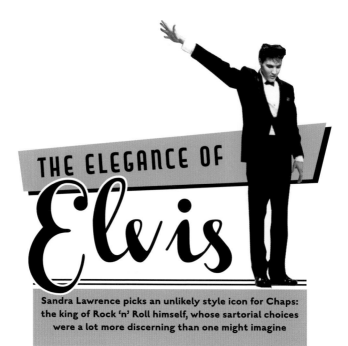

THE ELEGANCE OF
Elvis

Sandra Lawrence picks an unlikely style icon for Chaps: the king of Rock 'n' Roll himself, whose sartorial choices were a lot more discerning than one might imagine

Elvis Aaron Presley is one of the very, very few figures worthy of that ghastly, overused, underachieved word: Icon. Like the Byzantine images from which the word derives, his style is gaudy, mosaic-bright, shimmering, unmistakable. A golden face glowing with golden perspiration, golden medallions chinking against golden flesh, golden cape, swept in supplication to devoted disciples at a Vegas sellout like the halo of an Orthodox saint. But just as no-one in their right mind would start dressing like an 8th century Madonna and Child, Elvis's fashion choices are best left to the man himself. The Elvis Problem is not with The King. He made his own style, based on a heady mix of testosterone, popular culture, practicality and downright whimsy. Right up until that last couple of bloated, burger-barbiturates-and-bugaboo years, he looked great, however outlandish his choice of clobber. No. The Elvis Problem is with the misguided souls who try to copy him.

Born into dirt-poverty in Tupelo, Mississippi, Presley's prospects weren't great. He may be associated with denim, but he never wore it outside

movies; it reminded him of times when working-men's fabric was all he could get. Got a photo of Elvis in jeans? Chances are it's a film-still. He felt he owed his fans the respect of dressing smartly – they'd paid for their tickets; they deserved a show. And, right up to the end, he gave them one hell of a show.

When he was thirteen, Presley's family moved to Memphis, Tennessee. His was a predominantly black neighbourhood and Elvis became obsessed with the blues music that black hipsters were grinding out of Beale Street (above). He'd later base his career on the sounds he heard blaring from the road's honky-tonks, strip-joints, burlesques and wirelesses. But there was something else down Beale Street. Something cool. Lansky Brothers was already supplying fabulous, flashy clothes to the top stars of the day: Count Basie, Lionel Hampton, Duke Ellington, BB King: style-mongers to a man. Around 1952, Bernard Lansky started noticing a good looking young white guy hanging around his store, saucer-eyed as a poorhouse kid outside a sweetshop. Eventually Lansky invited the shy 17-year-old inside to look around. Elvis ogled the colourful shirts, baggy pants and sharp jackets, but couldn't afford more than the odd bolero. He told the shopkeeper "When I'm rich, I'm going to buy your store." Lansky replied "Don't buy me; buy from me." Right to the end the 'Clothier to the King' boasted he'd put Elvis in his first suit – and his last.

What made Presley different to other rockers of the 1950s was his willingness to find inspiration from wherever it came. At the same time as he was admiring the dapper style of the blues mavericks, he was seduced by the slicked-back, sideburned grease of the long-distance truckers passing through Memphis. Elvis didn't dye his dark-blonde hair black until the movie *Loving You* in 1957, but once he did, he never turned back. The sideburns were, throughout his life, an act of rebellion. He kept growing them, kept being forced to shave them off – first by the army, then by his domineering agent Colonel Parker, who needed Elvis to look squeaky-clean for maximum Hollywood cash return.

Parker was responsible for some of Presley's worst fashion faux-pas. A carnival showman, he knew everything about making a quick buck; nothing about style. *Fifty Million Elvis Fans Can't Be Wrong*, the album claimed, but Colonel Parker could be, especially after he and Presley were introduced to Liberace, another man with a unique sense of style, but not one anyone else should attempt to emulate, not even The King. Elvis hated the notorious gold lamé suit by Nudie of Hollywood. He liked bling, but there was a limit. After the cover shoot, he never wore those ridiculous sparkly pants again, instead pairing the jacket with plain black peg slacks.

A lot of Elvis's early clothes were surprisingly

fatigues were all fans would see of him for the next couple of years. Worried people would forget him, he recorded singles to be released while he was away, but to be extra-sure, he managed to make his first post-military appearance sporting his biggest quiff yet. It's still not clear how he circumnavigated the army haircut rules, but just listen to those fans going ballistic on the Frank Sinatra TV show and wonder at the gloss of the guy: slimline tux, floppy western bow tie, sharp pocket square, Cuban-heeled boots, enormous, jet-black DA. He looks fantastic. Sinatra looks like he's sucking lemons.

The early sixties were the movie years. The Colonel trussed his cash cow in increasingly unbecoming getups –

conservative. Black trousers, simple box-back sports jackets, bombers, knit tops. Denounced from the pulpit every Sunday by Bible-Belt preachers for those saucy hip gyrations, why would he need to be outlandish in the way he dressed? What Elvis excelled in, however, was the way he mixed the respectable with the unacceptable. A black suit with shocking pink shirt and socks. Western-style jackets with pleat-front trousers and white buckskins. A sensible-looking jacket opened to reveal a shirt with orange panelling or black lacing. A basic, short-sleeved shirt, sleeves rolled even further along those biceps and the collar turned up to hide a neck he was convinced was too long. It wasn't. Later, designers would keep the high collars as a way of framing that chubby, angelic pout.

It's hard to imagine the kind of society where a rock star would meekly sit while his trademark haircut was shaved before trotting off to do his share of military service without a whimper. Presley had already lost his quiff once – for *Jailhouse Rock*, where he also wore what, for anyone else, would have been a career-defining jacket. But this time it was serious. A flat-top brush cut and army aloha shirts, leis, 'nice-boy' prep, vaguely-naughty denim, but it was a policy of diminishing returns. The Beatles had arrived. The kids were moving on. Elvis was mainstream fodder and he loathed it.

The '68 Comeback Special remains one of the most extraordinary gigs music has known. Unplugged, jamming in front of a small audience, Elvis never sounded – or looked – so damn good. He'd been working with designer Bill Belew, who saw Presley's rangy style as a direct descendant of the dandies of Regency England and Napoleonic France. He designed a black leather suit based on American jeans/jean jackets but with a flair owing more to Beau Brummel than James Dean. High collar. Leather boots. Tight pantaloons. Mussed-up, brushed-forward quiff. Sideburns to rival Mr. Darcy and Lord Byron combined. The King was back.

Belew contined working with Elvis into the 70s. Paisley shirts, striped trousers, scarves; Presley made a half-hearted fist at flower-power but it really wasn't him. He needed a new look for a new, dynamic stage act he'd been developing. He'd first got into karate in the 1950s and now he was working funky Hong-Kong Fooey poses into the show. But the gigantic stadium audiences could hardly make him out in his old black stage kit. His glaucoma was playing up under the lights. And his shirt kept coming untucked with all those kicks. Belew's first jumpsuits were fairly plain affairs. White, sometimes red or blue. All-in-one, open to the waist, with wide belts and a little military braiding or fringing, twinned with yellow-glass shades based on the old motorcycling goggles of his youth. *That's The Way It Is*, filmed in 1970, shows Elvis the way he was. Slim, with post-coital haircut and sweat gleaming through a hussar-style shirt slashed to the waist, he is a cross between Napoleon, Marlon Brando and the Prince Regent. Unfortunately Elvis was just about to follow in all those giant figures' footsteps in a rather different way.

As the great man's whip-thin girth turned to spandex-stretching gut, Belew designed ever-more-elaborate jumpsuits to draw the eye away from his podgy popstar's paunch. Jewels, sunbursts, peacocks, tigers, even an American eagle, all embroidered by needlework maestro Gene Doucette. The belts got wider and wider; sparklier and sparklier. One day Presley went missing from Graceland, bowling up in the White House Oval Office several hundred miles away on a whim to

meet President Nixon. He was wearing a cape. It didn't work. Elvis's fans still adored every gyration, every karate kick, every toss of sweat-drenched satin scarf, but the rest of the world was beginning to find it all faintly ridiculous. We will never know what he might have come up with next. Would he have reinvented himself yet again? Or just turned into the caricature a million fat old Elvis impersonators perpetuate today in the name of keeping the King alive?

Nearly forty years after his death, whatever we may think of Elvis's style, it was his and his alone. I admire every hip-swivelling, quiff-combing, chest-baring, flare-flinging, lycra-louching inch of him. That does not, however, absolve anyone else from trying the same thing. Squeezing into a jumpsuit will not send you to Vegas without passing go. Donning a squashy motorcycle hat is more likely to get you a place in the Village People than the Jordanaires. And we all know what happens to superheroes that wear capes. For the love of the King, DO NOT TRY THIS AT HOME.

Am I Chap?

THE CHAP GIVES ITS READERS AN UNCOMPROMISING SARTORIAL ASSESSMENT.
PLEASE SEND YOUR PHOTOGRAPHS TO CHAP@THECHAP.NET

"It is with some trepidation," writes Roger Brook Bailey, "that I find myself in the slightly dubious position, after much coercion from ones chums, of having to concoct an epistle to your periodical merely to get clarification on a subject about which I have never had the slightest misgiving." Yes, your chums are quite correct: you do dwell in the darkest pit of Suburbia.

Loan Diaz is French, where things are done differently.

"Here is a photo of myself and my good Lady Stacey we really enjoy reading your spiffing magazine we are both into the 30s 40s and 50s eras the photo was taken in a 1930s railway coach of which we had a holiday in down in Darkest West Wales all the best Steve and Stacey" Didn't they have punctuation in the 30s, 40s and 50s?

"It is with regret that I feel obliged to inform you of an error in your otherwise sublime tome. The dog pictured with the Prince of Wales on page 39 of issue 86 is not a fox terrier but a cairn terrier. For your consideration I have attached a photo of Brian the fox terrier on my wedding day on the Isle of Harris wearing of course the holy cloth." Sir, we regret to inform you that you are not wearing Harris Tweed, if that is what you mean by "the holy cloth." Oh and your dog's got an erection.

"I have been out and about again," writes Simon Doughty, "so thought I would send you photos of my adventures for you to rip the piss out of." Thank you Mr. Doughty. Not wearing your favoured cloth on this occasion; are you searching for the nearest emporium of denim?

"I've just returned from my friend's hen weekend," writes Emma Oliver from Portsmouth, "where I got to try clay pigeon shooting for the first time. Turns out I'm a rather handy with a shotgun; does this make me chap?"
That isn't a shotgun, madam, it's a camera, or are you just pleased to see us? The outfit is rather splendid, however.

Clément Waquet appears to be some sort of Dadaist, on holiday in Communist China with his potted plants and his amplifier. By not even asking us whether he is Chap or not, he is.

"This is a photo of Mr. Harry Bamford, who we believe is a Chap of the highest order, we hope you agree."
A man who wears tablecloths and celebrates Christmas in the middle of June cannot possibly be taken seriously.

"This picture," writes Benjamin J. Fitch "was taken by a rather sweet young filly I bumped into when stumbling back to my cabin from the bar on the Orient Express. Needless to say I felt it was my duty promptly to turn around and escort her back to the bar. A lady, alone, on the Orient, Never!"
A shirt, with no studs, on the Orient Express? Never.

"I'm Antony Robbins. I'm one of the directors of the Museum of London. I take my job very seriously. But perhaps I should know better?"
We take our job very seriously too. And we're not that keen on French automobiles.

FEMME FATALIC
ATTRACTION

Sunday Swift delves into the immaculate conception of the everlasting image of Marlene Dietrich

O ur previous investigation for The Dandy Doctor was into the fluid and light-hearted Dandyism of Emma Peel. However, not all Dandies, nor indeed dandizettes, have the same light touch as Emma Peel. In this issue, we turn to German actress and singer Marlene Dietrich. Like Peel, Dietrich emphasised a surface image, a certain sophistication and intelligence; strength through gender ambivalence and affection for excess.

However, Dietrich's Dandyism emphasised an unattainable, world-weary glamorous ennui distinct from Emma Peel. Dietrich was mercurial, icy, distant and occasionally cruel. She was also a consummate Dandy who created an iconic and untouchable image: even today, she is still regarded as the epitome of 1930s Hollywood glamour.

You probably know Dietrich, even if you've never seen her classic films like *Morocco* (1930), *Blue Angel* (1930), and *The Devil is a Woman* (1935). Maybe you know her from her sixty-year music career, or for her 'legs, legs, legs'. Dietrich once insisted, 'I am not an actress, I am a personality.' And what a personality! Her love affairs are legendary, both with famous women and men: Greta Garbo, Joseph von Sternberg, Douglas Fairbanks, Joseph Kennedy, John F Kennedy, George Bernard Shaw, Edith Piaf and Frank Sinatra, to name a few. Dietrich is also famous for quips and epigrams: 'I am at heart a gentleman', she once said.

Or maybe you know her from her very bitter feud with Elizabeth Taylor: it was certainly memorable – not many people could get away with writing an open letter to Taylor saying,

'Why don't you swallow your diamonds and shut up?' Or, maybe you follow fashion and have an interest in women who break barriers in society; if so, you might know Dietrich for her androgynous and occasionally masculine attire.

Whichever version of Dietrich you might know, her image is, to this day, a striking and complex one. Absolutely aware of the importance of presence, Dietrich once said, 'I dress for the image. Not for myself, not for the public, not for fashion, and not for men.' For a Dandy, maintaining image is paramount. Dietrich created what Lutz Koepnick calls an 'impenetrable surface'. She solidified herself as a legend, not just because she created an iconic image that would outlive her, but because maintained absolute control over that surface image and the ability continually to reinvent herself when necessary.

Dietrich was a European who belonged everywhere and nowhere: Born in 1901 in Berlin, she abandoned life as a silent film star, cabaret singer and dancer in Germany for Hollywood in the 1930s. Germany effectively disowned her, due to her active support for US troops during World War II. Dietrich became an American citizen in 1939, and spent her life travelling around the world, residing both in America and France until her death in 1992.

Originally hired by Paramount as competition against Swedish actress Greta Garbo, both Garbo and Dietrich were enigmatic and exotic to American audiences. Eventually, Dietrich eclipsed Garbo's fame, and Dietrich's image came to represent sexuality and glamour in 1930s Hollywood.

Dietrich adapted well to Hollywood: or, more accurately, Hollywood adapted well to her. Back in Berlin, the fact that she wore masculine attire and was actively and unapologetically bisexual was hardly shocking – in fact, it was quite in fashion for the time. Hollywood was not so modern: a woman who wore trousers was outrageous enough – but a woman with such modern sensibilities when it came to sex was absolutely scandalous.

Even more astonishing, however, was Dietrich's cinematic introduction to America. With the support of director (and occasional lover) Josef von Sternberg, Dietrich utilised her gender ambivalence as a strength within her films. Von Sternberg pushed to release Dietrich's second film, *Morocco*, before *Blue Angel* because he wanted America's first experience with Dietrich to be a memorable one. Memorable and history making it was: *Morocco* is famous for two reasons: firstly, Dietrich wears a tuxedo in the film; secondly, the film contains the first cinematic kiss between women.

1930s Hollywood was aghast, and yet this Dandy flourished. Critic Kenneth Tynan argued that Dietrich 'Has sex but no positive gender. Her masculinity appeals to women and her sexuality to men'. In typical Dandy form, rather than quelling under Hollywood's ethics, she forced Hollywood to bend to her: Dietrich didn't follow trends: she set them. Instead of Dietrich abandoning her androgyny, women everywhere in America followed her example and started wearing trousers.

As such, Dietrich's Dandyism, Sapphic in nature, emphasises a gender ambivalence and playfulness to gender identity that have held the attention both of audiences and critics alike. Through psychoanalytic and Marxist theories, many critics have attempted to prise the image from the performer – all, in

short, in an effort to find the 'real' Dietrich behind the iconic image she presented. In their efforts to deconstruct Dietrich, they end up breaking her into pieces, writing essays focusing on her face, her voice, and her famous legs.

The problem with trying to see the 'real' Dietrich is that Dietrich was, first and foremost, a Dandy. Dandyism consists, ultimately, of creating, presenting and controlling a surface image to others. Dandyism intentionally avoids any depth: it avoids allowing others to see any real person beneath the façade. Focusing purely on surface and image, Dietrich created an idea of herself. Dietrich, the idea, was glamour and enigma; unapproachable and unknowable; a world-weary acceptance coupled with cold rebellion; a femme fatale in a tuxedo.

But Dietrich did not just create this persona: she also showed a flexibility to both alter and protect the image when needed. Although her icy and unattainable image was initially successful, she was considered box-office poison after several of her films failed in cinemas. Universal offered her a western with James Stewart called *Destry Rides Again* (1939). Dietrich re-invented herself, this time into the more attainable glamour girl with a sense of humour.

When the Second World War broke out, Dietrich transformed into a humanitarian World War II USO soldier. Returning to America post-war, she attempted to renew the femme fatale diva image – but by the 1950s, Hollywood's interest in her had waned. Las Vegas offered her the opportunity to re-invent herself once again, this time returning to her roots as a cabaret entertainer. The majority of the rest of her career was spent in Las Vegas in her famous bespoke 'nude' gowns, which gave the impression of revealing all and yet concealing her almost entirely.

Throughout all of these versions of Dietrich, one thing remained the same: she always represented glamour. Dietrich herself knew this was the key to her success, remarking, 'Glamour is what I sell, it is my stock in trade.' And in this currency, she was certainly wealthy. Through glamour, Dietrich ultimately became famous not for her films or cabaret acts in Las Vegas, but for being herself: Steven Back, her biographer, stated, 'We often think of her not as being an actress, but of being Marlene Dietrich. She became a legend, she knew she was a legend, she kept it alive for 90 years.'

Like many Dandies, Marlene's twilight years were spent in self-imposed exile in France until her death. In a 1984 documentary, Marlene, Dietrich's

daughter Maria says: 'Any decay of the Dietrich picture, the legend, was abhorrent to her, not because she was afraid of age, but because she was afraid of tarnishing legend. Dietrich did not become a recluse because she couldn't face her age. She became a recluse because the legend no longer was able to be re-embellished.'

Maria understood Marlene's Dandyism: the carefully constructed image of Dietrich, the idea, outlasted any real moment of Dietrich herself. This is Dandyism in its purest form: the image of Dietrich was pure spectacle: a visual representation of an otherworldly creature of glamour not to be objectified (for she already objectified herself), but to be consumed. Dietrich ultimately protected not herself, but the legend she had spent a lifetime constructing.

Jules Barbey D'Aurevilly wrote, 'The famous maxim of Dandyism: in society, stop until you have made your impression, then go.' Marlene Dietrich, the woman, did just that: she may have aged and gone, but she ensured that Dietrich, the legend, the idea – the Dandy – lives on.

The Butler
AT YOUR SERVICE

Mr. Bell is the Chap's resident butler, whose sole desire is to attend to your socio-domestic-sartorial conundrums

Gaston Bayard: *I am French and in need of some trousers. Can you advise me where to start?*

The Butler: Well Sir, I must admit this question did throw me slightly off, as it were! I had always assumed, Sir, that trousers were not part of a French chap's wardrobe? However, I am more than happy to help you in your quest to achieve appendage coverings. Firstly Sir, may I recommend the following webular sites? The notable www.old-town.co.uk has always been highly recommended and they do an excellent range of gentleman's attire in the trouser department! Then I would recommend the following retailers, also online but more than suitable for your needs www.darcyclothing.com and www.fogeyunlimited.co.uk. Before you commit to purchasing your first pair of trousers,

Sir, you may wish to consider how hard-wearing the material is and what sort of events you may wish to be using them for. A pair of lightweight worsteds will not do if one is planning to do some gardening, for example, Sir. Either way I wish you the best of luck in the trouser department, monsieur!

Arthur Copeland: *I recently attended Goodwood Revival and got completely soaked by the rain, which persistently fell throughout the entire Saturday of the festival. My question to you is this: is it acceptable to sit down to dinner while water drips from one's hat? And is it acceptable to wring out one's cuffs into the soup?*

The Butler: Oh dear, Sir! I did hear from other fine ladies and gentlemen who also attended that the weather situation was not exactly ideal! My first point, if I may

politely make it, Sir, is that in future, before taking one's seat at table, it may be advisable to remove one's hat, as it is generally frowned upon for gentlemen to wear hats indoors. I think the best thing I can offer in the way of advice for this sort of situation, should you be unfortunate to find yourself in a similar one in the future, is for Sir to pay a visit to the lavatory before sitting down at table, and use one of those mechanized blower things fully to dry oneself out as best as possible.

SHOE MAINTENANCE   TROUSER PRESS   ETIQUETTE   LAUNDRY   GROOMING   DINING   SMOKING

is named after a gentleman named Mr. Fitzroy Somerset, Lord Raglan, commander-in-chief of our forces during the Crimean War (during which another commander lent his name to the cardigan). Raglan had lost his right arm in the Battle of Waterloo, and some have speculated that the raglan style was developed because the sleeve fitted better on his armless side than a traditional shoulder and sleeve.

Benjamin Buckleigh: *Could you please advise on correct pocket watch insertion? I am unsure which of the four pockets of my waistcoat to place it in, and whether left or right, and which button in which to place the other end of the chain. I heard that Beau Brummell only allowed two links of his watch chain to show outside his waistcoat, but does this rule still apply?*

The Butler: Funnily enough Sir, I was only recently assisting a gentleman on the same question! To start with the basics, in regards to which pocket you put it in, the general rule of thumb is the bottom of the two, and then as for left or right, I would say whichever side you would normally wear a wristwatch. Generally this tends to be the left hand side, Sir, but obviously it is your preference! Indeed you are correct: along with many other elements of Beau Brummell's extreme attention to detail, only two links were ever displayed outside the waistcoat. Generally the only rules to follow are that if you have a double-breasted waistcoat, then stick with a single chain. If wearing single-breasted the choose a double Albert. I have Sir, included two pictures (above and below) so you can see the difference between the two styles. With regards to what position on the waistcoat to put the other end of the chain through, I always recommend at least four buttons up from the bottom, Sir.

Peter Wilkinson: *I have recently purchased a splendid 1940s belted tweed overcoat with normal padded shoulders as opposed to a Raglan sleeve. Is it okay to wear this over a tweed jacket, with its own padded shoulders, or will this result in me looking like some sort of action hero or American football player?*

The Butler: The coat may easily have enough padding on the shoulder area for that on its own, Sir! The only thing I can suggest is that you try the two items together and see how they look. If it does look as though you are trying to smuggle a door under you coat, then I would recommend a visit to your local tailor, to see what he can do! It would, I daresay, be a simple matter of adjusting the padding. As a final note on this question, some of our readers may be intrigued to know what exactly a Raglan sleeve is. The style

Olivia: *I work for a bespoke marriage proposal planning company called The Proposers. Over the past four years we have created over 850 marriage proposals across the world. From cats dressed as waiters serving afternoon tea, to hiring the speed boat used in James Bond, to abseiling into caves to set up a romantic dinner and hiring celebrities, each of our proposals are unique and tailored to that particular couple. What would you say is the ideal place for a Chap to propose marriage to his lady?*

The Butler: Generally the thought of marriage can send a chap running to the hills, Madam! Personally, I feel that a chap appearing on horseback wearing this best tweeds would be a splendid way to propose marriage. Then, should the lady (or gentleman for that matter) decline, at least the humiliated fellow can make a speedy escape.

SLIM JIM PHANTOM

Gustav Temple met rockabilly drummer Slim Jim Phantom
of the Stray Cats, to talk about rock 'n' roll, Jerry Lee Lewis,
hair products, bespoke tailors and the scarcity of Princess
Diana souvenirs in London. Photographs by Peter Clark

When you first chose the name Slim Jim Phantom and became the drummer in the Stray Cats, did you realise that you'd never be able to gain weight or lose your hair?

I have the same name as my father, as is the practice with the New York City Irish nobility. His nickname is Big Jim, so I became Slim Jim. When we got into rockabilly, everybody needed a nickname and mine stuck real good and tight. As for my Barnett Fair, we always said that we'd rather lose a limb than our hair.

The Stray Cats were an all-American rockabilly band, yet your big success only came once you arrived in England in the 1980s. What made it so difficult to break America?

Rockabilly was not a known genre around our neighbourhood in New York, and that style was non-existent. We were doing pretty well as young rockabillies and local eccentrics playing in the clubs, dressed to the nines 24/7, but we wanted the brass ring of making a record and to have an adventure. We had a few UK music mags and thought London was a good idea – we had heard about Teds and Punks and thought everyone was hip and cool there.

Back then, a scene was represented by a band with a sound; nowadays it's represented by a look. And you just find the music for the look. Whereas I always thought with a band like the Stray Cats, you play the music, then you find the look?

Yeah, and there was a bunch of different things that inadvertently added to our success here. One of them was that, when we came here, we fell in with a lot of people, and in England, especially London, everyone was something: you were a mod, or a ted, or a ska boy, or a rude boy. Everyone had something that they were. Whereas where we

were from, we thought anyone who had any style was in it together – it was us against the squares. So we mixed it all up. I remember one guy saying, 'You don't mix a black leather jacket with brothel creepers,' and we said, well why not? We had a pile of clothes in the corner, so whoever got the orange cowboy shirt and the leather trousers, that's what you had that day. As long as you were painting from the same palette, everything was cool. I see these rockabilly kids today and it all seems very traditional. I appreciate that angle but it isn't how we did it.

I liked that quote from the book about you going to your first punk gig in London, the Cockney Rejects, and a policewoman advising you to leave because you were teds.
That's right, and she saved our butts by doing that! In America you couldn't have found one person who knew what you were. I'm a musician, that was always the first thing. It wasn't like I found a good haircut then started to play the drums. We got pretty good at the music and then found a style that we fell in love with, not the other way around. And I also liked other stuff than pure rockabilly clothes. Keith

Richards had a velvet jacket and I thought, how cool to have a job where you get to wear a velvet jacket.

Did you use that stuff on your hair, Black & White Hair pomade? I remember it never washed out. I had to wait till my hair fell out to get rid of it!
I used to go to Kensington Market to get a haircut then not wash it for three months. They'd have to use Ajax to strip it down to dye it again. We used Murrays and then Nu Nile. That stuff was like gold back then.

Where did you first hear rockabilly music?
With me it started with the Beatles and the Stones; you look closely at the credits and think, who's C. Perkins? On blues records, you wonder who W. Dixon is from the Allman Brothers album we had. I had some older cousins and they had records; who can afford records when you're eleven years old? I'd borrow the records and look at the liner notes. It all comes back to what I call the nerding out; once I found my way into rockabilly, then I wanted to know who Elvis liked. You can go back as far as you like. I

think people sometimes get it wrong where they feel they have to take one instead of the other. I like the Rolling Stones *and* Gene Vincent. I like Buddy Holly and I like the Beatles. And I liked the Clash and then Adam and the Ants.

You started out listening to the old rockers like Jerry Lee Lewis and then, 20 years later, you're on a television show playing drums with Jerry Lee Lewis. Your description in the book of your first meeting with him, I think in a dressing room, was incredible.

Yeah, I was at the Jerry Lee Lewis gig in about 1983 with the English tailor Glen Palmer. He worked on Savile Row and then Granny Takes a Trip. He's a real character. You talk about these blues legends that will never happen again; he's the guy from the tailoring world that will never come again, you know, like Tommy Nutter, one of those guys. He's still around, I still speak to him – he's a character out of Dickens. He lives in America, he's a big Jerry Lee fan, and we're just in the audience like anyone else. Jerry Lee's tour manager came over and said, 'You the Stray Cats boy?' So we went backstage, knocked on the dressing room door, and this voice says, 'Come on in, it ain't locked!' It was a little dressing room and there he was, The Killer, with this big girl on his lap all dolled up like Marylin Monroe. And he just stood up, saying, 'Hey, it's the Stray Cats boy!' and she fell on to the floor. It was a very strange scene, man.

After our conversation he turned the lights off in the room, and I could hear the girl screaming, and I heard him laugh the devil's laugh, so I just felt my way to the door knob and got out. Then I didn't see him again for ten years. And then my friend Jerry Shilling, who had worked with Elvis for a while, was managing Jerry Lee, and he called me to be on that TV show. Then I didn't hear from him again for a couple of years and then he called me to go back on the road with them.

So was it Jerry Lee who made that decision at your first meeting that he wanted you to be his drummer?

I would like to think so, but I've met the guy ten times in my life, and every time I meet him I'm not sure that he knows who I am! Like when we did the tour, I'm not sure if he realised it was me who'd done the TV show a few years before that. And when I played with him a few years ago, I'm not sure he knew that I was the guy who used to go on tour with him. I'm just not sure.

He has got a faraway look in his eyes. Does he inhabit another dimension that we're not aware of, do you think?

Yeah, I think so. He's really showbiz. We were doing these gigs and there was no set list, no clock, no nothing. And at 59-and-a-half minutes he would kick the piano stool away, do the thing with his feet, then he'd leave the stage and the band would ride out the end of the song. I'd go in the dressing room and look at the clock: one hour and one second from when we'd started. And that's with no set list!

Today's hipster movement seems so far from the days when the Stray Cats were around. Has the age of rock 'n' roll passed us now? Is making artisan bread the new rock 'n' roll? Can you imagine Chuck Berry baking bread? Jerry Lee Lewis kneading sourdough?

I'm far too lazy for such domestic endeavors. I do like fresh bread, but there are some top notch bakeries on my patch – plus I can't imagine those original cats making their own sandwiches, let alone baking the loaf from scratch. There will always be rock and rollers; whether they're as cool as our favourites, I doubt it.

We're going to wind up with the most important topic, which is of course clothes. You mentioned starting out with lots of thrift store stuff, but do you now get clothes made bespoke?

As soon as I was able to have clothes made, I have. I met Glen Palmer, and he's made clothes for everybody; the Getty guys, Tom Petty, the Stray Cats, every rock 'n' roller around.

Has he got a specific look?

Yeah, well this is one of his, what I'm wearing

today. You know, rockabilly cowboy meets Doc Holliday, but he'll add some lamé somewhere. He's one of those cats who can make an outfit for Cher and then also make a shirt for Prince Charles.

Tommy Nutter used to make suits for beatniks and aristocrats in the same building.
Yeah, not just costume stuff, he's a skilled tailor. In the past I'd go to Glen and say, let's try to combine Hank Williams with Brian Jones.

So you would actually work with him, not just leave him to make all the decisions?
Yeah, but he'd always choose the lining or whatever.

If you go to a Savile Row tailor, they look at you and tell you what they'll make for you.
Sure. When I go to the doctor for an operation, I'm not going to tell him what to do! You just know you're gonna have the right surgery. And it's part of the fun, when you see that they chose orange lining for the vest – I mean waistcoat – something you might never have thought of.

I'm glad you called it a waistcoat.
Yes, I was very careful! Don't want to get in trouble with your readers. There's a British shoe guy too, called Colin Johnson. He makes bespoke shoes, but rock 'n' roll shoes. If you want green suede on top of a crepe sole, or if you want to get a Dr. Marten's sole with black patent leather, he can do it. Once they have your measurements, you just call them.

Is it a bespoke service, with prices like John Lobb?
Not really. They're only a couple of hundred bucks a pair. It's bespoke in the way that, a month later you'll get them and forgot that you ordered them. He's an eccentric. They're artists, these things take time.

There's a fun project I've started to do. There's this old shirt brand called Da Vinci, been around since the forties. There's a lot of historic evidence of Elvis Presley wearing their stuff, and Jerry Lee. They made those shirts that had a short sleeve, maybe a diamond on the pocket, maybe an Argyle pattern. We used to call them barbecue shirts.

Like a bowling shirt but smarter?
Right. They started in the forties and kept going into the sixties, when they made cowboy shirts that people like Clapton and Lennon would wear. So they've reactivated the brand, and they're remaking all the old patterns and fabrics, with some new stuff – and they've chosen yours truly to be the spokesman for them. I've seen some samples and it's really cool stuff.

That can sometimes go wrong, when you get an old company relaunched. Abercrombie & Fitch is the worst example. They used to make safari suits for Ernest Hemingway and now…
This English guy called Chris Wicks has relaunched another old company called English Laundry, and he really knows his history and he loves it. A lot of these English guys, like Lloyd Johnson and Pete Golding, love old juke boxes and Harley Davidsons and Corvettes, they love all the cool American stuff.

Is this why you did so well in London, because that interest in rockabilly was already here? Was Johnson's already down on the King's Road when you arrived? American Classics next door?
Lloyd saw us on the street and thought we were French rockers! He stopped us and we told him we were from New York, so we went to his store and became friends. That was 35 years ago and I'm still buddies with the guy.

So Da Vinci was originally founded by the Lansky Brothers, who made all the clothes for the original R&B guys, but Elvis sought them out because he was a hip guy; he was going on the other side of the tracks, watching what the R&B guys were doing, and he took those ideas to the other side of the tracks, mixed it with hillbilly – and the fashion as well.

[On the way to take the photographs, Slim Jim confessed to a liking for Princess Diana memorabilia, but had noticed a marked absence of it in any London souvenir shops]

Do you think there is some sort of conspiracy to write Princess Diana out of British Royal history?

I have always been a true fan of your Rose of England, and this observation is made from a place of genuine admiration. I would like to say, without any conspiratorial connotations, that Princess Diana merchandise is very hard to come by in traditional, mainstream outlets in central London. If this sounds like folly, I propose a challenge to Chap readers: look for a Princess Di postcard or tea towel in any souvenir shop and report your findings to fellow observant, my chum, Gustav Temple.

Later that day Mr. Temple discovered a Princess Diana mug in a souvenir shop on Portobello Road. It was posted to Mr. Phantom as a gift. Readers are invited to send photos of any Princess Di merchandise spotted on their travels to chap@thechap.co.uk

Thanks to Honest Jon's record shop, Portobello Road, for granting us photography permission

A STRAY CAT STRUTS, MY LIFE AS A ROCKABILLY REBEL by Slim Jim Phantom is published by Thomas Dunne Books

THE TIP OF THE ICEBERG

D onald Trump has too many sartorial flaws to list here, but if we limit ourselves to his neckwear choices, the situation is appalling. Mr. Trump always wears his tie extremely low, with the tip at least half a foot below his waistband. Extensive research has revealed that he is shooting himself in the foot with this approach, for this results in the rear tip of his tie not reaching the loop which is there to keep it from flapping about. This photo clearly shows Mr. Trump has used sellotape to fasten the rear tip to the back of the front tip. Which begs the question: why is the president of the USA going to so much trouble to maintain a ludicrous length of necktie?

We can only look to previous presidents for answers. John F Kennedy not only wore his ties at the correct length (one-and-a-half inches below the waistband) but also rarely wore his jacket

unbuttoned, so the end of his tie was never visible. If a president can be judged according to the way he wears his tie, *The Chap* is able to provide an exclusive insight into the new leader of the Free World: there is something fishy about him.

the LIP Weasel

Michael "Atters" Attree with his round-up of all things hirsute and occult

THE HIRSUTE HALL OF INFAMY

Here Be Beauty

Well it's slim pickings "beauty"-wise in this issue! I'd have bright red ears too if my beard and sides were that pedestrian. Still, it's a hirsute growth with a smile; thank you John Crams.

"For The Lip Weasel or Am I Chap?" You were shoved here, so that's the "Am I Chap?" bit answered. "The moustache tankard keeps my whiskers dry." I'm sure Mr. Mitchell's liver more than compensates!

Mr. Vine submits colleague Tristan "The Crow" with a goatee that's far from a masterpiece, but clearly Tristan loves himself so we'll pop it here. Your lip-fur (in the AWOLrus style) is nothing to crow about either.

Here Be Monsters

HAIR FORCE ONE

At his age, Jason Curd should be commended and encouraged to experiment; it's part of his hirsute-hood initiation. All the same, I find myself writing "could do better" in this Whisker Report (and expelling him).

"Lu-Pegs" explains: "There'll be hell toupee if it's "flaps up" on this flight." Sadly for Donald Trump, that's not a cat or he'd grab it with ease. Why not grab it for your own? (see Haiku).

This daguerreotype contrived a sickening, almost satanic nausea – until I realised the hairy maverick was simply playing with my mind. Within the tradition of numerous comic annuals – can you spot the difference, children?

THE PENTAGRAM OF ATTERS

It's as if Hollywood's animators consult the entrails of sheep (or the FBI), the way they predict future events while "sexing" us subliminally; however the "Holy Grail" of cinematic conspiracy references must surely be Kubrick's The Shining. Did Stan fake the moon landing/s? Observe those close-ups of Danny's Apollo T-shirt in the film, along with the curious designs on the hotel carpets (exactly mimicking the Apollo launch-pad layout) and one may be compelled to ask more. Lee Unkrich's film Toy Story 3 is the latest shrine to those Shining subliminal teasers. "237" appears repeatedly throughout his film, as does that same carpet pattern. To Kubrick aficionados, 237 is not only The Shining's hotel room number, but it denotes the exact number of miles from Earth to the moon. Having just taken our satellite's perigee and apogee into consideration, I'm happy to go with Kubrick fans there (regardless of NASA's website – the former are far more reliable).

£21,000.
THE BIGGEST WAGER
ON RECORD !

THE MAN IN THE IRON MASK

Jock Rawlings on an extraordinary Edwardian gentlemen's wager that sent a man in a helmet pushing a pram around Europe

O n the first chilly morning of the year 1908, a large, excited crowd had gathered together in Trafalgar Square. They were there to cheer on a rather mysterious gentleman who was about to begin an attempt to walk around the world. The nameless adventurer cut a strange figure among his fellow Londoners: to begin with, his head was entirely enclosed by an iron helmet. This peculiar millinery addition hadn't gone unnoticed by the more observant among the spectators; in fact, it was the cause of much interest. It had clearly once belonged to a suit of armour and came with a visor that completely obscured its wearer's identity.

The helmet wasn't the only strange thing about this proposed feat of endurance. The entire journey was to be accomplished while pushing a rickety child's perambulator. Who was this man and why was he about to circumnavigate the globe on foot? And why on earth was he wearing that helmet? The pram held all the answers: the helmeted gentleman had placed a hand written sign that explained everything.

It turns out that this whole endeavour was the result of an extraordinary wager. In fact, if you were to believe the sign, the largest bet ever made. £21,000 was at stake, around £1.5 million in today's money. The sign also laid out a set of conditions that must be fulfilled for the bet to be paid out. They included the following:
1. The man attempting this ridiculous folly must never reveal his true identity nor ever remove his helmet in public.
2. He should start out with only one pound in his

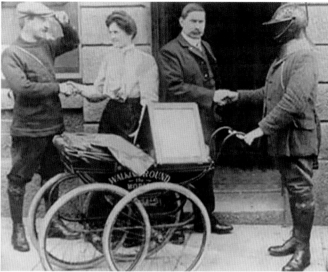

pocket – the expedition must be self funded from the proceeds of commemorative postcard sales.

3. He must visit 169 British towns and cities, collecting signatures from prominent residents as proof, before setting out on his world tour of 17 international capitals.

4. He would be accompanied at all times by an independent adjudicator who would ensure fair play. He was to take only one set of spare underclothes.

5. And finally, somewhere on his travels he must find and marry a woman. Without contravening the first condition.

The odds seemed frankly insurmountable. But our man was nothing if not game, and so, at precisely half past ten on that New Year's morning, in a blaze of publicity, he set off on the first leg of his adventure.

The origins of this curious episode can be traced back to the previous year, and a disagreement between two members of London's National Sporting Club. The two gentlemen in question were the famous American financier and banker, John Pierpont Morgan, and the club's founding member and president, Hugh Cecil Loather, 5th Earl of Lonsdale. Both men were fantastically wealthy, larger than life characters who shared a love of sport and adventure. One evening, the conversation quite naturally turned to the matter of circumnavigation and whether it could be achieved on foot and incognito. Lonsdale believed that it was perfectly possible, whereas J. P. Morgan remained sceptical. A wager was quickly proposed to test the theory. All they had to do was

find someone who was willing to accept the bet and spend the next few years pushing a pram around the world, while wearing four and a half pounds of iron on his head. Apparently it wasn't as difficult a task as one might imagine.

The Man In The Iron Mask, as he came to be known, was a big hit with the public and

Harry Bensley (left) unmasked

the press alike. His quixotic adventure had caught the imagination of an Edwardian Britain which had been brought up on precisely this sort of heroic nonsense. He drew crowds of admirers wherever he went; people queued up to meet the man and buy his postcards, and presumably he made some sort of a living. He even managed to sell one to Edward VII for a fiver when the pair met at Newmarket races. Apparently His Majesty pleaded with the masked man to reveal his true identity but this royal request was flatly refused.

And it wasn't just The King who wanted to unmask our hero; newspapers were desperate to get the scoop, offering rewards as high as £1,000 to anyone who could shed any light on the mystery. On one occasion, in an episode straight out of PG Wodehouse, a chambermaid hid under his bed in an attempt to get a glimpse of his elusive visage. But it was to no avail; The Man In The Iron Mask's secret held firm.

There were some close shaves, however. He was arrested in Kent for selling his postcards without the proper documentation. When he appeared before the local magistrate, he was ordered to remove his helmet and state his full name. Again,

he stood firm and refused. The magistrate was not amused and became insistent. But when the nature of the bet was explained to him, His Honour relented, allowing the defendant to enter a plea under his chosen sobriquet. The Man In The Mask was fined two and six and sent on his way.

But, as we know, celebrity is a fickle beast and, slowly but surely, the novelty began to wear off. The public grew bored of helmets and moved on to other distractions. But The Man In The Iron Mask's endless slog continued. For over six years he walked the earth, firstly around Britain and then further out into the world. He claimed to have covered 30,000 miles, pushing his pram, selling his postcards. Reports of his whereabouts, so numerous in those first months, had begun to dry up, and before long The Man In The Iron Mask had been forgotten.

Then in 1914 war broke out across the world and the strange man in the helmet suddenly resurfaced in England. According to his own account, he had travelled to twelve countries on the list and had reached Italy when he'd heard news of the fighting. With only six more countries left to visit, he found himself in something of a dilemma: should he go on and finish what he'd started, or should he call off the wager and return home to fight for king and country? Ultimately duty won the argument and he chose the latter.

When he arrived back in London he discovered that J. P. Morgan had died the previous year and that the Earl of Lonsdale was busy raising a 'pals' Battalion to send off to the war. Both parties agreed that the wager should be officially declared null and void and The Man In The Iron Mask was free to reveal his identity. His name was Harry Bensley.

Bensley had been 33 years old when he accepted the bet. He had a certain roguish reputation around The National Sporting Club and was known to have an eye for the ladies. Money was no problem for Harry, thanks to some clever Russian investments and an annual income that was rumoured to have been around £5,000. He was just the sort of chap Morgan and Lonsdale were looking for. It's difficult to understand exactly why a man in Bensley's position would agree to take on such an arduous Journey (even taking into account the huge sum of money at stake) but if you believe Bensley's version of events, he barely hesitated before agreeing to the terms of the wager.

Despite the fact that he was expected to find a wife somewhere along the way (he allegedly received over 200 proposals from women all over the world) Bensley was already married to a woman named Kate Green and had been since 1898. Quite what she thought of his six-year absence is anyone's guess, but the two were reunited upon his return. There were always rumours of other women, and perhaps even another wife but, like so much of Bensley's life, the truth remains a mystery.

Bensley joined the army and fought in the war but was discharged after being wounded in 1915. And then, two years later, disaster struck. The Russian proletariat rose up against their oppressors and almost overnight Bensley's investments were rendered worthless. He never recovered his fortune and spent the rest of his life drifting from job to job. He worked as a cinema usher and served as a local Labour councillor, but his life would never again be touched by the fame he had briefly enjoyed. He died in a bed sitting room in Brighton in 1956.

But perhaps there is one last twist in the tale. Before he passed away, Bensley apparently confessed to an illegitimate son that the wager had been a complete fabrication, and that the loss of his money had less to do with the Bolsheviks and more to do with a huge gambling debt. The story goes that he'd found himself out of his depth in a

Harry Bensley in later life

high stakes poker game with Morgan and The Earl and lost heavily, his finances left in tatters. Bensley, unable to cover his debt, was facing ruin, public disgrace and a possible prison sentence. But the two millionaires had other ideas, suggesting a possible solution in the form of a bizarre forfeit. And so was born The Man In The Iron Mask.

If this version is nearer the truth, then it might explain some of the more humiliating conditions that were laid down in the original wager – this was intended as a walk of shame, after all. But did The Man In the Iron Mask actually spend six years walking around the world as he had claimed? Did he, in fact, ever even leave these shores? Certainly his early wanderings around the southern counties of England are well documented, but when it comes to his travels farther afield, the world's newspapers fall strangely silent. Is it possible that a strange Englishman could walk around a foreign city wearing a knight's helmet without attracting any attention? I leave you to draw your own conclusions. Harry Bensley remains an enigma, with or without his iron mask.

For more information about Harry Bensley, visit www.mcnaught.orpheusweb.co.uk

RICHARD E. GRANT

Gustav Temple met The Doctor, The Scarlet Pimpernel, Withnail and Sherlock Holmes, all in one man, and that man is Richard E. Grant, who discussed his film roles, his range of scents, his alternative to drinking and his difficulty with hats

This year marks 30 years since the release of *Withnail and I*. While you were filming, did you have any idea that, 30 years later, fans would still be quoting entire sequences of your dialogue and watching the film at special themed screenings?

If only! The producer threatened to pull the plug half way through the first day of filming, saying we were already behind schedule and declared that he'd ripped the Bull scene from the script. All grand standing hogwash, and Bruce Robinson called his bluff and said he'd resign there and then. After which the stupid c**t left us alone. A man called Denis O'Brien, who embezzled piles of George Harrison's money and is still on the run. Without any stars, car chases, explosions and an unfathomable title, there were rumours that it would never get released, so the bonus of its subsequent cult status is beyond all imagining.

Was your perception of the role at all sympathetic, or did you play Withnail as an unlovable character – despite the fact that audiences went on to adore him?

I loved the character from his first line to his last.

He is so utterly selfish, rude, caustic, entitled and convinced of his own worth, underpinned by enormous self-loathing, so unapologetically 'himself', that it was a 'gift' to play him.

Did you learn much about Vivian Mackerell, upon whom Withnail was apparently based?

Bruce Robinson told me that *Withnail and I* was his homage to Vivian, who sadly died before he reached fifty. He eked out his days in a hospice, with a voice box due to his throat cancer, and a pipe attached to his stomach that he poured Scotch directly into. I never met the man, but everyone who knew him vouched for his scabrous wit and supreme sense of entitlement.

Was *Withnail and I* as much fun to film as it is to watch, or just very hard work?

The crew told us that we should value every moment of the shoot, as very few movies, in their experience, were as good to make as this one was. Having never made one before, I took their word for it. Peter Frampton and Sue Love, the make-up and hair team, were a non-stop laughter riot. Shamelessly politically incorrect, with a running commentary on proceedings that kept as laughing every day.

Kevin Jackson wrote in a tribute to *Withnail and I* for the BFI: "To pronounce oneself immune to the charms of *Withnail and I* is to declare oneself a philistine, a Puritan and a snob." Do you agree?
Indeed! Although its always interesting to meet people who make a point of letting me know just how much they either hated or 'didn't get' the film, like I could give a continental flying fuck! Haha.

> *"Social life in Swaziland was dictated by the three Bs – bonking, booze and boredom, so I was well educated in the arts of debauchery"*

However, a friend of mine with OCD found it impossible to watch, as he was so traumatised by the state of the Camden Town squat kitchen sink that he had to leave.

Was there any ad-libbing during filming, or was every line scripted from the start?
Everything was scripted and adhered to, including every comma and full stop. Bruce declared that he hadn't bust a gut writing a screenplay, to be improvised or messed around with.

How soon during filming was the original ending, where Withnail shoots himself, changed?
That suicidal ending was never in the screenplay, but was how the novella concluded which Bruce originally wrote in 1969.

Did you know anything about the lifestyle depicted in the film, having recently arrived from Swaziland when you began filming?
Social life in colonial Swaziland was dictated by the three Bs – bonking, booze and boredom. So yes, I was well 'educated' in the arts of debauchery.

The state of my living conditions at university and drama school were not a million miles away from Withnail's squat, as my flatmates will testify.

Have you ever met anyone quite as eccentric as Uncle Monty?
I knew an amateur play director, growing up, who was a real-life Monty, given to florid explosions of temperament and grandiose gestures and pronouncements. He also made a habit of using his shirt or jacket pockets as ashtrays and spoke in conspiratorial tones as if the world might end at any minute.

As the oldest actor in the cast, what did Richard Griffiths make of the film's success and its acquisition of cult status?
Richard loved the script, but loathed the fact that none of the cast benefited from any residuals from video/dvd sales or the endless showings on cable and terrestrial TV. So he was resistant to contributing to documentaries or anniversary screenings, as other people, unconnected with the production, were coining the proceeds.

Withnail made heavy drinking, having a posh background and wearing Savile Row suits fashionable, even cool. Are you as pleased at this as we at the Chap are?
Indubitably, indefatigably and unequivocally, yes!

You are fortunate enough to have worn some fabulous outfits for many of your roles, including the famous Withnail coat. Which was the closest to how you really like to dress?
As I began my film career 30 years ago playing Withnail, wearing a long turn-of-the-20th Century coachman's coat, I've had my fair share of frock coats, ranging from the 18th Century in *The Scarlet Pimpernel* to Victorian suits in *Dracula* and *Portrait of a Lady*. Plus Fours in *Twelfth Night*, formal gear in *The Age of Innocence* and *Downton Abbey*, with some slim-line shiny 90s suits in *Spiceworld* and a variety of sleaze-ball '70s outfits for *Dom Hemmingway*.
One of the bonuses of being an actor is that you get to dress in character clothes that you'd never wear in real life, so nothing that I've been in has much resembled my everyday clothing.

As Gordon Comstock in *Keep the Aspidistra Flying* you wore lots of tweed. Did the habit remain once you'd finished filming?

Indeed! The Withnail coat was Harris Tweed. Madonna gave me the suit I wore in her directorial debut *Filth and Wisdom*, which was a 1930s Herringbone three-piece tweed suit, which the Sydney Opera Company then used as a template for my suits in *My Fair Lady*, which I did in 2008. It's a quintessentially English look and very practical in the country. Love the smell of it when rained on!

There is no question that you look excellent in White Tie, as seen in many of your film roles. Are you as comfortable in full evening dress outside work and do you get many opportunities to don the Marcella bow tie?

I think that full evening dress and white tie makes any man look elegant and stylish, no matter what his size or height. The stiff collars and starched board shirts of yore are a pain to deal with and I am grateful that we no longer have to negotiate those, but award ceremonies and formal 'dos' offer the opportunity to get spruced, booted and bow tied up.

We have found very few, if any, photographs of you wearing a hat of any description, outside a film role. Is this because you are one of those men who simply doesn't need a hat, or is it perhaps a phobia of some sort?

Ha ha. Rumbled! My wife declared that as I have such an elongated head, with four acres of forehead, most hats sit atop my tombstone features with comical results. However, on a recent trip to Bath, I found a brilliant vintage shop that sells those Baker Boy caps that everyone wore in *Peaky Blinders*. The producers of *Can You Ever Forgive Me* gifted me a Borsalino hat, as I wore a similar one in the film, and I've taken to wearing it. And will do more regularly as my hairline recedes off into the Ether!

Can you tell us something about the film you are working on at the moment, *Can You Ever Forgive Me*?

It stars Melissa McCarthy as Lee Israel, the biographer of Estee Lauder and Tallulah Bankhead, who fell on hard times and began forging famous writer's signatures, then letters, which she sold for

"I've only worked with
one actor who drank
through the shooting day
and his career went awol
very quickly."

"Let me put it this way, if there's a 'Camberwell Carrot' on the go, I'll be the first to partake thereof!"

a tidy sum, until rumbled by the FBI. Working in collusion with a coke dealing, kleptomaniac ex-con called Jack Horton, whom I play. It's about two loners who form an unlikely symbiotic friendship that is both hilarious and finally heartbreaking. All shot on location in Manhattan. Working with Melissa proved to be the happiest experience I've ever had making a movie. Ever!

Is the costume designer making you wear polyester suits for your role as Jack Horton?
The costume designer, Arjun Bhassin *(Life of Pi)*, sourced clothes from the early 80s, even though the film is set in 1992, to dress me, as that was the era that was Jack's heyday. So, long coats, high waisted trousers, skinny ties and New Romantic shirts.

Your allergy to alcohol is well documented. You must spend a lot of time around people who are getting drunk. Do you feel you are missing out?
Osmosis takes place, so much so that people assume I am drunk, simply because you instinctively adapt to how hammered people are who you're in the company of.

Instead of alcohol, do you have any other way of getting pleasurably out of control?
Let me put it this way, if there's a 'Camberwell Carrot' on the go, I'll be the first to partake thereof!

Have you ever truly enjoyed the pleasures of Lady Nicotine outside of a film role?
I tried a Lucky Strike once in 1971, stood up and fell over. Every time I've had to smoke in a movie, which has been a pretty regular requirement, the props team has always given me Honey Rose ciggies, which have no nicotine.

Has the age of the "Hellraiser" actor passed? Is there still any room for the Oliver Reed/Richard Harris type of behaviour on movie sets?
Long gone. Movies cost way too much money for production to be held up by drink or drugs. Plus getting the actor insured is increasingly stringent.

The working hours are very long, so it's not conducive to being off your face. I've only worked with one actor who drank through the shooting day and his career went AWOL very quickly. Digital HD film is also very unforgiving – if you're 'bombed', it will be cruelly magnified on screen.

You launched your own scent collection, Jack. Please tell us where on earth one starts when creating a brand-new scent?
I've been led by my nose all my life and compulsively sniffed everything in sight. When I was 12 years old, I had a big crush on an American girl called Betsy Clapp, newly arrived in Swaziland. She chewed gum, spoke at bullet speed and taught me to French kiss. Couldn't afford to buy her scent for her birthday, so tried to make my own by boiling gardenia and rose petals in sugared jam jars, which I buried in the ground hoping for some magical osmosis.

Four decades later, I finally took the plunge and started my 'one man brand', mixing perfume oils in my kitchen and then working with professional 'Nose' Alienor Massenet, who converted my amateur experiments into a professional product that became an instant bestseller when Jack launched three years ago. As the scent bottle is 'sleeved' inside a vintage style Union Jack calico bag, I called it Jack. I chose a quintessentially British name in tandem with the Post box red packaging. The success of the first version has enabled me to produce Jack: Covent Garden and recently Jack: Piccadilly '69 – which has notes of petrol, amber, bergamot and leather.

You've played the Doctor, Kafka, the Scarlet Pimpernel, Withnail and Sherlock Holmes. Are there any iconic roles left that you still would like to play?
King Lear – when I'm *really* ancient and crotchety.

I hear they are looking for a new Bond – has the role ever appealed to you?
Absolutely. However, there is the very small problem that I don't have large muscles, wide shoulders or a bottomless supply of testosterone to fill those Bond shoes. ■

YOUTH TRIBES

Olivia Bullock on a radical street style that emerged under the dark shadow of the Vichy government in wartime Paris

Paris has long been a melting pot for the Avant-garde. Its coexistence of artistic tradition and radical unconvention has been well documented. Artists, writers, poets and musicians have flocked to the city and enjoyed its liberalism and acceptance. This was notably so during the interwar period, when many black Americans, fleeing racial tensions and segregation still prevalent in their homeland, took advantage of the city's laissez-faire attitude.

This migration brought a new culture and vibrancy, and with it a fascination for black performers and musicians known as the *Tumulte Noir*. Between 1920 and 1939, the popularity of jazz and swing, reinforced by these new adopted citizens, was increasing. Soon a vibrant jazz scene was established in the bars and nightclubs around Montmartre, endorsed by French musician Django Reinhardt.

The popularity of jazz and its absorption of black music personified an exuberant and carefree attitude. A style of dress, inspired by the Zoot suit-wearing musicians, was soon adopted by young men and women. This outward approbation of other ethnic groups was beginning to spark debate and controversy as to how France was to deal with racial and ethnic difference.

The association with black American culture was soon marginalised when, after the outbreak of war in 1939, and under the German occupation of France a year later, an enforced patriotism became mandatory. Yet, despite this, a group of young men and women would distinguish themselves as the very antithesis of this idealised French citizenry. Their total advocacy and solidarity with these new incomers was upheld in the face of authority. They were to be one of the first youth movements of resistance and rebellion. They named themselves the Zazous.

The strict conservatism implemented under the Vichy regime during the occupation saw dancing, among other liberal pastimes, prohibited. The gathering of Parisian youths made the Germans nervous, but dancing in particular was considered indecorous, considering that many young men were losing their lives fighting for their country. However, this morally conscious effort on the part of the regime did little to mask the motivation behind the ban, as the government began to enforce an increasingly tight supervision to control its citizens

> **"** Their hair was greased back in the *style Anglaise*, much maligned by the regime, and a little thin moustache *à la mode de Oxford*, accessorised with a Chamberlain umbrella, regardless of the weather. **"**

and also the media, who began to foment a virulent anti-Semitism, opposing any image that challenged an obedient homogenised French citizen. Jazz, and all associations of black America that had so delighted a young French audience, was now deemed degenerate and henceforth forbidden.

Goebbels issued an edict banning 'negro music' and the Montmartre jazz community were deported, interred or left unemployed. In less than a year the Zazous, discouraged by the regime's strict morality and ideology, rejected these values, and even consciously sought to celebrate and indulge in all things unpatriotic. They later adopted the phrase 'A Swing France In a Zazou Europe'; they were the most visible and flagrant in their displeasure and, as a result, were despised by the Nazis.

It is not certain how the name Zazous came about, but it is possible it was borrowed from a song by Harlem jazz musician Cab Calloway called *Zah Zuh Zah*. Calloway famously wore the controversial Zoot Suit – a colourful oversized suit, favoured by many Jazz musicians, which blatantly ignored government decrees on the rationing of clothing

fabric. The Zazous, as a gesture of solidarity (and ultimately a declaration of support) took inspiration from this outlandish apparel and created their own unique style.

Their distinctive appearance was no doubt a visual statement of defiance. Like the Zoot suit, men would wear oversized jackets cut to the knees, often in a bright checkered print (favoured by both sexes) and with several half belts; their trousers were loose fitting and tailored at the ankle to show off white or coloured socks. The shirts were high collared and kept in place with a pin, worn with a narrow tie in heavy cotton or wool. Suede shoes with thick soles were favourable, later nicknamed 'brothel creepers'.

Perhaps most controversial of all was their hair, which was left long, in a response to a government decree that all barbershops donate hair to the war effort to be manufactured into slippers and sweaters. Their hair was greased back in the *style Anglaise*, much maligned by the regime (their UK equivalent the Teddy Boys were much admired) and a little thin moustache *à la mode de Oxford*, accessorised with a Chamberlain umbrella, regardless of the weather. Women wore their hair curled to the shoulders or in braids. Bleached blond was preferable; otherwise a single lock was either bleached or dyed. They were rarely without dark sunglasses and red lipstick. Tailored check or stripe jackets with oversized shoulders were worn with short full skirts, ankle socks and, like their male counterparts, thick-soled shoes; a far cry from the wholesome maternal image propagated by the regime.

The Zazous were young, educated, often wealthy, and hence had time and money at their disposal, which contributed to their hedonistic lifestyle and outward rejection of the work ethic imposed on them. This objective soon spread throughout France, but it was the terrace of the Pom Pom cafe on the Champs d'Elysees and the *Boul Miche* near the Sorbonne that were to be associated as the venue of choice to assemble, and where it might be possible to observe an audible gesture of defiance such as their shouts of "Swing!" followed by a little hop, then a cry of "Zazous, hey hey hey Za Zazous!" with a slap on the hip and a turn of the head. Their more bohemian accomplices, with their sheepskin jackets and multi coloured scarves, preferred to gather in the Latin Quarter. Beer with Grenadine syrup, fruit juices and a trend for eating grated carrot salad in vegetarian restaurants were *de rigeur*.

> **"Most controversial of all was Les Zazous' hair, which was left long in a response to a governmental decree that all barbershops donate hair to the war effort to be manufactured into slippers and sweaters"**

As the Zazous increased in numbers, they encompassed all races and classes. The poorer associates stole cloth and participated in black market activities to obtain outfits, but all were complicit in their resistance to the Vichy/Nazi administration. Some Zazous would extend their defiance by joining resistance movements; others, in solidarity with French Jews, would wear the yellow Star of David with the words 'Zazous', 'Swing' or 'Goy' emblazoned on it. Some female Zazous, in recognition of the racial hostilities towards black Americans, would blacken their faces in an expression of solidarity. It was now acknowledged that the Zazous posed a very real threat to the nationalistic youth image demanded by the Vichy regime, who suspected them of having an apathetic, irreverent attitude to the war in general. The pro-Nazi newspaper *Gringore* described the Zazous as "perverted kids and idle little girls".

To further instil the moral fibre and productivity of an increasingly dissident French youth, the Vichy regime created the fascist youth organisation the *Jeunesse Populaire Francais*. Declaring the Zazous as enemies of the coalition, French officials mounted their most aggressive expulsion on the Zazous. On June 14th 1942, the Jeunesse Populaire, boasting the slogan 'Scalp the Zazous!', raided the cafes and bars on the Champs d'Elysses, the Latin Quarter and at Neuilly. The Zazous were rounded up, beaten and attacked with hair clippers. Some were arrested, many were sent to the countryside to work on the harvest.

This vehement reaction by the regime only magnified the Zazous' social influence. Those who managed to escape sought out a clandestine existence. Holed up in basement clubs and underground venues off the Boulevard Saint Michel and La Jeunesse Doree, and in more sleazy establishments near the Etoile, they would listen to 78s and talk in English slang, laying the foundations of a nightclubbing culture and giving rise to the birth of the discotheque.

In the countryside, the ban on more liberal pursuits was increasingly disregarded. Dancing and listening to jazz was enjoyed in remote barns, isolated houses and small towns across France; and yet, despite this dedication, the Zazou movement seemed to be losing momentum, eventually resulting in their demise in 1942. It is difficult to say when they disbanded, although it might be a fair to assume that the *Service du travail obligatore* imposed by the government in the same year, recruiting all able bodied men and women into forced labour, was reason enough to remain incognito, or otherwise go into hiding or avoid any circumstances whereby they might draw attention to themselves.

As disappointing and irresolute as this sounds, there is no doubt the Zazous represented a dissident minority, and their refusal to conform to a progressively compliant and acquiescent society distinguished them as a paradigm of youth counterculture. Their distinctive appearance, their decadence and dandyism and their confident rebellion, are all characteristics that constitute and maintain youth movements to this day.

Liberté, égalite, fraternité!

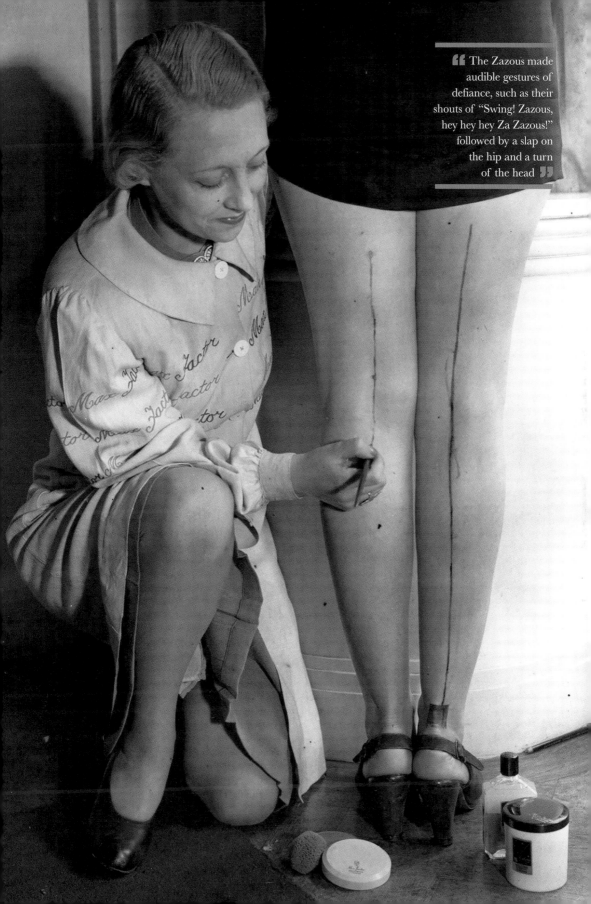

ROGER & ME

His Rogesty's top tip of how to get people to smile for a photograph – just before the click of the camera, murmur in your best Mooreish-croon, "witty titty sex"

The first time I received a birthday card from Sir Roger Moore felt like the end of all presents, and the beginning of a serene unending gratitude to the mysterious forces who govern this orb of wickedness and wonder, known to many of us as Planet Earth. I've always been amazed by the human capacity for belief. Whether you choose to worship a deity, devote yourself to collecting relics from the last days of Diana Dors or are only truly happy when immersed in the syncopations and rhythm of cricket on the radio, you know what it is for something to enlarge the sphere of your mind. The first time I saw Roger Moore, the frontier of my face dissolved

and I began to imagine a new path, one in which charm, empathy and generosity emerged as real contenders on the surface of aplenty shattered by one too many supremacy struggles. All I needed to do was grow a mole on my cheek and find out how to raise my eyebrow, and my journey into offering that little bit Moore could begin in earnest.

For Your Eyes Only was the first Bond film I saw at the cinema, in Bournemouth with my brother Will. It may not be Bond's finest but to me that film is a sacred doctrine. I distinctly remember the atmosphere in the Odeon as I, an eight-year-old with a pudding-bowl haircut drenched in navy corduroy, began to realize that choices need to be

made in this life. Is corduroy the answer? Could there be another fabric beyond corduroy? If that chap on the big screen who seems to know he is at best moderately good at his job, and happy to transmit this information to all but the sleepiest of us, could there be a way to seize this life and deploy one's personality? Could that, in fact, become a professional occupation? You'll have heard people criticize and praise Roger – and indeed Connery and Caine – for either being "the same" or "themselves" in movies, depending on our point of view. Either way, these three made a decent living dressing up and drinking, which seemed to me to be the best possible outcome to any scenario which didn't involve winning the lottery, inheriting a castle or marrying Princess Leia. Since none of those options were immediately apparent, I became a devotee of the Moore Method. Embrace what little skill you have, deploy it appropriately with relentless dedication and hope for the best.

Little by little, I advanced. From learning to order a signature drink betraying no irony, such as my fabled Malibu and Pineapple years (many bruises), to my discovery that wearing a safari suit in teenage years, while repelling 95% of love-interests, had a rare 5% hit rate which I regarded as evidence that this dress code could yet blossom into the uniform of a nouveau Casanova. It wasn't until I began to devise my own rare form of dress which invariably involved the clash of floral shirts with check jackets that things really started to look up

and I found myself thrown out of fewer and fewer television studios. And as they looked up, disaster struck: Roger Moore collapsed on stage in New York in 2003.

He was my hero and I was beset with grief that I'd never had the chance to thank him for the inspiration. My friend, director and animator Dan Chambers, created a short cartoon *'Roger Moore's Requiem'* to assuage my grief. It tackled, in rather a Verdi's *Requiem* sort of way, what may happen to Roger's eternal soul in the event that he had the effrontery to check out from this grubby galactic pearl too early. By the miracle of the Internet, the Requiem reached Roger who declared himself "tickled pink". It led to *The Fly Who Loved Me*, a short animation which Dan and I subsequently put together for UNICEF, in which Roger played the part of Father Christmas and I a fly who volunteers to pull the sleigh in place of his reindeer. I remember walking into the suite at the Hotel de Paris in Monte Carlo to record with Roger. The door slid aside, a bit part in this titanic meeting of worshipper and idol, and there he was, resplendent, genial, the self-deprecating 007 idol of my childhood, watching the French Open tennis. His first words? "Hang on lads, I'll just turn this crap off".

But here comes the twist. Within moments, the hero of my childhood became my hero for completely new and different reasons. Aside from his top tip of how get people to smile for a photograph (just before the click of the camera, murmur

in your best Rogery-croon "witty titty sex"), he spoke with gentle determination to help tackle issues that blight the lives of children around the world, from goiter to HIV, and equal education for girls and boys. Compassion, empathy, action, these are the engaging tributes that linger as I reflect on the sad loss of my dear friend.

In the years that followed, Roger was always evocative, immensely engaging and never less than a force ten terrific gust of goodness. He once told me over lunch of his years before the war, remembering "the sun beating down on the dust and the scent of a bakery in the distance". He revelled in language and his voice was the core of his presence and artistry. I remember meeting Roger backstage

at the British Library to hear him read Rudyard Kipling's *If*. His voice was astonishing in its richness – a never-ending carpet of opulence that slides deeper into eternity with every passing day. His comic timing, while used with considerable self-deprecation in the Bond films, is gently spectacular in *The Persuaders* and *The Saint*, always happy to let the scene, script and cast breathe gently and expand the life in the moment. His empathy and timing as an actor was one thing, but it was also a real tenet of his vastly generous spirit. Specifically, I recall his kindness in inviting my parents backstage at his recent touring show in Exeter when he declared to my Dad "Ha! You're even more Olly than he is!" My daughters will remember wander-

ing into my office to find me on a Skype call with him, believing me to be engaged in a top-secret communication with James Bond himself.

How to remember him? His signature recipe for The Moore Martini is a good enough start: add a teaspoon of Vermouth to a jug, discard. Pour in a bottle of gin, then decant into individual glasses placed in the freezer with a lemon twist. It has to be said, they do taste very Moore-ish, and of course he adored his food and drink. I remember lunching in Monte Carlo's Café de Paris with him when a health scare compelled His Rogesty to eat steamed fish, but he insisted I ordered and devoured his favourite liver and bacon on his behalf. He ate it with his eyes. But his influence on me stretches far beyond food and drink. For years growing up I practiced curling my eyebrow in the mirror – even today my two daughters are remark-ably adept at mimicking my quizzical stare over the breakfast table, as I croon in my best Roger voice on the status of their homework.

Roger was unfailingly courteous, charming, funny and considerate. He adored his wife Kristina and his children, Deborah, Geoffrey and Christian, along with Gareth Owen, his friend and mine, biographer and beloved assistant. From drinking Jack Daniels with Sinatra to having his toenails painted by Peter Sellers, Roger's treasury of memories is sadly lost, but their glimmer remains in those lucky enough to share his recollections. I remember, for instance, discovering his love of Sancerre, as he regaled me over a glass or two with tales of a trip to the Loire Valley with Michael Caine and Leslie Bricusse. One can only imagine the high jinks.

I was on my way to record an interview with Sir Michael Parkinson when my brother Will Smith, also a devoted fan of Roger, texted me: "Have you seen the news? Roger has gone to the great ski chalet in the sky". The day stopped along with my heart, but I was lucky enough to be able to share memories of Roger, a mutual inspiration, with Sir Michael. I was due to record a retrospective with Roger, an overview of his career to be broadcast on BBC Radio 2, to mark his 90th birthday. It will still be recorded, as a tribute to His Rogesty, with a line-up of his friends picking out tracks to recall key moments of his life. The news of his death stripped me; the twinkle in his eye that never failed to dazzle, snuffed. They say you should never meet your hero. But in fact you must. If they don't measure up to your expectations, they should never have been your hero in the first place. As far as Roger and me go, nobody did it better. I only hope there's a guest room in the great ski chalet in the sky. With lashings of Sancerre. ∎

MR. ERBIL

**Elizabeth Fitt meets the Kurdish dandies who are empowering a new generation,
one moustache comb at a time**

Relaxing over shisha at a cafe in the English Quarter of Erbil in Iraqi Kurdistan, the three founding members of Mr. Erbil are all smiles and a reassuring grasp of the English language rare in these parts. Ahmed Nauzad sports a rather fine navy waistcoat (bottom button un-done) with matching polka dot pocket handkerchief (Presidential Fold). Goran Pshtiwan and Omer Nihad are lower-key, in Italianate slacks and leather jackets. They sip black tea from small glasses.

Billed as the next Dubai, Erbil circa 2013 was booming – investors backed large scale development as the post-Saddam era, oil infused economy shook out its dusty feathers and strode Phoenix-like towards Independent Kurdish wealth and prosperity. Jump to April 2017 and that dream is in tatters. The economy of the Kurdistan Region puts one more in mind of a road kill crow, ravaged as it has been by budget cuts

from Baghdad and the continued influx of Syrian refugees and Iraqis displaced by the ISIS conflict, at a cost of US$1.5billion per year. On top of this, the fall in global oil prices has hit the Kurdish Region hard. Public services are woefully inadequate, with fewer than seven hours of national grid electricity per day, and the population is struggling with severe austerity measures and an unemployment rate of 14%. The reality of this has left public sector workers (a little over 50% of the total workforce of the region) facing pay cuts of up to 75% and salary arrears stretching to months on end.

What does one do when faced with such a situation? Well, according to Nauzad, what one doesn't do is rest upon one's laurels: "Sitting at home doing nothing won't help at all – you must be creative and take action," he states. And so began an initiative to take on these difficult times with

a stiff upper lip, a rather natty moustache comb (more of which later) and the desire to inspire a new generation of Kurdish people to take pride in their heritage and shape their own destinies.

Mr. Erbil is a gentlemen's club. Nauzad and Pshtiwan explain that, among other things, the purpose of their club is to change attitudes to Kurdish

> "We are never involved in religion or politics. We have many different religions in our gentlemen's club – it doesn't matter, we accept everyone, as long as they are human, that is all"

products and culture, both within Kurdistan and globally, while motivating Kurdish youth to take their own initiative and build the future they want to see. Now in their late twenties, the three founders have known each other since their school days. They have a long standing passion for the finer points of gentlemen's attire, rooted initially in admiration for Florence-based Pitti Uomo. They sought to emulate their Italian contemporaries, but with a twist – viewing men's fashion as a means to gain traction with a broad audience and do good (as well as an excellent means to the end of looking rather splendid, naturally).

The members of Mr. Erbil, some 30-odd in number, come from all walks of life: mechanics, engineers, doctors, barbers, civil servants and tailors. This is a deliberate strategy, according to Nauzad, who points out that, in order to change attitudes, people must first feel connected. Broadening the variety of

members broadens the scope of those who can relate to Mr. Erbil. Pshtiwan adds, "We are never involved in religion or politics. We have many different religions in our gentlemen's club – it doesn't matter, we accept everyone, as long as they are human, that is all."

Splendidness aside, the economy, human rights and the environment are the three areas closest to the heart of Mr. Erbil. The hook may be sartorial in nature, but the desire to inspire and support others to instigate and further their own change in these three areas goes deeper. They intend, through channelling their new-found fame into creating a global platform from which to raise awareness, to put Kurdish culture and products on the map.

Their penchant for the sartorial has led Mr. Erbil to design their own line of gentlemen's attire. Their clothes are inspired not only by the styles they loved so much growing up, but also the unique local fabrics of the Kurdish region. All their pieces are made up by tailors in their home town of Erbil and fabrics are sourced from Kurdistan, lending much needed support for the local economy. For the time being, their designs are limited to personal use by a lack of start-up capital. However, they hope to launch a gentleman's necktie range this month. The stuff of which these ties are made is called Krr. Made from goat hair taken from village goats clipped seasonally, Krr is found nowhere else in the world; this neckwear is one of a kind.

Mr. Erbil members are also rather taken with discreet male grooming and have launched a beard care range called Rishn (meaning Beard in Kurdish), complete with both beard and moustache combs. They aim to equip the bearded and/or moustachioed gentleman with everything required to maintain luxuriant yet cultivated facial hair

What would Mr. Erbil like to say to followers of The Chap? "London Chaps have always been an inspiration. It's never about the cut of the suit; it's about the cut of the heart."

growth with pride. If their own beards are anything to go by, Rishn products are something no be-whiskered gentleman should be without. The profusion of perfectly coiffed beards in the room is really quite mesmeric. Initially their Rishn products and neckties will be available only locally. Shipping costs from Iraqi Kurdistan remain prohibitive for the time being, with postage fees considerably surpassing the cost of a tie.

Among other humanitarian activities, the members of Mr. Erbil are passionate about women's rights, specifically in raising awareness of Kurdish women active in their local communities and empowering them to further develop their own businesses. This is not limited just to those in Kurdistan, but open to Kurdish women all over the world. Their Thursday Inspiration slot regularly features inspiring Kurdish women who have settled in other countries, as well as those resident in Kurdistan. The effects of the Thursday Inspiration slot are

sometimes profound for the businesses featured – a couple of teenage jewellery designers in the nearby town of Sulaymaniyah found themselves deluged with months' worth of orders in a matter of days.

In an area where sexual equality is not a priority and the absence of equal rights remarkable, for an inherence so ingrained as to render invisible the very idea that one's rights as a woman may be compromised, this sort of thing is important. That is not to say that the women here are all overwhelmingly oppressed; they are not. But little credence is given to the concept of women as equals.

Nauzad says there's little chance of changing the attitude and practices of older Kurds regarding the environment, but certainly hope for younger generations who are currently ill informed about the impacts of their lifestyle choices. In an effort to combat this, Nauzad, Nihad and Pshtiwan have begun by organising a campaign centred on Newroz (Kurdish New Year) celebrations in March. Kurds make for

the mountains for celebratory picnics with friends and family at this time, which invariably results in areas of natural beauty becoming littered with plastic and other detritus. Mr. Erbil intends to highlight the unsightly and negative environmental impacts of such behaviour and instil more of a sense of pride in this beautiful region. Armed with pride, the hope is that Kurdish people will also take responsibility and provide more careful guardianship of their homeland.

The passion and energy with which these gentlemen pursue their aims is admirable – having faced seven months and still counting of no pay check appearing in his bank account, Nihad, who works full time at the Erbil Stock Exchange, could certainly be forgiven were his form to appear a tad sub-par. On the contrary, with absolutely no discernible tremor of the upper lip, he talks excitedly about hopes for the future and gives off an air of expansive positivity that is contagious. Nauzad has likewise experienced the backlash of the economic crisis first hand and,

having recently become separated from his role with a private sector equipment company, intends to embrace the work of Mr. Erbil on a full-time basis. Pshtiwan, who is currently in the final throes of a Business Management degree, is equally sanguine.

Nauzad elaborates on his hopes and dreams for the future of Mr Erbil, "I want Kurdish people to have pride in the quality of Kurdish products. And for our products to sell worldwide, in America and Europe. We need to show big businessmen here that importing is not the only way; we can export as well."

And then he tilts his head, smiles and mentions a certain hankering for a gentlemen's club headquarters, "With a coffee salon, a barber, a tailor, everything a gentleman needs to look after himself well."

I had one last question for the members of Mr. Erbil – What would they like to say to followers of The Chap? And their reply was this "London Chaps have always been an inspiration. It's never about the cut of the suit; it's about the cut of the heart." ∎

Pictures: Mustafa Khyat and Shwan Blaiye

THE GREY FOX COLUMN

David Evans, author of Grey Fox Blog, on viewing the source of Harris Tweed, Kempadoo hats and Acassi gentlemen's bags

This column has a distinctly tweedy and leathery feel to it, as befits the shortening days leading us towards autumn and early winter. Earlier this year I visited the Outer Hebrides as guest of the Harris Tweed Authority, to find out more about this wonderful cloth. Surely almost every reader of this august journal owns something made from Harris Tweed, giving the impression that this is a common product made in volume? In fact, Harris Tweed is woven in relatively small amounts in the homes of islanders on Harris and Lewis.

Its colours reflect the diverse colours of the landscape; misty blues and greys from sea and sky, mossy greens, peaty browns, creams from the white sand beaches and yellows and purples of the gorse and heather. Its water resistant and durable nature makes it an ideal cloth for British weather. Indeed, tweed was the original technical sporting fabric,

keeping outdoor workers and country sportsmen and women warm, comfortable and dry in all weathers.

To earn the Harris Tweed 'Orb' label, the cloth must have been woven in an islander's home. Cloth made in a mill or outside the Hebrides cannot legally be named Harris Tweed. I visited the mills that prepare and dye the wool, spin it into yarn that is warped on to beams, which are then sent out to the weavers for the cloth to be woven. The weaver adds the weft to the warp and returns the cloth to the mill, finally to be washed and checked, stamped with the Orb and distributed around the world. This isn't a mass-produced product; it's a home-made cloth that contains the essence of the islands in which it is made.

As a slightly older man, I used to regard tweed caps with caution. To my earlier generation, they were worn by older men (many of whom nowadays seem sadly to have adopted baseball caps),

so I avoided them. However, as ever in search of British-made menswear, I recently tried a corduroy cap from Kempadoo Millar, whose caps are made in Yorkshire. I loved its style and practicability and was bereft when I left it in a taxi. Luckily it was soon replaced and it's a much-worn item that has encouraged my hat-wearing (and elsewhere in this journal I may be found wearing some excellent British-made hats from Laird Hatters).

Founder Rhian Kempadoo Millar told me about her company: "The inspiration for Kempadoo Millar caps often comes from lyrics and landscapes. I'm lucky enough to live in Yorkshire with its heather, dry stone walls, bracken and green fields – the colours are beautifully subtle. My family live in the Caribbean so I like to add a little flash of Tobago sea turquoise or a vibrant Immortelle tree orange under the peak. It's a nice way to design from the two influences.

The caps are manufactured in Yorkshire using traditional methods, hand finishing and using locally sourced fabrics and tweeds from the many remaining textile mills. It's an exercise in 'localisation' – spending the time & energy to find the people and skills from our local area… we are interested in each element of the cap being made with honesty – ensuring the process is just as impressive as the final product."

My cord cap is an attractive ginger called a 'Parkin'. Those of you with northern tendencies will know that parkin is a sticky ginger cake. It takes me back to my childhood, when a tea of parkin and dandelion and burdock was seventh heaven. Style with a gabardine jacket to keep you warm and dry as the weather changes.

And on to more tweed: Acassi is a British brand making bags for men. Launched in 2016 by founder Julie Paisley, it uses British made and

sourced materials, including Harris Tweed, high quality leathers and solid brass hardware. Julie abandoned her career as a photographic stylist after a holiday to Harris opened her eyes to the beauty and craftsmanship of Harris Tweed, and she decided to make bags incorporating this colourful and iconic cloth. Determined to develop a brand of her own, rather than other people's, she worked on blending colours of tweed with high quality leathers. She visualised her brand being British-made, using the best quality leathers in amazing colours. She designed her first bag and Acassi was born. "It is important to me," Julie told me, "that the manufacturing of my products remains in the UK, keeping alive traditional skills, supporting British manufacturing and, very importantly to me, being able to control the ethical side of my brand. To help preserve the traditional heritage of UK Industries, to avoid the 'Fast Fashion' of today and to ensure the makers of my products have safe working conditions".

The bag I have is beautifully made; the leather soft and the Harris Tweed full of colour. Inside, it's roomy, with plenty of nooks and crannies for belongings. This is a high quality piece of British leather work. While they are sold as men's bags, they'd be ideal for anyone and useful for business or leisure.

When it comes to leather, oak bark tanning is probably the oldest method of treating hides to make leather. Using oak bark, the raw hide is converted to leather after around 12 months of the tanning process. There is a market at the top end for shoes and leather goods such as Tim Hardy's oak bark belts, which he makes by hand. Tim explained the process to me: "Oak Bark leather uses a completely natural tanning process as practised two thousand years ago at the same site in Devon, which keeps all its natural blemishes, beauty and

patina and handles, cuts and works wonderfully well, with the final product moulding to its owner and maturing like a fine wine".

The leather is tanned at J. & F.J. Baker & Co of Colyton, whose website contains a fascinating video of the process. Like all good leather, the belts ages slowly but beautifully – a bit like older gentlemen of course. Style with flannel or corduroy trousers, a chunky fisherman's jumper and matching leather brogues.

Another leather product made in the UK is this pair of vintage-style cycling shoes from REW Reynolds, England. The business was founded in 1921 to make bicycles, but later diversified into cycling shoes and these remain their main product. Made for men and women, they are the product of Northampton shoemaking skills, being Goodyear welted and produced from full-grain leather for the uppers and a leather sole. They are for flat pedals but REW Reynolds make other models for those who like to clip in with cleated shoes. Style with a tweed cycling suit.

As a blogger I should never work with animals. Over the last few months I've received several e-mails addressed to 'Dear Harry', asking if Harry would like to try a pair of socks, visit a restaurant to review its food or wear a knitted silk tie on Instagram. Harry is my four-year-old Labrador retriever. ∎

Links:
The Harris Tweed Authority:
www.harristweed.org
Kempadoo Millar: www.kempadoo.com
Acassi: www.acassi.co.uk
Worcestershire Leather Co: www.timhardy.com
REW Reynolds: www.reynolds-england.com

www.greyfoxblog.com

AM I CHAP?

SEND PHOTOS OF YOURSELF AND OTHER BUDDING CHAPS AND CHAPETTES TO CHAP@THECHAP.CO.UK FOR INCLUSION IN THE NEXT ISSUE

"On my way out to the office," writes Laurent Mather, "I note that my cuffs are unfortunately hidden, but that sartorial faux pas aside, do I pass muster?"
If only it were that simple. If we 'put that sartorial faux pas aside' all the time, we would be Vice Magazine or the Beano.

"This is a photograph of my better half, Mr. Cory Warren," writes John Sawyer, "who is celebrating a recent court victory with a bespoke tweed suit and a glass of Scotch. What does The Chap think?"
Sir, congratulations, though what we think depends on the victory being celebrated. Not sure we'd approve if Mr. Warren got off an armed robbery charge. If he successfully sued the News of the World for poor journalism, then cheers!

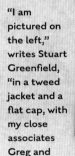

"I am pictured on the left," writes Stuart Greenfield, "in a tweed jacket and a flat cap, with my close associates Greg and Grant. As a British expat in the U.S., I feel I have to keep the British end up and that the smartest way to do so is with a tweed jacket and waxed mustache. My American friends would also like to have their chap credentials assessed."
So you decided to 'go native', by wearing pinstripes with tweed, fastening your watch chain absurdly high and spelling 'moustache' incorrectly. The food looks weird as well.

"This picture was taken with my freshly married wife on our wedding day last year," writes Christopher Wall. "Could I be considered just a little bit Chap?"
Sir, we presume the wedding continued into the evening, when you switched from Morning Dress to the Evening Dress pictured? We had to employ technical wizardry to ascertain that the hem of your coat is in the correct position with regard to your waistcoat. Your good lady may sleep soundly in the nuptial chamber, for it is.

"I don't know whether you would consider any submissions from Germany," writes Andreas Mandrysch, "but we are earnestly doing our best to keep up with the civilized countries." Sir, your trouser cuffs fall short of their destination, namely the surface of your shoe. Your chum also displays garter, but for the correct reasons. Is he German too? Probably not.

"Miss Verity," writes her father Ian Hawkins, "wishes to know if she qualifies as a Chapette. Her apologies for the omission of a scarf but it had snagged and torn on a blackthorn shrub! However, she hopes the quality of the tweed will make up for that."
Tweed was made to withstand plants like blackthorn and hawthorn, so your daughter is already one step ahead. We can only congratulate her on looking sharp despite being *sans foulard*.

"Here I am cycling the Morecambe promenade on my 1930s ex-police Raleigh bicycle," writes Simon Doughty (rather smugly), "Wearing 'Patterson' blazer, Epoch straw hat, Universal Works waistcoat, Old Town collarless shirt, Dr. Martin leather/canvas combinations, and yes, actual pantaloons de Nimes." Not only does old Doughty have the nerve to keep sending us photos of his denims, but now he seems to be operating some underhand marketing strategy for his chums in the clothing trade. Still, keep 'em coming Simon!

"Whilst out and about, a friend of mine took some pics. Am I chappie enough?" writes Keith Roper-Hitches. Out and about sans chapeau and jacket? Not even close, though your pet looks a bit like the dog on the labels of 'Chappie' dog food.

"Are we chap?" write Emmanuel and Anne-Sophie Prunevieille (meaning 'old plum' in French). "Fromage France with love!"
You look very nice, and very French, but you really need to finish getting dressed before sending us your photograph.

"I am writing to determine whether I am a chap or not," writes Louis Newman. "I was told by a friend that I should most definitely send an email to your website. If you need to know what brands they are, I can happily tell you."
No thanks.

"Stephen here in leafy Leicestershire; may I ask indeed am I a chap?" writes Stephen Smith.
It used to be the case that submissions showed people trying a bit too hard to be Chap. Nowadays they're not even trying at all. Whatever next, photos taken of shop dummies?

Ah, thank you, Auriel Roe, for confirming that.

Alex Thornton-Smith is proud of "eschewing the modern trend of donning garb akin to that of a 'Power Ranger' to ride one's motorcycle; I have instead decided to put my faith in the safety of tweed (the gentleman's sporting cloth of choice)."
Thank goodness for that, someone actually making an effort. Cufflinks while motorcycling – now that indeed is Chap.

LOZ SCHIAVO

Gustav Temple spoke to Loz Schiavo, who styled hair and make-up on Tarzan, the Look of Love, Anthropoid and many other films, and she also styled the hair and make-up on Peaky Blinders, for which she received a BAFTA nomination in 2015

"When Cillian Murphy first sat in my chair for his first haircut on Season 1, I gave him a typical 1920s haircut and it just looked boring. So I graded his hair from a number 4, to a number 3, then 2 and then one, and gave him that line. So it really individualized that haircut"

you did the hair styling for all the cast on peaky Blinders – was it just the male actors?

Well, I've been the hair and make-up stylist for seasons 1-4, for male and female members of the cast. I designed all their hair and did all their make-up.

So stylists are expected to do both? Everyone assumes it's one person for hair and another for make-up.

In America it's like that, but over here you need to do both.

That's a lot of work. How much of it is in the preparation, before you start filming?

Basically you get four weeks prep.

Is that all you got at the very beginning of Peaky Blinders, when you had to come up with the hair styles from scratch?

I got even less! For the first season I only got three weeks' prep. Or maybe even just two weeks, and I was thinking, how the hell am I going to do this? I come from a film background, so doing a TV series was a bit daunting.

How much of a brief did you get at the start, on how their hair should actually look?

At my first meeting with the director, he said to me, I need someone who can do out-of-the-box hair-cuts; something that doesn't look quite right. I want something that nobody has ever seen before on screen. So my initial idea was that as soon as they put their Peaky caps on, all you see is skin all around, and the moment they take their caps off, they've got an individual haircut.

Each of the four brothers has a unique hair-style, so that must have been difficult, with the constraints of the period?

Well, even though we wanted something a bit out

of the box and a bit odd, you still have to design each hairstyle around the actor's face.

Does each actor's hairstyle change at all, over the seasons? I noticed that in Season 3, the back of Tommy's hair looked a little longer than in previous seasons?

When Cillian Murphy first sat in my chair for his first haircut on Season 1, he said, 'We need to do this in stages'. So I gave him a typical 1920s haircut and it just looked boring. And this show isn't boring, so we need something to push it. So I graded his hair from a number 4, to a number 3, then 2 and then one, and gave him that line. So it really individualized that haircut.

When we got to Season 3, Cillian said, 'I want it a bit longer through the back and the sides, to show that my character is growing up. But don't tell the rest of the boys.'

"Arthur, even though he's a Peaky Blinder, still has to break every rule there is. The director, in season one, wanted him to have a big walrus moustache, and over the seasons we've shortened it. But this season he grew his own, which made it much easier to style..."

What about Arthur? I noticed that when he gets a bit heated and angry, his hair flops about a lot on the top. That's all designed, is it?

Again, Arthur's hair, when he's got his cap on, is a Zero Guard. When he came to me, he already had longer hair, so I wanted to work with that hair. There's a book which is my bible on this series, called *Crooks Like Us*.

Yes, I've got it! I love that book!

There's a hairstyle in there very similar to Arthur's.

I made it shorter through the sides and longer on top. Arthur's character is a bit goofy; he's a bit messed up, so the longer hair really works.

So was *Crooks Like Us* a big inspiration for you?
Yes, we all looked to it for inspiration, but varied it according to the person. What's important about the Peaky haircut is it's definitely not an undercut. In a GQ Magazine article, they did an article about 10 Things you didn't know about Peaky Blinders. They didn't ask us, they didn't come to the source. They went to some barber and asked him how to do a Peaky cut. And he said, 'It's an undercut.' But it's nowhere near an undercut!

What is an undercut, exactly?
It's where it's really short underneath then longer on the top, so it flops over. You have to style the hair to suit the character. You're not going to give Arthur a really clean-cut, short goody-two-shoes haircut.

Did you also get involved in Arthur's moustache?
Arthur, even though he's a Peaky Blinder, still has to break every rule there is. The director, in season one, wanted him to have a big walrus moustache, and over the seasons we've shortened it. But this season he grew his own, which made it much easier to style, but he didn't like having to take it home with him. 'Loz,' he said, 'I'm not walking around with a Peaky haircut *and* a moustache!'

Since the series aired, have you seen many people with a Peaky hairstyle?
Oh yeah, I see it everywhere. When I first cut the boys' hair in Season 1, they went out on the street after filming and people were staring at them like they were complete weirdos: 'What hairdresser's done that?' But from Season 2, it just seemed normal. No-one looked at the boys' haircuts when they were walking around, because everyone else had it. It didn't look so menacing any more.

If you do the make-up as well, does that mean you get involved in the cast's tattoos?
Yes, we design all the tattoos.

Did you base them on real tattoos that people from the period would have had?
No, we made them all up. We use a company called Tattoo Now, and I give them a picture of what we want, and they replicate it on to tattoo paper for us. I talk to Cillian about what he wants; each tattoo has a special symbolism. So the one on his chest of sun rays was based on a real tattoo with a Jesus figure inside the sun rays. So we took the Jesus away and kept the sun rays.

Tommy wouldn't have Jesus on his body, would he?
No, exactly! He's not that type.

With Tom Hardy's character, Alfie Solomons, was it more a question of covering up the actor's actual tattoos?
Yes, he is very heavily tattooed. We might have just seen an arm, so we had to cover that up.

Would the character of Solomons not have any tattoos, being Jewish?
We gave him some hand tattoos. Although Jewish people traditionally aren't supposed to have any inkings on their skin, Tom said, 'Look, I'm not a traditional Jew.' Tom's really up for changing character. So I decided from the beginning to give him psoriasis, making his skin red and blotchy around the neck, beard and hairline.

Was that your idea or was that written into the script?
No, it was actually my idea! From Season One, Alfie Solomons has lung cancer, but we wanted something else that showed physically on the exterior. Obviously psoriasis isn't a sign of lung cancer, but it's not a sign of good health either. You know something's going on. But Tom's great at remembering details like that. When we started on Season 3, he said, 'Loz, I'm sure you gave me more psoriasis last time?' So we slapped a bit more on, and he saved the continuity.

Peaky Blinders, series four, is on BBC Two

AN ENGLISH CHAP IN NEW YORK

Excerpts from Mr. B the Gentleman Rhymer's meticulously kept leather-bound diary during a recent trip to the United States

TUESDAY 10TH SEPTEMBER

*G*etting oneself a U.S. visa is enough of a lark, for starters. Months of trying to prove myself worthy of work (pardon my French) across the pond, with press cuttings and letters of recommendation from friends in high places, led me eventually to my interview at the American Embassy on Grosvenor Square. When I turned up for my 10 o'clock appointment, it was clear that I was not the only one. The queue snaked right around the square, so I joined the back and waited patiently. Once I'd got about five people from the entrance, an official asked if I had my field telephone with me. I replied in the affirmative and was promptly sent off to a chemist's on Bond Street to pop it in a locker for the duration of my visit. I returned and joined the back

> "The hockey flyer depicted a silhouetted lady and read 'Get Your Booty on a Tuesday.' "How dare you!" I said as I handed it back. "I am an Englishman. I get my booty on a Wednesday"

of a now much longer queue. Shortly after, a rather wild-eyed chap joined the queue behind me. Oddly enough it turned out to be Mr. C from 90s psychedelic rave pop types the Shamen. I wondered quietly to myself whether it was 'letters day' at the Embassy, and I would soon be hearing a gruff voice shouting, "I ain't

getting on no plane" from a bit further back. Anyone under 40 might not get that reference.

When I finally made it to the little booth where my interview was to take place, I was merely told by my interviewer that I had a "magnificent moustache". I thanked him and he asked me if I ever read *The Chap*. I told him I that not only was I an avid reader, but that I occasionally wrote for it as well. "I shall be approving this!" he joyfully exclaimed and stamped my documents with something of a flourish.

SUNDAY 13TH OCTOBER

Upon arrival at JFK airport, the wait for customs was customarily long, but the customs chap was unexpectedly pleasant, the moustache working its magic on officialdom again. That and my newly acquired 'Alien Of Exceptional Ability' visa. The yellow cab journey through Queens opened my eyes to the myriad of New York's spectator sports, such as mixed weight vehicle jostling and fistfights between truckers and cab drivers.

My first evening in the city was spent in Gramecy at the launch of *I Am Dandy*, the splendid book by Rose Callaghan and Nathaniel Adams. The Big Apple's finest and dandiest were in attendance,

I got my first New York show done without a hitch and a splendid night was had by all.

I awoke the next morning, just a tad the worse for wear and jetlag to find your humble author's fizzog squeezed between photographs of Kanye West and Sandra Bullock on the front page of the US Guardian's website. They move fast over there, you know. Chap-Hop had officially arrived.

I spent the next couple of days as the last of the unknown international flaneurs, perambulating about the place, enjoying the general rambunctious-ness of the locals and taking part in an 'Ice Hockey test', which turned out to be a lesson in hyperbole and raucousness. Outside the stadium I was handed a flyer that depicted a silhouetted lady and read 'Get your booty on a Tuesday'.

"How dare you!" I said, handing it back. "I am an Englishman. I get my booty on a Wednesday."

SATURDAY 19TH OCTOBER

After a week of solid 'flanning' (I have decided that that is now a verb) it was time for my show at the Way Station in Brooklyn. A perfect place for some Chap-Hop, with its eccentric knick-knackery and toilets that were accessed via the frontage of a full-sized

Tardis. I was dined and interviewed by a well-dressed chap from a nerd-based website before the show, then played the show in two halves. They do like value for money in NYC, you see. During the break I was enjoying a tipple when I noticed blue lights flashing outside, so went to investigate. Apparently someone had fainted during the first half of the show and had whacked their bonce on the Tardis door. I noticed the stretcher being loaded up, and then recognised its contents as being the prostrate figure of my new chum who had been interviewing me not an hour previously.

"A horrible reality dawned upon me, making my blood run cold... Where was my banjolele?"

After the show I enjoyed a few drinks with Rose Callahan and her husband Kelly, then we took in a late night meal in a café opposite the apartment where I was staying. We eventually exited at about 4am, and as I swerved my way across the street I stopped halfway, as a horrible reality dawned upon me and made my blood run cold…

Where was my banjolele?

I realised that not only had I left it in the back of the taxi, but I'd also left my all merchandise and other bits and bobs in there too. To compound my problems, we'd gone and flagged the cab on the street and paid cash, so there was no way of tracing it. The rest of my US tour was going to be somewhat light on the old signature twanging. After much fretting and phoning of taxi companies, I gave up and returned, somewhat crushed, to my digs. The next day I met up with my New York cabaret chums Legs Malone and Donny Vomit, and we set about replacing my beloved instrument. Banjoleles are less than prevalent in the Big Apple, but we eventually found one in a music shop in Fort Ridge (who still send me spam every ruddy day) and I was back on the road again, as it were. When I got back to base camp I found an email from the cab driver telling me that he'd found my gear in the 'trunk' of his cab and could I arrange its return?

I arranged for said cabbie to meet me on the street with the goods, and when he arrived I paid his fare and tipped him twenty dollars. He looked at the notes with an air of disappointment, paused for a moment and said "…ok", so I gave him another ten. Again he looked disdainfully at the wedge and repeated his little 'ok' mantra, so I thanked him again in as jolly a fashion as I could now muster, closed the door and took my leave. "A beautiful moment sullied by avarice,"

thought I. Then again, perhaps I shouldn't have told him that he'd "saved my life" when he arrived.

SUNDAY 20TH OCTOBER

I took my banjolele back to the music store the following day to get a refund, only to find that they couldn't refund that much in cash and had to 'cut' me a cheque. After much to-ing and fro-ing, I had to accept said useless piece of paper. My dear chum Legs came to the rescue and did some sort of signing-over thingy, the mechanics of which I can't quite remember, and even if I did would make a terribly dreary paragraph. Suffice to say she saved the day and I got the dosh back.

The Sunday was spent at the Brooklyn Tweed Ride, which was a magnificent display of style and endurance, as it was bitterly cold. I skipped the cycling bit and headed straight to the bar, which was the final destination of the whole event. I am happy to report that our betweeded brothers and sisters across the pond are as splendid and welcoming as anywhere in the world. I do sometimes have to pinch myself to think that my silly mucking and plucking about had led me to places like this: a large bar in Brooklyn, with a bagpiper from Niagara extolling the virtues of what I do among a throng of some of the most immaculately dressed coves I've ever clapped eyes on. I salute them all.

My last show in New York was at The Lower East Side's legendary Slipper Room, an opulent underground den of cabaret and Burlesque, after which we headed to Times Square at 3 o'clock in the morning to polish off the filming of my videogramme *Hip-Hop Was To Blame After All* with Rose and Kelly. As luck would have it, we found ourselves there on the night before the Thanksgiving Day parade, so the roads had been cleared of all traffic, giving the impression that it had been cleared just for us. This would have been most pleasing, had I not been concentrating on trying not to freeze to death.

Before heading home, I was invited to Donny and Legs' place for Legs' birthday party, which was again full of colourful types, including a dominatrix who nearly broke my delicate banjolele-playing fingers with a handshake, and a satisfying number of chaps with splendid lip weasels. I was invited to stay over, so after the party ended myself, Donny, Legs and the dominatrix watched the film version of *Sgt. Pepper's Lonely Hearts Club* band, which inexplicably starred the Bee Gees being chased about by Frankie Howerd while singing Beatles songs.

Donny regaled me with the story of how, a few weeks previously, he'd been mugged near his apartment in Fort Ridge while listening to *Tinkerty Tonk* from my *Tweed Album*. Apparently the song played on his headphones throughout the whole ordeal.

"It's still my favourite Mr. B The Gentleman Rhymer track," he assured me. ∎

> **❝** Bond's brown barleycorn tweed hacking jacket in Goldfinger has taken on something of a divine status in the community of sartorial appreciation. **❞**

TWEED ON FILM

**Nick Guzan looks at the role of tweed jackets in cinema,
from slick British secret agents to sporty San Francisco cops**

During the early decades of cinema, tweed was just as ubiquitous on the silver screen as it was in real life, often worn by honest, homespun gentlemen of taste. Think James Stewart in one of several tweed suits during George Bailey's fateful Christmas Eve in *It's a Wonderful Life* (1946) or John Wayne's Irish tweed sports jacket making a positive impression when his character returns to his ancestral home in *The Quiet Man* (1952). Lovely examples, to be sure, but nothing groundbreaking in terms of how it was worn.

Even the more villainous tweed wearers of this era were still urbane chaps with traditional inclinations toward the art of dressing, from Clifton Webb's scheming snob Waldo Lydecker sporting a double-breasted tweed suit in *Laura* (1944) to James Mason's charismatic Philip Vandamm donning a series of odd waistcoats with his grey tweed suit in *North by Northwest* (1959).

Then came the 1960s. Every era has looked to the future to some extent, but the swinging sixties was one of the first decades in modern

> *"Old school members of 007's circle such as gadgetmaster Q had worn fine traditional examples of tweed, but it wasn't until Goldfinger in 1964 that Sean Connery's sophisticated spy wore tweed on screen"*

history where youth was taking the lead across the globe. The less informed may consider tweed to be professorial or old-fashioned, which is certainly not to the fabric's detriment, but this rugged sportswear was rejuvenated in 1960s cinema, for a brief but brilliant flash, as the suiting of choice for youthful rogues on both sides of the Atlantic.

In Hitchcock's *The Birds*, (above) released in 1963, Rod Taylor's Mitch Brenner is a successful and swaggering Bay Area lawyer, the type who

Warren Beatty wears a brown herringbone three-piece tweed suit in *Bonnie and Clyde,* 1967

has a family home a few hours up the coast in the smaller coastal hamlet of Bodega Bay. Though he wears a wool suit in the city, Mitch sports tweed in this more bucolic, homey setting, donning a fine mixed grey tweed suit worn with a white shirt and silk tie for his younger sister's birthday party. The jacket blends American tailoring with sporty English details with its "shapeless" sack jacket, structured shoulders, slanted flapped hip pockets and ticket pocket, close three-button front, and short double vents.

The following year found James Bond sporting tweed on screen for the first time. It wasn't the

> **"Bond's hacking jacket in Goldfinger is one of the few garments in more than one film, Connery also wearing it in Thunderball"**

debut of tweed in the James Bond series, of course; how could such a quintessentially English franchise not feature tweed in its first two films? Old school members of 007's circle, such as the gadgetmaster Q, had worn fine traditional examples of tweed, but it wasn't until *Goldfinger* in 1964 that Sean Connery's sophisticated spy wore tweed on screen.

Bond's brown barleycorn tweed hacking jacket in *Goldfinger* has taken on something of a divine status in the community of sartorial appreciation. Of course, it may help its case that Connery wore it during some of the film's most iconic scenes, from a statue-shattering encounter with Oddjob to piloting his gadget-laden Aston Martin DB5 through the mountains of Austria. Nonetheless, the jacket is one of the few of 007's garments to appear in more than one film, as Connery would wear it the following year in *Thunderball.* Both films feature the jacket with a beige shirt and brown silk tie – knitted in *Goldfinger,* grenadine in *Thunderball* – with taupe trousers and high-top brown suede derby shoes.

At this point in the series, Sean Connery's

Steve McQueen in a brown herringbone tweed sports jacket in 1968's *Bullitt*

THE QUIET MAN

John Ford's cinematic love letter to his ancestral home remains a perennial St. Patrick's Day favorite, even if it is a somewhat overly sanitized depiction of Irish life in the 1920s.

Based on a 1933 short story by Maurice Walsh, *The Quiet Man* stars Ford's favorite actor John Wayne as Sean Thornton, a former boxer from Pittsburgh who is returning home to reclaim his family's land in Ireland. The setting, Inisfree, is fictional, but much of the movie was filmed on location in western Ireland around the village of Cong, County Mayo.

With his tweed jacket, flat cap and flannels, Sean Thornton looks every bit the native Irishman when he arrives by train at Castletown. "He didn't have the look of an American tourist at all about him," Father Peter Lonergan (Ward Bond) remarks with approval in his narration.

Many of the costumes were tailored by the O'Máille family, who continue to sell Irish country clothing at their shop in Galway. Their web site proudly states that John Wayne and Maureen O'Hara both visited its store for their characters' costumes, making it highly likely that John Wayne wore authentic, locally hand-woven Irish tweed for his role in this most Irish of movies.

Sean's tweed is a herringbone twill weave of beige and light brown yarns to create an overall tan effect, with a slight cast toward taupe. The single-breasted jacket has notch lapels that are often worn with the back collar flipped up for a touch of insouciance. The notch lapels and the welted breast pocket have 'swelled edge' seams. The jacket also has straight-jetted hip pockets in line with the lowest button. Although Sean's tweed jacket is pure Ireland, his button-down collar shirt, striped tie, and v-neck jumper are indicative of his Americanization.

Both Ford and cinematographer Winton C. Hoch won well-deserved Academy Awards for their work on *The Quiet Man*.

Bond had established a uniform for himself of a two-button lounge suit – often in shades of grey – tailored by Anthony Sinclair, with a pale blue Turnbull & Asser 'cocktail cuff' shirt and navy grenadine tie. The hacking jacket in *Goldfinger* marked one of his first deviations from this uniform, though Bond remains generally true to his usual taste, wearing solid colors, side-tab adjuster trousers, and grenadine or knitted ties.

Tweed thus became more commonly seen on fashionable male figures of the mid-sixties, from 007 to Michael Caine's eponymous character in *Alfie*. A sophisticated secret agent and a playboy in swinging London are natural candidates as style icons, but it's hard to imagine bestowing a similar honour on a small-time Texas desperado during the Great Depression. Yet Warren Beatty's larger-than-life interpretation of the criminal Clyde Barrow in Arthur Penn's stylized drama *Bonnie and Clyde* (1967) featured the gang leader in a variety of natty duds that shared little in common with the backseat wardrobe of the real-life hoodlum.

Costume designer Theodora Van Runkle dressed her protagonists in an intentionally anachronistic fashion, evoking the 1930s but adding modern touches, which would speak to audiences of the late '60s who embraced the look and attitude of the 'romantic' outlaws. A standout of Beatty's wardrobe appears midway through the film, as the gang takes over a bank for a smooth and successful heist. The setting is a summer afternoon in a dusty small town in Texas, yet Clyde strides into the bank beautifully attired in a brown herringbone tweed three-piece suit, complete

with half-belted 'action back' jacket, Panama hat, spectator shoes, and green polka-dot tie. Despite the weather, tweed appeared to be the fabric of choice for the male members of the gang that day; Clyde's brother Buck (Gene Hackman) sports a taupe birdseye tweed three-piece suit, and juvenile lackey C.W. Moss (Michael J. Pollard) diverts from his usual denim in his plaid tweed sports jacket.

"Every Dirty Harry movie would feature Clint in a stylish new tweed jacket, though the Bullitt days of a cop in cool rollneck and boots was out"

The great Van Runkle was only getting started. After the success of her costume design debut in *Bonnie and Clyde*, her next project would showcase an outfit considered by many to be the pinnacle of 1960s cool: the shooting jacket, rollneck and suede boots of Steve McQueen's eponymous detective in *Bullitt* (1968). When we first meet Lieutenant Frank

Bullitt of the San Francisco Police Department, he looks rather unremarkable – particularly for McQueen's standards – in a dark navy lounge suit, light blue shirt and olive foulard tie. Both his attire and the film's narrative refer to the police procedural of the previous decade's *Dragnet* and *M Squad*.

The next day, we realize this is something different. Bullitt glides down the iconic streets of San Francisco in a highland green Ford Mustang GT390 fastback, stepping out in a rich brown herringbone tweed sport jacket that remains a sartorial point of interest fifty years later, with its American sack cut, 3/2-roll button front, ticket pocket, short double vents and irregular tobacco-brown suede elbow patches. McQueen insouciantly eschews a traditional shirt and tie – even when on duty – and instead opts for a navy knit rollneck jumper, charcoal flannel trousers and snuff-brown suede crepe-soled playboy boots from Hutton. Joe Friday's wardrobe this surely is not.

After a decade of charming cads who flouted criminal codes and conventions, American cinema in the 1970s saw a return to venerating law and order. Pragmatic police officers like Bullitt were out, and a new breed of laconic lawmen like 'Dirty Harry' Callahan were in, upholding the truth and

nothing but the truth. Though they serve the same great city of San Francisco, Harry Callahan's manner of wearing a herringbone tweed sports jacket is a business-friendly, conservative ying to Frank Bullitt's freewheeling yang.

In the first scenes of *Dirty Harry* (1971), Clint Eastwood set an iconic standard for this uncompromising detective by donning a contemporary grey tweed jacket over a pale blue shirt, deep red sleeveless sweater and a silk repp tie in navy and red to bring both garments together, uttering "Do you feel lucky, punk?" while aiming his .44 Magnum at a – spoiler alert – ultimately lucky bank robber. The palette is no coincidence, as Inspector Callahan is presented to us as a 'red, white, and blue' all-American lawmen at the height of the Nixon era.

Every subsequent *Dirty Harry* film would thus feature Clint in a stylish new tweed jacket, though the days of the cool cop in a rollneck and boots was out, replaced by a dedicated detective in an office-friendly button-up shirt, tie and brogues.

They say fashion is cyclical, and tweed appears to be making a revival in the current decade on both sides of the criminal fence. The Shelby family in *Peaky Blinders* conduct their violent business in natty tweed three-piece suits and caps, while Benedict Cumberbatch drapes his incarnation of Conan Doyle's greatest invention in a long Irish tweed greatcoat in *Sherlock*.

It's not just the Brits who are continuing this legacy of tweed as the preferred fabric for defiant characters. While dressing Ryan Reynolds' insouciant gambler for *Mississippi Grind* (2015), costume designer Abby O'Sullivan informed me that she took cues from the rebellious all-Americans played by Paul Newman, Robert Redford and Steve McQueen in the 1960s and 1970s. The jacket she envisioned (pictured above) would be "an idealization of a certain type of man and visually complex enough to stare at on screen for long periods." What did she eventually choose? A micro-checked sports jacket in hand-woven Harris Tweed. ∎

KING OF THE UNDERWORLD

Chris Sullivan founded and ran Soho's Wag Club for two decades in the 1980s and was frontman for Blue Rondo A La Turk. He explains how his chappish look evolved during the 80s, at odds with the fashions of the time

A while back, purely because I was very prominent in the 1980s and ran landmark clubs during the so-called New Romantic era, some chump on that social media malarkey would not accept that, at that time, I was not wearing copious amounts of make-up. I of course defended my corner as, being 6 foot 2 and 14 stone with a noticeably broken nose and a few facial scars to boot, blusher and eyeliner were not entirely ideal. He also said that I must have sported frilly shirts and big shoulder pads. Luckily for us both, I didn't know where he lived.

Yet this is a common misnomer about the 1980s: many pundits who were not there think that that utterly ridiculous portmanteau was *de rigueur* for anyone who went to any groovy club in the early eighties but, if truth be told, it was anything but. And yet, I don't blame said inconsequential for assuming such untruths, as the epoch was defined by a few outrageous camp and entirely overt queens who grabbed the limelight, struck a pose at the drop of a hanky and thus tarred us all with the same mascara brush.

The truth however is that, the likes of yours truly sported a look that was entirely 'chap' and

"VHS meant you could pause the recording at pivotal moments and check out the kit. You could check whether the jacket had a bi-swing or Bayer back, whether the pants had regular or reverse pleats and so on. Now you could get it 100% correct"

had no truck with such ladylike adornment. At times, I sported a monocle, jodhpurs, three-piece New Edwardian suits, spats and a boater (but not at the same time) and garnered influence from Bertie Wooster, D.W. Griffiths, Erich Von Stroheim and Fritz Lang, as well as Robert Mitchum, Yves Tanguy, Frank Lloyd Wright and James McNeill Whistler. Indeed, I had no time for futurism, as I was still very busy dealing with the past, purely because there is so much of it.

I also emulated characters from British comics, throwing in a Desperate Dan or a Buffalo Bill from time to time, and on an off day I will admit to having recreated Plug. In fact, my whole *raison d'être* came from a few years previously in 1977 when I and a few friends from Wales – Mark Taylor and Mark Stevenson, who lived in London – were so appalled by the uniformity that punk had become that we embarked on a style dictate we christened Boys Weekly Rockers, whereby we dressed as our favourite characters from British comics like the *Hotspur* and *The Valiant*. Of course, taking the Michael 100%, I'd turn up at punk gigs dressed as Biggles in flying jacket and helmet, goggles, breeches and boots, Mark Taylor dressed as Sinbad the sailor in flowing Eastern robes, while Stevenson looked like Dennis The Menace on rather strong LSD. Everyone thought we'd lost the plot.

Fast forward to the Blitz Club in 1979. I still had the kit. I still liked the look. And so I persevered. But what was so useful back then was that, to further my endeavour, all I had to do was visit jumble sales. I'd buy the *Ham and High* and *The Camden Journal* and methodically hit every jumble sale in the vicinity. Lest we forget, this was 1979, so much of the mufti had belonged to men who had recently passed away aged, shall we say 75, so the kit was, if you were lucky, from the thirties, possibly postwar and almost definitely from the fifties and sixties. We'd chance upon military wear worn in India during the Raj, duffel coats sported in WW2 and collarless shirts that we'd marry up with stiff starched collars from Denny's in Soho. On a good day we'd find Huntsman suits, Hawes and Curtis shirts and Lobb footwear, and on a bad day we'd get properly elbowed by old ladies, a prehistoric scone and a cold cup of cha.

Coming from Wales, where the riches were few and far between, I was overwhelmed by the sheer quality on offer, but the richest haul we ever had was when one of my fellow students at St. Martins announced that his mother – who

Left to Right: Chris Sullivan, Christos Tolera, Ceryth Wynn Evans, Robert Elms, Daryl Humphries

worked at Charles Fox the theatrical costumiers near Charing Cross – had told us they were having a sale of 'everything.' So, as one would expect, we all – most of us St Martins Fashion Students resident at a Warren Street squat – went down there *en masse* and bought the bloody lot. Kim Bowen bought a floor length white fur coat; I, a complete Argentine Gaucho outfit plus many items that didn't fit, Christos Tolera a beautiful Edwardian lounge suit, while George O'Dowd bought their whole supply of Leichner face paint, in an array of colours that kept him going for a decade.

Shortly after this day of days, the Blitz Club started going downhill, purely because too many blusher and lace types were getting in and dancing like simpletons to electronic music. It was the silly season. My reaction was to start my own night in the St. Moritz, where we played music that was deliberately old and decidedly decadent: Marlene Dietrich, Lotte Lenya, Billie Holiday etc, and it took off. Before you knew it futurism was dead, and looking like a silent movie star wasn't. I recall two regular patrons who dressed like 17th-century English Puritans and sat nursing their bibles and water all night, while certain ladies dressed 100% Louise Brooks in *Pandora's Box* or Theda Bara in *La Belle Russe*.

I was big on the look sported by the King of the underworld played by Gustaf Gründgens in *M* directed by Fritz Lang, which was bowler hat, leather

gloves and a leather coat. Undoubtedly, we were all hugely influenced by movies that we saw at The Academy Cinema in Oxford Street, as afternoon screenings were less than the price of a half of lager.

Then in 1980 I spent the summer in Manhattan and, thoroughly disenchanted with this camp two blokes in make-up behind a synthesizer nonsense, decided to start a big band that used real instruments to play funk and Latin, and I designed these big suits that I had made by tailor Chris Ruocco of Kentish Town. I grew a goatee, pulled out the beret and the pork pie hats and listened to jazz and Latin. Soon I saw a similarity between my suits and zoot suits and, considering that said suit had sparked riots and disorder in 1941, decided that I would sport them for the band that I named Blue Rondo a La Turk. A year later I signed a £500,000 deal with Virgin, had a Top 30 record, appeared on the cover of *The Face*, the *NME*, *Sounds* and every other music mag in the country, sparking a nationwide trend for 40s kit and all that went with it, causing Armani to copy it and make himself a fortune.

But films were an even bigger influence for that look, especially after 1982, when VHS recorders became affordable. I checked the likes of Vincente Minnelli's *Cabin in The Sky*, Andrew Stone's *Stormy Weather* and film noirs like *The Glass Key* and *The Big Combo*. Now, not only could you could record great movies, but also you could pause the recording at

pivotal moments and check out the kit. You could check whether the jacket had a bi-swing or Bayer back, whether the pants had regular or reverse pleats and so on. Now you could get it 100% correct.

Another big effect on us UK style mongers in the early 80s was the cheap flights to the US of A. I'd fly to LA for a few hundred pounds and pick up hand painted ties for a buck apiece, Pendleton shirts for $5 and Eisenhower jackets for a score. No-one wanted them. Now, the supply of large-sized classic Californian leisure wear of the early fifties has almost dried up, apart from at huge gatherings like the Rose Bowl, where the likes of me almost pass out in delirious excitement.

Of course, one always remembers certain occasions when one was dressed to the nines. My favourite was when, in the middle of August 1980, I turned up dressed in a three-piece Edwardian suit, spats, gloves, cravat and walking stick to thoroughly underground gay club The Paradise Garage. The largely black and Hispanic clientele were dressed in shorts and slashed T-shirts, even headbands, for goodness' sake. Thus, dressed as I was, I brought the place to a complete standstill. And then the legendary DJ Larry Levan played *Do What you Wanna Do* by T Connection and I took to the dance floor, pulled out a selection of my best moves, as perfected in Wigan Casino or the Soul Boy clubs of mid-70s London – fast steps sixteen beats to the bar, eight

spins on the run, a back drop, the splits and back up for more absurdly fast footwork. While I was on the verge of a coronary, the crowd erupted into applause. Later as I, sweating like Giant Haystacks, sat down to nurse my thumping heart with a fruit juice and a downer, Levan came over with Frankie Knuckles and sat and just looked at me. I could see in their eyes that they thought that someone might have spiked their drink and I was just yet another apparition. Levan, perhaps lost for words, said, "I never knew Sherlock Holmes could dance like that!"

"Never judge a book by its cover," was my reply but I instantly regretted saying it, as one really should. As Confucius said, at 3.37 am on the 22nd April 502 BC, "There is no greater giveaway than a chap's kit and especially his footwear!"

I still carry the torch, wearing the clothes that I want to wear, and have never felt the need to be either fashionable or trendy. This attitude has stood me in good stead through the years running my club, The Wag, as a style pundit and even now as I lecture at St Martins. As far as clothing is concerned, I have only one motto which is, 'To Thine own self be true,' while Oscar Wilde's comment "Fashion is a form of ugliness so intolerable that we have to alter it every six months," still has a place in my soul. ∎

Rebel Rebel: How Mavericks Made the Modern World, by Chris Sullivan, is published by Unbound

ACROSS THE ALPS BY SPACE HOPPER

Gustav Temple meets Steve Payne, the self-styled gentleman adventurer whose voyage across the Alps by Space Hopper is one of many eccentric and perilous journeys. Photographs by Olivia Bullock

What made you want to bounce across the Alps on a Space Hopper?

I've been doing crazy adventures each year for the last few years, each involving a different method of transportation. My first was a walk to Canterbury from Southampton, following the route of the Continental mediaeval pilgrims to the feast of Thomas Beckett in Canterbury Cathedral.

"Trans-Alpine bouncing has never caught on as a form of gentlemanly or even mass-transportation. It's just too difficult"

I dressed in authentic 14th-century clothing and took original food recipes from the period with me.

When I reached Winchester, a homeless man came up to me saying he'd seen an interview with me in a newspaper, and gave me a pasty that he'd bought me. It turned out he'd only had £3.60 in all the world and he'd spent £2.80 on the pasty for me. When I asked him why, he said, "You're like us, you're sleeping rough in the middle of winter, and we look after each other."

During that trip I met a few other homeless people and got some good advice on how to keep warm. It turned from a historical journey into one that was raising awareness for homeless people. I left home with 12 followers on Facebook; by the time I reached Canterbury I had 182,000 followers.

A year later I crossed Wales by river in a Coracle, a small round Welsh fishing boat, following the pilgrimage of Saint Brendan the Navigator.

How do you navigate? SatNav or traditional maps?

Neither. I just followed the river. I was doing the journey exactly as St Brendan would have done it in the 5th century, in the same clothing. I told the river authorities where I'd be. They said, 'Not a good idea but ok. We'll make a note of it.'

I'd love to see that note! 'Man in fifth-century garb crossing Wales by coracle'.

When it capsized and floated off, I had to phone the police and report it, but I was only four miles from the end of the journey so I just walked the rest of the way. So I'd done a journey on foot and one by boat, and I needed a third form of transport for the next journey. I had used the first two journeys as ways of raising awareness for homeless people; while sharing the pasty with the chap in Winchester, he spoke of the difficulties of how he was living. When I asked him what it was like living on the streets, he said, "It's like trying to cross the Alps on a Space Hopper. It's a completely ridiculous way of doing things."

And I thought – there's my next journey. I'm going to cross the Alps on a Space Hopper.

So once you had the motivation, how did you plan the trip across the Alps?

I had to investigate 50 or 60 possible routes across a portion of the Alps. I knew it would be a substantial trip, because you can't cross the Alps anywhere without covering at least 60 or 70 miles, and I needed a route where there was an emergency shelter at least every five miles, because 5.2 miles was the world record for a singe journey on a Space Hopper. I found a place called Bardonecchia in Italy, which advertises itself as the 'Gateway to the Alps' on the Italian side, to Grenoble, which advertises itself as the 'Gateway to the Alps' on the French side. It was a trip of about 76 miles.

I did eight months of practice in Wales to see what kind of terrain the Space Hopper could handle. It copes very well with grass, packed earth, stone, but it doesn't like small, sharp flints. Fortunately the Alps is mainly limestone, so you don't get a lot of sharp igneous rock. I did some practice on the snow at Christmas and found that Space Hoppers don't perform very well on snow, so I knew it would have to be a summer trip.

I hadn't factored on it being the hottest summer for 100 years and I was wearing a tweed suit and a pith helmet and getting through 16 bottles of water a day. You don't need much more than energy bars when you're bouncing all day long. I slept in emergency shelters, where for 15 Euros you get a space on the floor to sleep on.

I once had a go on my son's Space Hopper and it isn't an easy thing to master. It doesn't strike me as an efficient mode of transport?

That's why Trans-Alpine bouncing has never caught on as a form of gentlemanly or even mass-transportation. It's just too difficult. Generally speaking, I was climbing for the first four days, and I was slowly descending for the next fourteen days. I worked out a route in which all the climbing was at the beginning. Some of the inclines were quite steep; there were a few rock faces I had to climb up. I had to deflate the Space Hopper and put it in the backpack. At one stage I took a wrong turning and had to climb a 40-foot cliff face. I used my umbrella to catch hold of ledges and pull myself up.

Did you have any spare Space Hoppers, in case of accidents?

I took four with me. I named them after famous people who had crossed the Alps: Hannibal, Napoleon

– he burst on day five and became Napoleon Blown-apart. Nellie, in honour of the elephants, blew away off the top of a mountain on day 14. I was so tired after bouncing up an incline that I literally fell off the Space Hopper and fell asleep. I think I was probably asleep before I hit the ground. When I woke up, Nellie was gone. I couldn't think of a name for the fourth one, so I put it out on the Internet and they came up with 'Bouncing McBounceface'.

How did the locals react to you?

I had to learn the phrases for "Because I am an Englishman" and "Why wouldn't you?" because they'd come up to me and say, "Why are you doing this?"

What will your next voyage be?

I'd like to recreate the flight of Eilmer of Malmesbury. In 1018, exactly a thousand years ago, he invented a flying machine. He climbed 80 feet up Malmesbury tower and leapt off, strapped to a pair of leather and wickerwork wings. You'd expect that story to end with crushing death on the stones below, but he became the first person to fly, achieving 220 yards. He crashed into the roof of the bakery, fell to the ground and broke both his legs, but survived.

I thought I'd build a pair of leather and wicker-work wings to recreate that flight, but I couldn't find a building 80 feet tall that they'd allow me to jump off. I might try it off the end of Bognor Pier, which is 40 feet up, and then I'd land in the sea.

The other opportunity is the wreck of Henry V's flagship, the Grace Dieu – twice the length of the Mary Rose but a good 300 years earlier. It sank at the bottom of the River Hamble in Hampshire and has never been raised. During the middle ages they did underwater exploration in submarines made out of barrels. So I could build a submarine out of barrels and explore Henry V's flagship.

How does that work?

You put a whole barrel over your head, with weights on the bottom of the barrel. Then you stand inside it, as there's no bottom, and get lowered down on a rope. You take a breath, have a look around, then come back into the barrel for more air. You've only got about four minutes before all the oxygen turns into carbon dioxide. I could have an air supply in the barrel, but then I'd have to register it with the British Scuba Diving Association. If you just jump into the water with a barrel, it's up to you.

There are so many rules about what you're allowed to do these days. If you want to cross the Alps on a Space Hopper or set off across Wales in a Coracle, before you start, you've got to think, who's going to prosecute me and what for? ■

SUBSCRIBE TO THE CHAP
FOR HALF PRICE

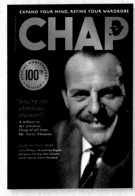

*T*his year The Chap celebrated 20 years of anarcho-dandyism and the publication of our **100th edition.**

As a special introductory offer to readers of Best of The Chap, we are offering an annual subscription for half the usual price, at just £14.00 instead of £28.00.

Subscribers receive four quarterly editions per year, which they receive before copies reach the newsstands. The Chap is also available at most branches of WH Smith in the UK. To take up the half-price offer, Simply visit our online subscriptions page and use code **BOTC19**

www.thechap.co.uk/subscribe

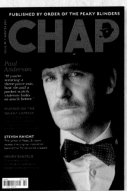

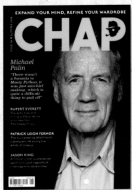

THE CHAP SHOP

Visit The Chap Shop to view our range of grooming products and gentlemen's accessories.

As well as shaving brushes, safety razors, shaving soaps and aftershave from the best British brands, The Chap has produced Flâneur, a classic men's eau de cologne, and a range of art deco-inspired pocket squares.

All these products are available exclusively from our online store at www.thechap.co.uk

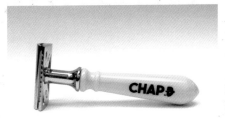

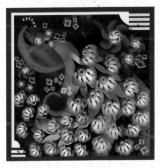

ACKNOWLEDGEMENTS

A special thank you to the following designers, who turned The Chap from a
random collection of fancy words and pictures into an object of beauty:
Rachel Barker, Carina Dicks, Katie Moorman, Mikaela Dixon, Rian Hughes,
Joe Gardiner, Charlotte Cooper, Tom Watt, Vic Darkwood and Caroline Lindop.